THE ENGLISH MODEL FARM

The English Model Farm

Building the Agricultural Ideal, 1700–1914

Susanna Wade Martins

WIND*gather*
PRESS

The English Model Farm:
Building the Agricultural Ideal, 1700–1914

Copyright © English Heritage, 2002

Published by: Windgather Press, 29 Bishop Road, Bollington, Macclesfield, Cheshire SK10 5NX, UK

Distributed by: Central Books, 99 Wallis Road, London E9 5LN

British Library Cataloguing-in-Publication Data
A catalogue record for this book is available from the British Library

ISBN 0 9538630 5 0

Typeset and originated by Carnegie Publishing Ltd,
Chatsworth Road, Lancaster
Printed and bound by The Alden Press, Oxford

Contents

List of illustrations   vii

Acknowledgements   xiii

1. Beauty, Utility and Profit   1

2. Landlords, Tenants and the Farming Framework   8

3. The Philosophy of 'Improvement', 1660–1790   34

4. Patriotic Improvement, 1790–1840   68

5. Practice with Science, 1840–1875   112

6. Retrenchment, 1875–1939   170

Epilogue   198

Appendix: County Synopses   203

Notes   224

Bibliography   231

Index   237

List of Illustrations

Figures

1. Block plans to show the development of farm layout, 1750–1900. (Phillip Judge)   6

2. Loose boxes at Cronkhill, Shropshire (Jeremy Lake)   21

3. Block diagram to show by decade the date of construction of model farms to which references were found during the survey. (Phillip Judge)   22

4. Graph to show the level of wheat prices, 1770–1900. (Phillip Judge)   23

5. Graph to show movements in rents, 1690–1914, from Turner 1997, 149. (Phillip Judge)   24

6. Map to show the percentage of farms per county (pre-1974) over 300 acres in 1851, from Overton 1996, 175. (Phillip Judge)   25

7. Maps showing the landscapes of the Thorney Level in the Cambridgeshire Fens and Example Farm at Cromhall, Gloucestershire. (Phillip Judge)   26–7

8. Maps showing the distribution of located and dated planned and model farmsteads in England built before and after 1840. (Mapping by Gisela Sunnenberg, School of Environmental Sciences, University of East Anglia, and Phillip Judge)   28–9

9. The School of Practical Farming and Agriculture, designed by the Scottish architect, Adam Menelaw, and Nicholas L'vov and built near Pavlovsk in 1798. (Society of Architectural Historians of Great Britain and Alexey Makhrov)   32

10. Block diagram to show the number of parliamentary enclosure acts passed for each five-year periods, 1650–1850, from Turner 1980, 60. (Phillip Judge)   36

11. Seventeenth-century maps showing farm layouts. Channons Farm, Tibbenham (Norfolk Record Office MC1777/1). Cranley Hall, Eye (Suffolk Record Office SRO IHD78).   38–9

12. Plan to show the layout of Sir Thomas Parkyn's new farmsteads at Bunny and Bradmore and photograph of one of his fine barns. (Mike Williams, photograph and Phillip Judge, plan)   40

13. Bank barn at Townend Farm, Troutbeck, Cumbria. (Jeremy Lake)   41

14. Andreo Palladio's illustration of Villa Dicani. (Redrawn by Phillip Judge)   42

15. W. Pitt's plan and elevations of a farm published in 1788. (Redrawn from *Annals of Agriculture*, **9**, by Phillip Judge)   44

16. Arthur Young's plan of a farm yard, published in 1770. (Redrawn by Phillip Judge from *A Farmer's Guide to Hiring and Stocking Farms, 2*)   45

17. Drawing of Arthur Young's feeding system ((1770), from *A Farmer's Guide to Hiring and Stocking a Farm.* (By permission, Syndics of Cambridge University Library)   46

18. A selection of Daniel Garrett's farm plans of 1747. (Redrawn by Phillip Judge)   47

19. John Carr's stable ranges at Street Farm and Park Farm, Hornby, North Yorkshire. (Michael Williams)   50–1

20. Foal Park Farm, Constable Burton, North Yorkshire. (National Monuments Record, English Heritage)   52

21. Drawing of the Gothic screen at Raby Castle Farm, from Young's *Northern Tour* (1771), **2**, 440. (By permission, Syndics of Cambridge University Library)   53

22. Robert Adam's plan for the Home Farm at Kedleston, Derbyshire. (Judith Appleby)   55

23. Circular layout for the Home Farm at Kedleston, Derbyshire. (Judith Appleby)   55

24. Plan for Culzean Castle, Ayrshire. (Redrawn by Phillip Judge)   56

25. Plan of Cadland Farm. (Redrawn by Phillip Judge from Sir John Soane's Museum, 64/6/41)   58

26. Plan and perspective reconstruction of Burley Farm, Derbyshire. (Judith Appleby)   60

27. Plan and perspective reconstruction of The Home Farm at Sandon, Staffordshire. (Judith Appleby)   61

28. Barn façade of Hatch Farm, Thorndon, Essex (1777). (Redrawn by Phillip Judge)   62

29. Drawing of a sheep cote from Lightholer's *Gentleman's and Farmer's Architect,* 1762, 24. (By permission, Syndics of Cambridge University Library)   63

30. The house at Bunkers Hill Farm, Greystoke, Cumbria, with the granary/ stable buildings to the rear. (Michael Williams)   65

31. Kent's plans for Norfolk Farm and Flemish Farm, Windsor Great Park, Berkshire. (The Royal Archives. The Royal Collection, copyright Her Majesty, the Queen).   70–1

32. Kent's design for a carthouse and granary to be erected at the Flemish Farm, Windsor Great Park. (Redrawn from Royal Archives Addl. mss. Geo./15. The Royal Collection, copyright Her Majesty, the Queen by Phillip Judge).   72

33. A plan for a farmstead with a water-powered barn from *Communications to the Board of Agriculture,* 1797. (By permission, Syndics of Cambridge University Library)   73

34. Loudon's plan of an octagonal farmstead. (Redrawn by Phillip Judge)   74

List of figures

35. A plan from Charles Waistell's book, *Designs for Agricultural Buildings,* 1827 (Plate V and VI, by permission, Syndics of Cambridge University Library).   76

36. Photograph of workers' housing, East House Farm, Chiswick, Northumberland. (Michael Williams)   81

37. The horse-engine house at Longdyke Farm, Shilbottle, Northumberland. (Susanna Wade Martins)   83

38. The buildings at East Brizlee, Hulne Park, Alnwick, Northumberland. (Michael Williams)   84

39. Plan and elevation of steadings at Outchester Farm, near Bamburgh, Northumberland, built for the Greenwich Hospital estates. (Redrawn by Phillip Judge)   86

40. Map of the newly-enclosed farmland around Sledmere Park, East Yorkshire. (Phillip Judge)   87

41. Block plans of the Sledmere farms, East Yorkshire. (Phillip Judge)   88

42. Sykes design for Maramette Farm, Sledmere, and photographs of the present buildings. (*Country Life* and Michael Williams)   89

43. Day House Farm, Staffordshire, from James Loch's *An Account of the Improvements on the Estates of the Marquis of Stafford,* 1820. (Redrawn by Phillip Judge)   91

44. Block plans of a selection of the Marquis of Stafford's farms in Shropshire and Staffordshire. (Phillip Judge)   93

45. Tearn Farm, Ercall Magna, Shropshire. (Mike Williams)   94–5

46. Wyver Farm, Belper, Derbyshire. (Michael Williams)   97

47. Drawn details, bird's eye view and photographs of Dalley Farm, Belper, Derbyshire. (Graham Douglas and Michael Williams)   98–9

48. Schoose Farm, near Workington, Cumbria, from J. C. Curwen's *General Hints on Agricultural Subjects,* 1809, frontispiece. (By permission, Syndics of Cambridge University Library)   101

49. Maps of Woburn Park, Bedfordshire and Holkham Park, Norfolk, within their agricultural landscapes. (Phillip Judge)   102–3

50. Robert Salmon's plan for Crawley Heath Farm at Woburn, Bedfordshire. (Redrawn from Bedford Record Office R. Box 818 Bundle 18/4, Bedfordshire and Luton Archives, with kind permission of the Bedford Settled Estates, by Phillip Judge)   104

51. Drawings for the sheep house at Park Farm, Woburn. (Redrawn from Bedford Record Office R Box 818 Bundle 18/11, 23 and 26, Bedfordshire and Luton Archives, with kind permission of the Bedford Settled Estates, by Phillip Judge)   106

52. Plan of the Great Barn at Holkham, Norfolk. (Plan redrawn from R. N. Bacon, *Norfolk Agriculture* (1844) by Phillip Judge)   108

53. Wheycurd Farm field barn, Wighton, Norfolk. (Michael Williams)   109

54. Aerial photograph of Leicester Square Farm, South Creake, Norfolk. (Derek Edwards, Norfolk Museums and Archaeology Service) — 110

55. Drawing of the machine room of a barn, from Copland's *Agriculture, Ancient and Modern*, 1866. — 113

56. A Lancashire dairy farm, illustrated in J. Binns, *The Agriculture of Lancashire*, 1851. (Redrawn by Phillip Judge) — 114

57. Designs for farms by John Gardner. (Redrawn from originals in Northamptonshire Record Office c/1410, by Phillip Judge) — 119

58. Langton near Spelby, Lincolnshire (Redrawn from *Farmers' Magazine,* **12**, August 1839, by Phillip Judge) — 122

59. Enholmes Farm, Patrington, East Yorkshire. (National Monuments Record, English Heritage) — 123

60. Covered yards at Knapp Farm, Herefordshire as illustrated in the *JRASE* in 1853. — 124

61. John Elliott's entry to The Royal Agricultural Society's farm prize competition as illustrated in the *JRASE* in 1850. — 125

62. Covered yards at Park Farm, Bylaugh, Norfolk. (Michael Williams) — 126

63. Chancellor's plans and elevations for Model Farm, Graffham, Cambridgeshire. (Essex Record Office D/DQn29) — 128

64. Northbrook Farm, Kirtlington, Oxfordshire, from J. B. Denton's *The Farm Homesteads of England*, 1863, plate XX. (By permission, Syndics of Cambridge University Library) — 131

65. Plan of Egmere Farm, Norfolk. (Phillip Judge) — 132

66. Model Farm at Holkham, Norfolk, as illustrated in Deane's *Selected Designs for Country Residences etc.*, 1867. — 133

67. Eastwood Manor Farm at East Harptree, Somerset. (National Monuments Record, English Heritage) — 134–5

68. Home Farm at Apley Park, Shropshire. (Michael Williams) — 136

69. Details of the buildings at Home Farm, Apley Park. (Michael Williams) — 137

70. Olliver Farm, Aske, North Yorkshire. (Michael Williams) — 140

71. The 'poultiggery' at New Horton Grange, Northumberland. (Michael Williams) — 141

72. Block plans of Christopher Turnor's Lincolnshire farms. (Phillip Judge) — 142

73. Christopher Turnor's Lincolnshire farms. (Michael Williams) — 144–5

74. Lower Farm, Millbrook, Bedfordshire. (Michael Williams) — 148–9

75. Beara Farm, Milton Abbot, Devon. (Michael Williams) — 150

76. Block Plan of Kilworthy Farm, Tavistock, Devon. (Phillip Judge) — 150

77. The new farms on the Thorney Level, Cambridgeshire Fens as illustrated by J. B. Denton, 1863, Plate XXI. (By permission, Syndics of Cambridge University Library), with examples of surviving detailing. (Michael Williams) — 152–3

List of figures

78. The map shows the boundaries of the new parish of Exmoor and the farms within it, with a detailed plan of one farmstead, redrawn from the *JRASE* (1856). (Phillip Judge)   154

79. Farmstead at West Sevington, Wiltshire. (Michael Williams)   156

80. The Home Farm at Greystoke, Cumbria. (Michael Williams)   159

81. Whitfield Example Farm, Gloucestershire. (Michael Williams)   161

82. The Dairy Farm, Windsor Park as drawn in Morton's book *The Prince Consort's farms* 1863. (By permission, Syndics of Cambridge University Library)   162

83. Flemish Farm, Windsor, from J. B. Denton, 1864, plate X. (By permission, Syndics of Cambridge University Library)   163–4

84. Shaw Farm, Windsor, illustrated in Deane's book of 1867.   165

85. Mechi Farm, Blennerhassett, Cumbria. (Michael Williams)   166

86. Upper Yatton Farm, Herefordshire. (Michael Williams)   172

87. Redrawing of 'Experimentia' Farm, from the *JRASE*, 1879. (Phillip Judge)   175

88. Professor John Scott's designs for a complete corrugated iron farmstead, from *Text Book of Engineering*, 1885. (By permission, Syndics of Cambridge University Library)   176

89. Scott's three-storied 'American Barn', from *Text Book of Engineering*, 1885. (Redrawn by Phillip Judge)   177

90. Plan from J. P. Sheldon's book *On British Dairying*, 1908. (Redrawn by Phillip Judge)   179

91. Farm buildings at Ferney Lea, Tiverton, Cheshire from a survey of 1790. (Cheshire Record Office DTW 2477/B/27)   180

92. Block plans of some of the Duke of Westminster's farms, designed by John Douglas. (Phillip Judge)   181

93. Plans and elevations of Cheaveley Hall, Huntington, Cheshire. (Redrawn by Phillip Judge with kind permission, from drawings in the Eaton Archives 122M02807)   182

94. Plan and photographs of Saighton Lane Farm, Saighton, Cheshire. (Michael Williams, photography, and Phillip Judge, with kind permission, from drawings in the Eaton archives 122M02152)   184–5

95. Details of farms on the Duke of Westminster's Cheshire estates. (Michael Williams)   186

96. Plans and photographs of The Pines, Little Ponton, Lincolnshire. (Michael Williams, photography and Phillip Judge, drawing.)   187

97. Tramway and stalls at Home Farm, Culford, Suffolk. (Michael Williams)   189

98. The buildings at Tyntesfield, Somerset. (Michael Williams)   190–1

99. Chancellor's drawings for College Farm, Finchley. (Essex Record Office D. F8. A37)   192

100. The buildings at Aston Wold, Northamptonshire. (Michael Williams)   193–4

101. Drawings submitted to the *JRASE* competition of 1908.   195

102. The Ovaltine Dairy Farm, Hertfordshire. (Reading Museum of English
Rural Life, Rural History Centre, University of Reading)   196

103. Water End Farm, Eversholt, Bedfordshire. (Michael Williams)   206

104. The Home Farm at Coleshill, Oxfordshire. (*The Builder*)   218

105. The Home Farm at Longleat, Wiltshire. (*The Builder*)   221

Plates (between pages 114 and 115)

1. Old Hall Farm Betley, Staffordshire. (Michael Williams)

2. Water wheel, Betley. (Michael Williams)

3. Interior of sheds, Betley. (Michael Williams)

4. Barns and stables at Taynton, Gloucestershire. (Michael Williams)

5. Arbour Hill Farm, Hornby, North Yorkshire. (Michael Williams)

6. Barn, Fort Putman, Greystoke, Cumbria. (Michael Williams)

7. Trebartha Barton Farm, Cornwall. (Susanna Wade Martins)

8. Park Farm, Hulne Park, Alnwick, Northumberland. (Michael Williams)

9. Stable block, Croome House Farm, Sledmere, East Yorkshire. (Michael
Williams)

10. The landscape around Belper. (National Monuments Record, English
Heritage)

11. The Great Barn at Holkham. (Michael Williams)

12. Stevens Farm, Chignall, Essex, elevation. (Essex Record Office D/DQn 29)

13. Stevens Farm, Chignall, Essex, plan. (Essex Record Office D/DQn 29)

14. Interior of covered yards, Stevens Farm, Chignall, Essex. (Michael
Williams)

15. Covered yards, Home Farm, Apley Park, Shropshire. (Michael Williams)

16. Olliver Farm, Aske, North Yorkshire. (Michael Williams)

17. Covered yards at Kilworthy Farm, Tavistock, Devon. (Michael Williams)

18. Manure chambers, Kilworthy Farm, Tavistock, Devon. (Michael Williams)

19. Warren Farm, Exmoor, Somerset. (Michael Williams)

20. Dovecot, Cheaveley Hall, Cheshire. (Michael Williams)

21. Aldford Hall, Cheshire. (Michael Williams)

Acknowledgements

A book such as this, which looks at buildings across the whole of England, inevitably relies on help from a wide variety of sources. As a result of appeals in journals and professional publications, many people wrote in with examples of planned and model farms known to them, but some experts were particularly helpful. Dr Edward Peters shared his wide knowledge of the West Midlands and David Neave, his research on East Yorkshire. Local archaeological, conservation and SMR officers set me in the right direction in their areas and took me to some of the sites known to them. Amongst others, Anne Holden in Essex introduced me to the farms of Frederick Chancellor, Ruth Gibson, the farms of the Bedford estate, John Healey those in Cheshire and Ann Bond those of the Duke of Grafton.

Owners, agents and tenants too were also generous with their time, taking me to sites, answering my questions and allowing me to search records. Everywhere I was courteously welcomed and cups of tea and coffee were always generously offered and most welcome. My memories of the response of the farming community to this project will always be a pleasure to me. The photographer, Michael Williams was also given permission to visit many of the finest farms, and it is the co-operation of farmers and owners which has made it possible to illustrate this book so fully.

The work has also involved visits to many record offices, most particularly in Bedford, Chester, Cheshire, Matlock, Shrewsbury, Stafford, Newcastle, Berwick, Essex and North Yorkshire where I was given all the help I needed. The Royal Archives at Windsor and private collections at Alnwick and elsewhere were made available to me, for which I am most grateful.

Dr Judith Appleby has kindly allowed me to quote from her thesis and use some of her illustrations. Nicola Bannister provided information from her unpublished research on the Birdsall estate.

Martin Cherry and Bob Hawkins have read early drafts of this book and given much valued advice. Paul Barnwell and Colum Giles, now with English Heritage but formerly with the Royal Commission for the Historical Monuments of England, gave me access to their farm records in advance of the publication of their book. Andre Berry from the Countryside Agency, and Keith Falconer have also read and commented on the final draft.

Friends at the Centre of East Anglian Studies, University of East Anglia, particularly Dr Tom Williamson and Dr Richard Wilson, have taken an interest in this project and have provided stimulation through our discussions. Despite all the help I have been given, any omissions or shortcomings remain my responsibility.

The photographs were taken by Michael Williams, who always seems to be able to make the sun shine on farm buildings, and the drawings are the work of Phillip Judge.

The book would not have been possible without the interest of Richard Purslow, Publisher at Windgather Press, and the financial support of English Heritage and the Countryside Agency. My particular thanks are due to my editor, Jeremy Lake at English Heritage, who initiated the project, and who has worked so hard on the text, especially during the final, and often tedious stages of its production.

Finally I would like to thank my husband, Peter, who has put up with domestic disruption and cheerfully taken numerous diversions on our regular journeys up the A1 to take in farms on the way.

CHAPTER ONE

Beauty, Utility and Profit

....

'It exactly answers my idea of a fine country house because it unites
beauty with utility'.

Edward Ferrars in Jane Austen, *Sense and Sensibility,* 1811

The planned and model farmsteads of the English countryside provide a lasting
testimony to the role of the landlord in the agricultural revolution of the
eighteenth and nineteenth centuries, when British agriculture led the world.
They are the products of the landlord-tenant system of capitalist farming,
whereby the landlord provided the fixed infrastructure for the farming enterprise, and the tenant worked the farm, providing the stock, seed and machinery.
When Arthur Young remarked, after his travels in France at the end of the
eighteenth century, that 'Banishment alone will force the French to execute
what the English do for pleasure – reside upon and adorn their estates', he was
drawing attention to what was regarded as a uniquely British system.[1] The
strength of this landlord–tenant relationship grew through the eighteenth
century, reached its height in the 'high farming' period of the 1850s and
remained unbroken until the onset of depression from the 1870s leading to the
great land sales after the First World War. As models for technical innovation
and the improvement of estates, designed to encourage tenants and enhance
the social standing of agricultural pursuits, farmsteads demonstrate the 'spirit
of the age' as manifest through their planning and design. They also reflect
a diversity of motives and philosophies, from the ideals of the gentlemen
intellectuals of the eighteenth-century Enlightenment, who aspired to the unity
of beauty and utility in ordered and cultivated landscapes, to the conflicting
aims of nineteenth-century Romantics and Utilitarians. It is the aim of this
book to look at these exemplary structures and consider the motives behind
their construction, their intended use and relationship to farming progress.

Model farmsteads were consciously built and planned as complete units,
whether to the designs of architects, engineers, landlords or their agents. For
present purposes, a model farm is defined as a steading built for a landowner
who wanted to set an example to the tenantry on his estate and society at
large, invariably in addition to satisfying his own taste for classical or picturesque buildings. The origin of the term 'model farm' is not clear, and does
not appear to have been used until the mid-nineteenth century when it was
applied to new buildings built as home farms or exemplary tenant farms on
estates. Here the latest techniques would be displayed to impress both the

tenantry and the owner's friends, often enhanced by the work of an architect of national or regional repute. Other planned farmsteads were built for tenants along more purely functional lines as part of enclosure or land reclamation schemes, often in association with the schools and cottages that form part of distinctive estate landscapes. Sometimes they incorporate an earlier barn, but in contrast to the great majority of other estate farmsteads, their creation was invariably seen as part of a total reordering of the agricultural landscape. The fact that these farmsteads were usually built on large estates, by well-run estate offices, means that documentation revealing the thinking behind them often survives, enabling our understanding of the buildings themselves to be greater than is often possible elsewhere.

The period of the traditional agricultural revolution (*c.* 1740–1870), of which these farmsteads were very much a part, was probably the period of most rapid agricultural change before the late-twentieth century. By the mid-eighteenth century rising rent levels, particularly on enclosed land, was stimulating a desire for 'improvement', encouragement for which was coming from the very top of society. George III saw agriculture, 'that greatest of all manufactures', as 'beyond doubt the foundation of every other art, business and profession'.[2] This movement for change also had its propagandist authors, among the most prolific of whom were Arthur Young, William Marshall and Nathaniel Kent, who travelled the country writing of what they saw and making sometimes exaggerated claims of the profits that could be made as a result of these changes.

The phrase 'capable of improvement', which frequently occurs in estate surveys of the 1780s and 1790s, is strongly indicative of the almost moral sense of purpose – rather than purely any cost-benefit analysis – which motivated many landowners in their efforts to exploit their estates' potential to the full. Agricultural propagandists saw untilled land as waste where human labour could restore the beauty and order of Eden. John Houghton saw Hampstead Heath as a 'barren wilderness in urgent need of cultivation'. Arthur Young wanted to bring the 'waste lands of the kingdom into cultivation and to cover them with turnips, corn and clover instead of lyng.'[3] In 1774, Thomas De Grey, managing the dry Breckland estates in Norfolk for his brother, wrote that the 'great expense [of land reclamation] would but ill answer, unless there was real satisfaction in employing labourers and bringing forth a ragged dirty parish to a neatness of cultivation.'[4] This was not a question of putting utility before beauty. A productive landscape *was* beautiful. God had created the land 'to the end that it should by culture and husbandry, yield things necessary for man's life'. Cultivation was a symbol of civilisation whereas 'wild and vacant lands', 'encumbered with bushes and briars' were like 'deformed chaos'.[5] The pastoral setting of many of the Bible stories also promoted the image of farming as a virtuous occupation. The Earl-Bishop of Derry wrote to the agricultural commentator, Arthur Young, 'I love agriculture because it makes good citizens, good husbands, good fathers, good children; because it does not leave time to plunder, and because it bereaves him of temptation'.[6]

Furthermore, the pursuit of agricultural progress, particularly in times of war, was increasingly regarded as a patriotic as well as profitable occupation. Writing as early as 1699 Lord Belhaven stressed the humanitarian and patriotic duty of agriculture. 'The scarcities of the previous few years ... I must impute in part to our great neglect of Husbandrie ... so it ought to be an Incitement to all those whom God hath blessed with Estates to Double their Diligence in the Improvement of their Grounds'. He asserted that good and productive farming would both help to keep starvation at bay and render foreign wars unnecessary; 'Husbandrie enlarges a Countrie and makes it as if ye have conquered an other Countrie adjacent thereto. And I am sure a conquest by the Spade and the Plough is both more just and of longer continuance than what is got by Sword and Bow'.[7] It was, moreover, an insurance against the threat of famine, which was still seen as a real possibility into the eighteenth century. Whilst the famine that devastated parts of Scotland in 1697 and 1699 was the last to occur on the British mainland there were certainly periods of savage dearth in the 1730s and early 1740s, marked by a combination of poor harvests, bitter weather and cattle disease. Finally, the Napoleonic scarcities and the potato famine of 1846–7 provided a salutary reminder of how easily famine could re-emerge.

The Enlightenment literature that served to promote this unity of beauty and utility drew heavily on the writers of classical antiquity.[8] Foremost amongst these was Virgil, who in his *Georgics* advocated their patriotic combination of beauty and utility. Land ownership and commerce were regarded as operating within a strict, but benevolent social hierarchy.[9] In his down-to-earth way, the agricultural and political agitator, William Cobbett could also pronounce, 'I have no idea of picturesque beauty separated from the fertility of the soil'.[10] Similarly, at Raby Castle (see pp. 51–3), Arthur Young described Lord Darlington's home farm within the parkland landscape in glowing terms. Not only was the view of it across the valley 'very fine', but more practically the buildings worked well. 'All his cattle are tethered in the winter, producing a vast quantity of dung. The liquid manure is run off into a cistern'. The language of the landscape designer and modernising farmer were thus juxtaposed in the same paragraph.[11] Young was not alone amongst the agricultural writers to express an aesthetic as well as a farming interest. The same mixture of sentiments can be found in many of the county *General Views* commissioned by the Board of Agriculture from the 1790s as well as contributors to Arthur Young's *Annals of Agriculture* such as Thomas Ruggles.[12] Ruggles was not only a Suffolk landowner-magistrate with great concerns for the plight of the poor who, between 1793 and 1794 wrote a *History of the Poor,* but also an enthusiastic tree planting landowner. He wrote regularly on the subject of 'picturesque farming'.[13] He described in glowing terms 'The farm yard on a winter's evening, when the threshers are closing their barns, and the cribs are filled with provender for cattle, which, whilst feasting themselves are producing a source of future plenty ... A well-appointed homestall exhibits such a sense of rural comfort and plenty as might excite the sluggard to labour'.[14] The farmyard, he said, must be in the most convenient place and surrounded by useful and necessary buildings. 'Use and convenience must in this department be allowed to take the lead of taste'.[15]

Many eighteenth-century landlords, their architects and landscape gardeners could thus choose to emphasise their systematic and planned attitude to estate management as one that regarded the rural landscape as the repository of virtue. Others, especially those conscious that expensive schemes might never pay for themselves in increased rents, placed more emphasis on their purely functional qualities. The tension between the desire for architectural display and the functional and economic viability of buildings is clearly reflected in the exhortations of the land agent and virtual founder of the profession, Nathaniel Kent. He recommended owners 'not to build anything that is not really useful',[16] thus reflecting the views of those charged with running their employers' estates at a profit. At Windsor, where he was employed by George III to reorganise the Great Park, he used recycled materials from existing buildings for his rebuilt farmsteads. Both beauty and profit were served by his proposals for proper management of the trees and the rationalisation of the arable, to which George III readily concurred. In his *Journal* Kent wrote critically of the trees deprived of their beauty because of lack of management and the impractical patches of arable scattered through the park 'intersecting the fine views'.[17] Francis Blaikie, the agent to the publicity-conscious Holkham estate in Norfolk in the early years of the nineteenth century, was typical of his profession in his efforts to restrain his employer from extravagant schemes.[18] In contrast, at Alnwick it was the Duke of Northumberland himself who set down a list of criteria for the building of new farmsteads on his estates. In the terms of the appointment of his estate architect, David Stephenson, in 1806, he stated that all new plans should be approved by him personally and expenditure on new buildings coinciding with the granting of a new lease should not exceed five years' increase in rent.[19]

Georgian commentators invariably wrote for an aristocratic audience to whom deference was due, a fact reflected in the tone of their writing and the dedications of their books to their patrons. Whilst many landlords, however, were interested in agricultural improvement, and indeed regarded it as a patriotic and moral duty, there were certainly others who neglected their estates. Copland wrote in 1866: 'If the landlords knew their own interest, and cared for that of their tenants, they would not neglect making permanent improvements. But the indifference they display ... affords little prospect [of this]'.[20] As the increasing complexity of land agents' work made them indispensable to their employers they became more outspoken in their opinions. Writing in 1862 specifically about home farms, Mr Browick, the agent at Stoneleigh (Warwickshire), commented, 'model homesteads, although to be met with in most counties, are not essential to the system. They are all very well in their own way, but ... rather let the estate bear a quiet and unassuming aspect, its buildings being plain but sufficient ... neatness and order should alike prevail'.[21] The agricultural engineer, George Andrews, wrote that farmers were generally against model farmsteads as they associated them with 'the practices of those gentlemen who, having pockets which overflow with wealth derived from other sources, erect the most costly places imaginable, and carry on their agricultural operation regardless of the great question whether it will pay or not.'[22] These contemporary views of model farmsteads have also been echoed by modern scholars. To Stuart Macdonald they were 'essentially a fashion, and exhibited the characteristics typical of a fashion in that they were expensive, trivial and ultimately ephemeral. At no time was the model farm of any great significance as a means of influencing even the effective innovative leaders'.[23]

Some model farmsteads fell into this category, but the historical importance of the building type as a whole and the innovative spirit which it represented must not be underestimated. The survival of many examples into modern times is an indication of their practicality and adaptability as well as their architectural merit. They demonstrated the potency of landed wealth, whether inherited or acquired through the fruits of industry and commerce, and the diverse motives of their builders. Just as the Georgian farmsteads with their classical proportions epitomised the aspirations of the Whig landowners who built them, so the monumental, flamboyant and optimistic designs of the Victorians attest to the triumph of the new industrial age. They formed the back-cloth to such publicity stunts for improved agriculture as the Holkham and Woburn sheep shearings and so helped to give interest in agricultural improvement the high profile which it achieved in Britain uniquely amongst European countries. Later examples were widely illustrated both in professional journals such as *The Builder* and the *Journal of the Royal Agricultural Society*, and in the more widely read *London Illustrated News*.

The increase of mechanisation and other labour-saving techniques, in addition to the scientific understanding of livestock and fertilisers, can all be followed through the changing design of planned and model farmsteads (Figure 1). Ideas on appropriate types of shelter for animals, in order to promote their speedy fattening for market and the conservation of manure, had developed in tandem over the 150 years after 1750. At their most sophisticated, as used around 1850 on the Duke of Bedford's Devon estates and the Earl of Radnor's farmstead at Coleshill (p. 127), they did not find general acceptance for another hundred years. Ideas promoting the efficient flow of goods and materials, first developed in the textile industry and applied to farm building design by Arthur Young in his text book of 1770[24] (see Figure 17), also assumed greater importance. They were developed, for example, on the farmsteads that were built by the Strutt family to supply food for the workers in their Derbyshire textile factories (see pp. 168). Schemes involving water, steam and wind-powered barn machinery, as well as tram lines for transporting stacks and feed, were all pioneered from estate offices by ingenious agents such as Robert Salmon at Woburn and architects such as Samuel Wyatt at Shugborough and elsewhere from the 1790s. New building materials, such as concrete and cast-iron and laminated timber trusses, alongside new uses for old ones such as slate, were also first applied to farmstead design by estates and their architects and agents. Some proved to be impractical, but it was only wealthy landlords who could afford to make these experiments and so help push forward the frontiers of agricultural engineering, thus encouraging

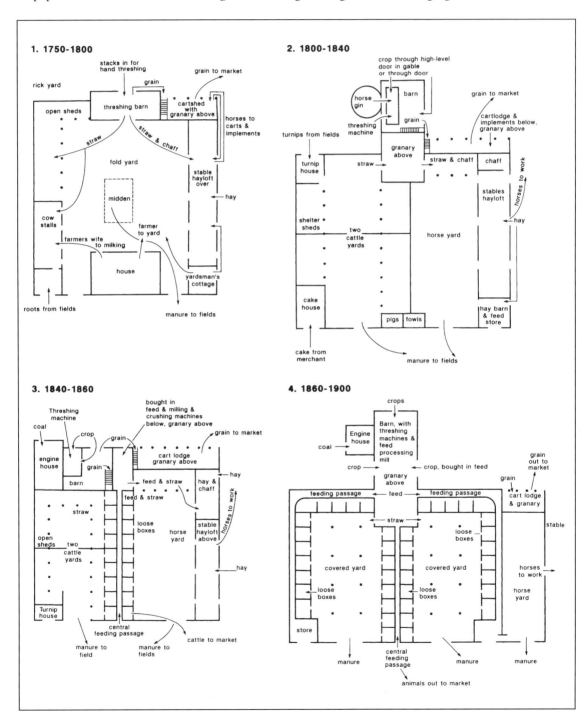

an increasingly scientific approach to agriculture. If many ideas were not taken up by contemporaries because of their high expense and the onset of agricultural depression in the 1870s, the upsurge of demand from the 1950s has ensured that many innovations, submerged for over seventy years, have reappeared.

FIGURE 1 (*opposite*). **The development of farmstead layout, 1750–1900.**

All farm buildings have certain basic functions, the first being the provision of shelter for animals and the produce of the farm. Secondly, they provide the means of processing that crop either by removing the grain from the stalk ready for sale or preparing fodder for livestock. Thirdly, and of increasing importance, was the role of the farmyard as a factory for the production of manure, before it was spread on the fields.

1. 1750–1800.

A courtyard plan with the house on one side and barn opposite with stables and livestock sheds down either side, often with a midden in the middle.

Here the house was very much part of the farmyard and was placed centrally with the end walls of the stables and shelter sheds forming matching frontages on either side. The threshing barn formed the north side of the yard and was used for hand threshing. The farm relied on manpower rather than machinery and home-produced animal feed and manure for the fields.

2. 1800–1840.

'E'-shaped plan, often with a barn at right-angles to the long range.

Mechanisation, using horse, water or steam power was increasingly part of the plan. The barn was frequently placed outside the main range and at right angles, so as to allow for the power source to be alongside it. The livestock buildings still needed to be connected with the barn as they relied on the waste products (straw and chaff) for bedding and feed. Livestock yards were now divided up to allow for the fattening of smaller groups of cattle. Although some feed and artificial fertiliser was being bought in, farmyard manure and home-grown fodder crops were still of major importance. As the farmer's lifestyle became more affluent, his house was likely to be a short distance away from the buildings.

3. 1840–60.

The Industrial Farmstead.

As imported feeds became more important, farm machinery was used not only to thresh corn, but to prepare feed, and feed processing was located at one end of the barn. Yards were divided up to allow for more individual feeding of stock. Advances in the methods of livestock fattening coupled with an understanding of the advantages of protecting manure from the rain meant that covered yards and loose boxes became standard in model farmstead design.

4. 1860 onwards.

The livestock and dairy farmstead.

The improved standards of living and the drop in cereal prices after 1870 meant that model farmstead designers concentrated more on livestock and dairying. More loose boxes were incorporated in the design and covered yards became universal. Feed preparation took over from other barn functions. Increased labour shortages and costs encouraged the search for labour-saving layouts and devices such as tramlines to move feed about.

CHAPTER TWO

Landlords, Tenants and the Farming Framework

....

> He gave it as his opinion, that whoever can make two
> ears of corn or two blades of grass grow upon a spot of
> ground where only one grew before, would deserve better
> of mankind and do more essential service to his country
> than the whole race of politicians put together.
>
> Jonathan Swift, *Gulliver's Travels*, 1726

In this quotation, we have one of the earliest literary references to the high regard in which the improvement of farming was held. Swift could well have had in mind his contemporary 'Turnip' Townshend who, even while a Secretary of State, was developing his estates in Norfolk and encouraging his tenant farmers – activities for which he is perhaps better remembered than his political career.[1] On all but the best soils, the yeomen and farmers who relied entirely on farming for their income could not afford to try new ideas until their viability had been proved beyond doubt by others. As Arthur Young advised, it was invariably to the gentry and greater landowners that they looked for this guidance: 'let the landlords try experiments, and if, a few years prove them to answer, the tenant will adopt them'.[2] 'Thus, through the efforts of country gentlemen first and foremost, initiatives were taken to spread innovations to the end of the realm'.[3]

Landlords such as Townshend, usually classically educated and often well travelled, were in control of much of the rebuilding and reorganisation of the countryside. Planned and model farms began to appear in increasing numbers through the eighteenth century, coinciding with a period of sharp decline of the small owner-occupier farmers and the consolidation of the landed estates whose owners were determined to capitalise on rising agricultural prices. The Act of Settlement of 1688 had enshrined the power of property, and the strict entailing of estates ensured that they were passed from generation to generation largely intact. Political stability, colonial expansion and with it mercantile wealth, as well as industrial and agricultural development, combined to sustain an enormous increase of between 40 and 50% in the wealth and disposable income of the gentry and aristocracy during the eighteenth century. By 1790 there was a group of about 400 great English landowners with incomes of over £10,000 a year who probably owned up to a fifth of the cultivated area of England and Wales. Below this were about 800 families, mainly baronets, but some knights and untitled gentry with incomes of between £10,000 and £3,000 a year. Lesser gentry with incomes of between £1,000 and £3,000 a year were much more numerous.[4] This wealth could be derived from military or naval service, political office, coal mines, industry, trade and plantations as well as from agriculture, and allowed landowners, both old-established families and newcomers, to construct fine country houses in increasing numbers and take a leisured interest in farming.[5]

The development of land tenure

One of the important differences which distinguishes medieval from later farming systems is the way in which land was held, and this in turn had a direct influence on the landscape and its buildings. As the hold of the landowner over the land became more secure, the division of responsibility for the provision of capital was becoming formalised. It was the duty of the landlord to provide the fixed capital in the form of farm buildings and farm layout, and of the tenant to provide the working capital for the farm as well as maintaining the land and buildings.

Until well into the sixteenth century most tenures were based on systems developed directly from feudalism. Money rents had replaced services, but the degree of security of tenure on the one hand, or control that the receiver of the rent had over the land on the other, was often unclear. This, coupled with the communal rights over commons and some open-field systems, meant that the influence of the landlord over his tenants was limited. Whilst this was the case, developments in agricultural techniques were associated with the farmers rather than the landlords, and the seventeenth and early-eighteenth centuries were the period sometimes identified as the 'yeoman revolution'.[6] By the nineteenth century all this had changed. The majority of farms were held under fixed term leases which often stipulated the type of agriculture practised. Farmers were expected to follow a rotation, they were not to plough up pasture, reduce the potential fertility of the land by selling manure, or the capacity of the land to carry stock by selling hay. The duties of landlords as providers of necessary buildings and tenants as to their maintenance were laid down. Most common rights had also been eliminated, often, but not always associated with the enclosure of land. The landowner's control was almost complete, and thus the changing shape of the countryside and its buildings over much of the estate-dominated part of Britain could be determined by him.

As part of these changes, agriculture was becoming more commercial. In the years up to 1870 Britain was normally self-sufficient in grain in spite of the fact that its population had increased by 6.5 million over the previous hundred years, a testament to increasing productivity and commercial organis-ation. It has been estimated that in the early-sixteenth century 80% of farmers were only growing enough for the needs of their families, whilst by 1850 the majority were farming for the market.[7] London, whose population increased by 70% between 1650 and 1750, and London prices, dominated the market. *The Mark Lane Express* published the prices paid at the London Corn Exchange and with the increase in provincial papers from the early-eighteenth century, these figures would be quoted nationally. The grain trade by sample began in London in the 1720s and was general by the 1750s. However, even if the trade was by sample, the main crop still had to transported off the farm, and access to good roads or waterways was of the first importance. The rent of a farm could be affected by its distance from a good road, and road building was one of the improvements expected of a landowner. The increasing sophistication of marketing during the seventeenth century meant that the role of middlemen and merchants who bought by sample had gained in importance. By the middle of the eighteenth century the great merchant house of Coutts Brothers had been founded on the grain trade and employed agents to make purchases in Northumberland and five Scottish counties. A transport system based initially on coastal traffic and improved inland waterways meant that a national market (defined as one that reacted fairly evenly to price movements) was 'strongly emergent' by 1750.[8]

Similarly droving was becoming increasingly highly organised, as more and more cattle were driven south as stores to be fattened in yards and stalls and then moved on to Smithfield for final sale. In the 1840s prices at Smithfield could be twice those at a provincial market, and this motivated farmers to send cattle there; for example, droves of cattle went down to London every week from Norwich. The coming of the railways opened up London to a national supply of meat. The Norfolk farmer, John Hudson, claimed that his beasts had lost 28 pounds in weight on the walk to London, and sheep seven. With the railway the journey was completed in less than a day with no loss.[9] Inevitably, farms near a railway line were now at an advantage and so would command high rents, especially if they could partake in the London milk trade as well. One of Frederick Chancellor's finest farms was built for the Express Dairy Company in the 1880s on the edge of London (see Figure 99).

The speed of change varied greatly across the country, but the decline of customary tenancies in favour of leasehold, the establishment of private property rights replacing communal systems, and the development of individualistic commercial farming were all radical developments in the conditions under which farming was carried out. All of them could increase the influence and control that the landlord had over farming as well as providing him with a financial incentive for improvement, through the possibility of increasing rents on successful commercial ventures. Although there is little doubt that this change began some time after 1550 and was completed by 1850, accurate estimates on a national scale are more difficult. Research in specific areas of the country suggests that a landlord-tenant system was already usual in some areas by the late-eighteenth century, but in others, particularly on the pastoral fringes, it was not.[10] Generally, however, the change was well under way by the late-seventeenth and early-eighteenth centuries. It is from then that landlords became more involved in the overall running of their estate as distinct from their demesne (or home) farms.

Increases in estate size

Although the years of the Commonwealth did not result in a revolution in landholding, and most Royalists were able to claim their lands back after the Cromwellian confiscations, many were heavily in debt and some forced to sell. The period 1660–1760 was conducive to the accumulation of medium and large-scale estates. Rents, land and agricultural prices were low, encouraging smaller owners to sell to those who were making money through government office, law or commerce, and needed land to increase their prestige. Strict settlements, preventing the break-up of estates, were more likely to affect large rather than smallholdings, again encouraging the already existing trend.[11] It was the larger estates which were more likely to have money to invest and so this trend too, alongside the formalisation of conditions of tenure, would encourage increased landlord capital going in to land improvements.

There is agreement that there was an increase in estate size during the 300 years from 1550 to 1850, but the extent and precise dating of the change is difficult to ascertain. Statistics are unreliable, but it has been suggested that at the end of the seventeenth-century landowners of over 10,000 acres controlled about 20 per cent of the cultivated land. By 1870, this had only increased to 24 per cent. The number of estates of under 300 acres was in decline. In the middle category of owners of 300–10,000 acres there was almost certainly an increase in the proportion held by those towards the top of this band. However, it is clear that changes were in the form of a gradual drift towards larger land holdings, rather than a major landslide.[12]

These generalisations hide great regional differences even within single counties. By 1850, for example, a contrast between the small, mainly dairy farmers of the Vale of Gloucester and the larger arable holdings of the Cotswolds was obvious.[13] Similarly, Caird commented of Devon, 'There are two classes of farmers in the county, one consisting of men with small holdings, little elevated above the condition of the labourer, the other of educated agriculturalists holding large farms, into which they have introduced improved methods of husbandry.'[14] Other areas of small dairy and mainly pastoral farms on heavier lands include the classic 'ancient landscapes'.[15] These included north and west Wiltshire, where 'green fields with lofty hedgerow trees, winding roads … succeed each other for miles along its [the Avon] fertile valley',[16] the areas of small, early enclosed fields over much of south Norfolk and central Suffolk and the Weald of Kent and Sussex. These farms, often controlled by small 'manorial' estates, were in close proximity to the recently enclosed farms on the lighter soils of south Wiltshire, north-west Norfolk and the South Downs.

The security of a long lease could provide the necessary stability to encourage the tenant to embark on a long term programme of land improvement, whilst husbandry covenants were designed to encourage the use of innovative rotations and prevent bad practice. Leases were sometimes seen as instrumental in improvement. Arthur Young, for instance, saw them as a mainstay of 'Norfolk Agriculture'[17] and Nathaniel Kent wrote, 'Leases are the first, the greatest and most rational encouragement that can be given to agriculture'.[18] In Cumberland, one of the main reasons for the great improvements in agriculture in the forty years after 1770 was thought to be the granting of 21 year leases, 'by which means the tenants of capital were encouraged to make those great exertions from which such advantages have resulted ... from the very increased produce, and the superiority of its quality'.[19] By the mid-nineteenth century commentators were more cautious. James Caird thought that leases were needed to bind bad farmers, not good ones,[20] and more recent historians have tended to follow this line, arguing that leases often did little more than enforce local conventions.[21]

No such doubts were voiced by contemporaries over the providing of the infrastructure for improved farming, in the form of a well laid-out farm of enclosed fields with the house and buildings suitably placed for the working of the land. Arthur Young regarded this as the most important function of the landlord.[22] The most expensive and significant improvement was enclosure, and the work of the owners in the Yorkshire and Lincolnshire Wolds was commented upon by the authors of the county surveys, published by the Board of Agriculture. Of the Sledmere estate in East Yorkshire (see pp. 85–90) an observer wrote, 'in the short space of thirty years [Sykes has] set such an example to other owners of land, as has caused what was a bleak and barren tract of country to become one of the most productive and best cultivated districts in the county of York'.[23] A frieze in Sledmere Hall illustrates this work of improvement and shows the high esteem in which such endeavours were held. Enclosure had an immediate effect on rent levels, which, providing that there were tenants available, could bring a return on landlord investment of between fifteen and twenty per cent.[24] In Northumberland, rents on many estates more than trebled between 1770 and 1813.[25] Following on enclosure, good buildings, including good houses, would help attract as tenants the 'men of capital' that every landlord was looking for. He knew that the prosperity of the estate, and thus the level of rents that could be expected, really depended on the calibre of tenant rather than any restrictions which might be imposed in leases.

It is impossible to assess the importance of tenant pressure rather than landlord initiative in new building, but there is some evidence to suggest that it was not insignificant. The Duke of Northumberland was well aware that requests for new building often came from the tenant. He made it clear in the terms of the appointment of the estate architect in 1806 that 'whenever it becomes necessary to build a wholly new homestead, the architect, the bailiff of the district and *the tenant of the farm* [author's italics] shall have a consultation whether the whole site is in the properist place for its renewal or whether the general and material interests of my estate may not be benefited by its removal to a more proper site'.[26] At Holkham, the agent Francis Blaikie was anxious to dissuade the tenants from asking for expensive buildings: 'It would be greatly to the advantage of the tenant as well as the landlord, and much to the credit of the former if they would condescend to be guided by the sound advise that I give them in regard to their buildings on their farms.'[27] It is noticeable, moreover, that the provision of farm buildings came way down the lists of improvements advocated by the journalist/land agents such as Nathaniel Kent, William Marshall and those authors who compiled the county reports for the Board of Agriculture, with often no more than a page devoted to them. Of the land agent/journalists, only Arthur Young published a farm design of his own[28] (see Figure 16).

The provision of land drainage had arguably the greatest influence on landscape change from the late-eighteenth century, bringing large areas of bog into cultivation. The drainage of the Marquis of Stafford's estates is described by James Loch in his book published in 1820. His work in Kinnersley and Weald Moors in Staffordshire resulted in the creation of arable land for the newly created neighbouring farms of Dayhouse, Crudgington Leasowes and Tibberton Grange (see pp. 90–4). The regular field boundaries and straight roads such as the Duke's Drive leading back to his residence at Lilleshall are evidence of this activity. Digging drains and the filling of them with stones and bush to allow water to percolate through into them and then down to a main drain, was heavy, labour intensive work, made easier by the introduction of machine-made clay pipe drains in the 1840s. Field drainage within the farm was often a tenant's responsibility until the mid-nineteenth century, but with the introduction of pipe drainage and the availability of government loans, it became a long-term investment which was carried out by the landlord, who in some cases was able to charge the tenant 5% interest on the cost of the work.

After drainage, the land needed deep ploughing, marling (or claying) and liming, evidence for which can be seen in the many marl pits and lime kilns to be found on the early editions of Ordnance Survey maps. The expense of this might also be split between landlord and tenant. The result was that huge tracts previously dominated by heath and rushes were brought into cultivation. However, much of this land was not ideally suited to cultivation, and as grain prices fell after 1870, drains were not cleaned and liming ceased, resulting in reversion to a more natural state, although still within the regular boundaries created by the improvers.

The process of agricultural improvement was very much one of partnership, and the role of the tenant must not be underestimated.[29] Once the landlord had provided the infrastructure, it was up to the tenant to make what he could of his farm. The implementation of new husbandry methods, the purchase of good stock, feed and fertilisers as well as machinery were his responsibility. An analysis of the *General Views* would suggest that a county's farming might be led by about 60–70 'professional farmers', most of whom would be tenants. These were the 'men of capital' required by the landowners to work the newly enclosed farms and pay the greatly increased rents. They men were literate, experimental and astute businessmen who established themselves in county society. As a class they were very much a creation of the agricultural revolution and differed from the sort of men who farmed the open fields.[30]

Landlords and 'improvement'

The position of landowners as leaders in agricultural change was always emphasised by writers on agricultural matters, at least until the early-nineteenth century – after all their livelihood depended on the patronage of the gentry who were the main purchasers of their books. Landowners were reported as amateur scientists, observing and experimenting on their home farms, and their activities spearheaded an increasingly scientific approach to agriculture. The pages of the *Annals of Agriculture,* published from 1784 are full of its subscribers' often bizarre findings and results. With a few notable exceptions, it was not so much members of the peerage who were significant contributors to the progress of agriculture, but rather the gentry, substantial owner-occupiers and larger tenants. However, the *Annals'* proprietor and editor, Arthur Young, was always disappointed by its limited sales, and patronising contrast between the 'illiterate husbandman' and 'scientific farmer' was one noted by another agricultural commentator, William Marshall.[31] The few aristocratic representatives of the 'landed interest' such as Lord Somerville and Earl Spencer lamented the limited interest taken by those they termed 'ordinary farmers' in reading .[32] Only a minority of farmers had the time to indulge in academic pursuits, although analysis of the authorship and readership of the first 25 volumes of Young's *Annals* suggests that Young was unnecessarily pessimistic. There were 316 different contributors and a readership of perhaps 3000 – a not insubstantial number of 'progressive agriculturalists of substantial means, which must have extended beyond the 2000 owners of more than 3000 acres which made up the landed gentry and aristocracy', to the 'farming interest' across Britain'.[33]

Britain was unique in the proliferation of its clubs and learned societies through the eighteenth century, all of which played a critical role in the diffusion of new technologies at the highest social levels. Clubs such as the Lunar Society were crucial as forums for discussion between the early inventors and entrepreneurs of the industrial revolution. Samuel Wyatt, the architect-friend of Matthew Boulton whose contacts also ensured his contribution to estate architecture (see below, pp. 58–62), dined there. Agriculture too was served by its societies and their membership was dominated by the landed interest. The Royal Dublin Society for 'Improving Husbandry, Manufacture and other Useful Arts' was founded in 1731, its members being expected to choose a particular subject for study and experimentation and then report back to the society. The membership of the Royal Society of Arts, after its foundation in 1756 was, in the early years, very concerned with farming matters. Its membership was mainly drawn from landowners, who were themselves involved in the establishing of local agricultural societies. One of the earliest of these was the Bath and West, founded in 1777, whose meetings were held in and around the fashionable spa resort. As one of its members wrote, 'Let agriculture be studied by gentlemen of landed property, on philosophic principles; let it be taught to their tenants; and the happy consequence will soon be apparent throughout this island'.[34] By 1800 there were few counties without some kind of organisation for agricultural improvement.[35] With 35 such societies in 1800, the number had grown to 95 by 1835 and mushroomed to 700 by 1855.[36] The Royal Agricultural Society, founded in 1839, was also dominated by the landed interest: so much so that the London Farmers' Club was founded in 1842 as a specific forum for farmers themselves. Many of the new institutions founded in the 1840s and 1850s were clubs rather than societies. These clubs were of a local nature, often serving a group of parishes rather than a county and drawing their membership from farmers rather than landowners. They were more ephemeral in nature, many of them only surviving for a few years and amalgamating or coming to an end in the farming depression after 1870.

The role of the landlord in promoting agricultural change has been much debated by historians. Traditionally, it has been the key role of men such as Charles, second Viscount ('Turnip') Townshend of Raynham and Thomas William Coke of Holkham (both in Norfolk) which has been stressed.[37] However, as more evidence from smaller estates becomes available, it is clear that these great names were merely some amongst a great number of smaller, less well known and documented landowners.[38] Much of the evidence for the great landowners as improvers comes either from their own writings or those seeking to influence them, and there is no doubt that their role has been exaggerated in the past, even in those regions most strongly associated with the large estates. For example, as early as 1787, William Marshall, writing of Norfolk as 'the cradle of the Agricultural Revolution', acknowledged the importance of the independent yeomanry, stating that 'In East Norfolk alone we are to look for that regular and long established practice which has raised deservedly the name of Norfolk husbandmen'.[39] The east of the county contained the best soils and was occupied by small owners and farmers who operated outside the boundaries of the large estates. Good soils had made them prosperous and given them the freedom to experiment, even though this was often within an open field context. New seeds were adopted and crops introduced. Similarly much of Suffolk, away from the light western soils, was dominated by a rich yeomanry – 'a most valuable set of men, who, having the means and the most powerful inducements to good husbandry, carry agriculture to a high degree of perfection'.[40] Their farms, mostly sited within old enclosed fields on the clay soils, were surrounded by thick hedges where both pasture and arable were important. They were characterised by substantial yeoman houses, with large multi-functional buildings behind to house and thresh their grain as well as to shelter their livestock. As yields increased in the eighteenth century, the animals were moved out into new buildings and the area of the barn extended. On the edge of the grazing marshes of the Norfolk Broads bullock sheds to house both cattle and their feed in the form of turnips were built. These expensive buildings for intensive fattening impressed William Marshall greatly when he visited the area in the 1780s.[41] These are the type of farmers described by Robert Allan as partakers in the 'Yeoman Revolution' which considerably raised output before the main period of enclosure and landlord investment in their estates.[42]

Important progress could therefore be made on naturally good soils by intelligent farmers practising the new techniques being recommended in the growing library of agricultural text books. On poorer soils, however, more capital intensive land improvement in the form of draining and marling was needed if the owners were to take advantage of increasing prices at the end of the eighteenth century. It is with the enclosure of these soils and their reclamation that landowners were primarily concerned. This is as true on the light soils of west Norfolk described by Marshall in 1787 as 'open sheep walks, extensive heaths …; or newly enclosed country, in which no general plan of management has yet taken place',[43] as over much of the wolds, moors and fen further north. By 1820, the picture had changed dramatically, with the creation of the 'planned landscapes' so vividly described by Rackham.[44] Regular fields, hawthorn hedges or drystone walls, well-laid out isolated new farmsteads and impressive houses designed to attract the men of capital needed to farm these hungry soils had sprung up over much of eastern England.

There is no doubt that landlord involvement varied greatly from estate to estate. Nevertheless, some landlords and their agents did indeed see themselves as able, and indeed duty bound, to remodel the economic and social fabric as well as the landscape of their properties. Power could be displayed through 'improvement'. Initially the term was mainly applied to agricultural reorganisation through enclosure, but by the end of the eighteenth century it covered not only a variety of progressive farm practices and parkland development, but also had gained wider social and moral connotations.[45] There were, indeed, those of a traditional Tory persuasion with romantic sensibility towards the idea of rural continuity who were opposed to a narrowly commercial approach to the countryside.[46] For others, a commercial approach was a matter of survival, as with the royalist supporters exiled during the Commonwealth who had come back to impoverished estates with ideas gained from what they had seen in Flanders, where heathland had been improved by crop rotations. 'When books were read by gentlemen and parsons then only the first step had been taken towards transferring theories into practice. Their continuing spread depended upon gentlemen instructing, or bullying, their stewards and bailliffs and – less often no doubt – prevailing upon their tenants. The home farms of the gentry were the spearheads of agricultural improvement'.[47]

The role of the agent

Employed by this band of enthusiastic landowners were members of the emerging profession of land agents. Although the more canny of the landowners might have been wise to follow the advice given to his son by Henry Percy, ninth Duke of Northumberland, to 'understand your estates better than any of your officers',[48] there is no doubt that the importance of agents increased greatly during the eighteenth century. One of the first books for their guidance was that published by Edward Laurence in 1727. It was originally intended for the 'tenants and stewards of the Duke of Buckingham' and laid down 'general rules and directions for the management and improvement of a farm.'[49] The book describes how 'the art of husbandry is of late years greatly improved', but admits that there is a great discrepancy between developments on the best and worst managed estates. Laurence considered that small farms were not suited to the large-scale and expensive draining and liming that was necessary before new forms of husbandry could be adopted. Amalgamation was a slow business as it was only possible when farms fell in hand, 'for it would raise too great an odium to turn poor families into the wide world by uniting farms all at once'.[50] Laurence illustrates a Herefordshire farm in a bend of the River Wye. The irregular shape of the fields, enclosed by thick hedges and including two orchards suggests early enclosure. The buildings are in the centre of the farm and although loosely grouped around a court are of an unplanned layout.

Certainly agents were likely to take a more utilitarian attitude to farm building than the architects seeking the patronage of the gentry. One of the first such men was Nathaniel Kent, who had started his working life as a minor government official in Brussells. In the late 1760s he began to find work in East Anglia, advising on land improvements, and set up the first firm of land agents in London with his nephews William Pearce and John Claridge. They were responsible for producing elegantly bound and extremely detailed surveys of several Yorkshire estates such as those at Harewood and of the Earl of Egremont with suggestions for improvement.[51] Kent's reputation was enhanced by his publication in 1775 of *Hints to Gentlemen of Landed Property.*

In 1791 he took on the prestigious task of reclamation and remodelling of Windsor Great Park for George III. His belief in improved management for 'beauty and profit' was a theme echoed by others following this new profession. When William Young, the factor for the Sutherland estates of the Marquis of Stafford and Duke of Sutherland, retired in 1816, he wrote that his 'favourite object through life has been to drain moors and improve wastes',[52] a sentiment which would have been understood by his counterparts to the south. Young's place was taken by James Loch, who with the wealth of one of the richest men in England behind him, was also responsible for re-organising the southern estates of the Marquis of Stafford in Shropshire and Staffordshire. He drained marshes and built new farmsteads, and in Sutherland he undertook a radical re-organisation of the entire estate. He wrote that 'the property of a great

English nobleman must be managed on the same principles as a little kingdom, not like the affairs of a little merchant'. Huge estates with great wealth at their disposal could afford to 'look forward fifty years to make the most of the present'.[53] Loch's son, George, was still working for the Sutherland estate in 1858 and made very much the same point when writing to the Duke on the question of building a new farmstead. Whilst he did not want to involve the Duke in unnecessary expense, 'there are occasions when expenditure is wise and provident ... It is as one of a class of wealthy landlords, like the Duke of Bedford or Lord Leicester or Lord Yarborough, or many others, that the Duke of Sutherland can make improvements on his farm buildings ... the great capitalist can anticipate events and can command success'.[54]

As well as the promoting of grand schemes, some agents, such as Robert Salmon at Woburn, were engineers and inventors. His background was typical of many in this emerging profession. He had come to Woburn as a clerk of the works under the architect Henry Holland who was working on the Abbey. In 1794 he was appointed resident 'architect and mechanist' and in 1806 he was promoted to agent.[55] The estate records are full of his notes and designs for farm buildings, including a horse mill to be built at Woburn and a variety of machines such as a system for moving stacks in trolleys.

Agents such as Salmon were drawn from a surveying and architectural background, and may have learnt their skills allotting land after enclosure acts. Their duties could well include the laying out of new farmsteads. Others were the sons of farmers or the owners of small estates who spent time working with well-known improving landowners and farmers as part of their training. An applicant for the position of steward to the Gateshead estate had spent time with Messrs Culley of Fenton (famous livestock breeders in Northumberland in the late-eighteenth century), besides working in East Yorkshire.[56]

The early-eighteenth-century land agent's responsibilities were mainly limited to managing the legal relations between landlord and tenant: the family lawyer could normally cope with this. But by the nineteenth century the estate office became the centre of a complex and often diverse business.[57] As well as controlling thousands of acres of agricultural land, it might handle mining, housing, and dock interests, which could involve the loss of good farming land. The duties of the agent now involved farming, building and managerial skills. On the efficiency of the agent depended the smooth running of the estate. Although some of the most famous, such as James Loch, were drawn from the ranks of lawyers, others were practical men of farming stock. Prominent amongst these were Francis Blaikie, agent to Lord Chesterfield (Derbyshire) before he moved to Holkham, Andrew Thompson, agent to Ralph Sneyd (Staffordshire), John Yule, agent to Sir James Graham (Northumberland) and John Matthew, recommended by the agricultural writer, James Caird, to Sir Robert Peel.[58] Most land agents learnt their trade either from their fathers, or as students in an estate office. As the nineteenth century progressed, fewer and fewer landowners managed their own estates and the firms of agents became more important. East Yorkshire landowners employed firms based in London, Hull and York, the heads of whom were either solicitors or surveyors.[59]

The main responsibility of the agent was to see that his employer's estate produced a profit. This could mean that he might try to keep some of the owner's more extravagant ideas in check, and here they could be in conflict with the architects whose grandiose schemes might well appear attractive to their patrons. The existence of pattern books meant that many agents, such as John Gardner, working for the Duke of Grafton, were able to adapt published plans to their own purposes. The plain classical steadings around the family seat in Northamptonshire are examples of well-proportioned, functional designs which would have provided very adequately for the requirements of their farms (see Figure 57, pp. 119). Many of the designs published by the engineer and inspector to the Land Improvement Companies, John Bailey Denton, in his beautifully illustrated book, *The Farm Homesteads of England*, published in 1863, were the work of agents rather than architects.

The home farm

Many estate owners were at pains to point out that they had the interests of their tenants at heart. 'A good understanding between landlord and tenant' was a toast regularly drunk at the sheep shearings and audit dinners at Holkham Hall in Norfolk. In reality however, their economic interests were different. The tenant's aim was to win the maximum production from the soil during his tenancy, whilst the landlord was more concerned with the long-term value of his property.

There were various ways in which landlords and their agents could influence farming techniques and boost productivity on their estates, most notably through the husbandry clauses of their leases and the provision of an improved infrastructure in the form of enclosures, roads, drainage, houses and farm buildings. For some landlords, this was sufficient. The fictional Mr Brooke in *Middlemarch* was thus keen to belittle Sir James Chettam's enthusiasm for taking 'one of the farms into my own hands and see if something cannot be done in setting a good pattern of farming among my tenants'. Brooke's view, which was no doubt shared by many of Elliot's readers, was that it would be 'a great mistake ... going into electrifying your land and making a parlour of your cowhouse ... no, no – see that your tenants don't sell their straw, and that kind of thing; and give them draining tiles, you know. But your fancy farming will not do – the most expensive sort of whistle you can buy. You may as well keep a pack of hounds'.[60]

Many home farms, however, were regarded as not simply convenient sources of fresh food for the great house but as places where the interests of landlord and tenant converged, and where new techniques and machinery could be demonstrated to both tenantry and fellow gentleman farmers. The very best served to elevate the social status of agricultural pursuits, seen in the public eye as far removed from the ignorant farmers and bucolic squires so ridiculed in early-eighteenth-century literature. Arthur Young recognised that 'farming gentlemen' could be divided into two sets: those who needed to make a profit from farming and 'those whose fortunes are so considerable as to be above attention to economics' For these men, the home farm provided the opportunity to experiment and thus 'render pleasure subservient to the public good'. 'A gentleman of large fortune practising farming without improving upon the customs of his neighbours, instead of deserving praise, merits nothing but disgrace ... profit ought not to be the aim of these pursuits, but the good of mankind'.[61] John Lawrence, writing in 1801 urged that the home farm, and the park around it should be used as a 'theatre for the display of all notable varieties of experimental husbandry'.[62]

If home farms were intended to set an example to the tenantry, then the activities of the monarch were an example to other landowners. As we have seen, the land agent, Nathaniel Kent, was employed by George III in 1790 to improve Windsor Great Park. He stressed the need for 'men of distinction' to set an example. Having set out his plans, he commented: 'A farm of the kind here described, situated so near the Capital would excite attention, challenge imitation and be productive of great good to society'.[63] When, sixty years later, plans were being drawn up for the rebuilding of the Home Farm at Frogmore, Mr Turnbull, the architect at Windsor, wrote in 1852: 'Situated as they [the buildings] are in the very centre of the Queen's private walks, they are naturally an object of much interest and ought to be such as Her Majesty could herself visit with comfort and might have some satisfaction in showing her royal and other visitors'.[64]

Most home farms were run at a loss, and the Duke of Bedford was unusual in hoping to make a profit at Woburn. He expected his bailiff to produce a 5% return on capital invested, because he thought it would be a bad example to the tenantry if they saw that he lost at farming.[65] When improvements at Sandon (Staffordshire) had established a working home farm, there were yearly meetings between the owner, Nathaniel Ryder, and the farm bailiff to examine profits. In 1791, they were lower than Ryder had hoped, amounting to only £120. This was explained by the fact that the marling of a 15-acre field had cost more than expected and that it had been a difficult hay-making.[66] In 1796 Sir Ralph Sneyd of Keele took the running of his home farm into his own hands 'because it is to be my amusement as well as my employment and the living when in absolute idleness is what I cannot do'.[67] Other than the showpiece events such as the Holkham and Woburn sheep shearings, home farms might be visited by the tenants at least once or twice a year to pay their rent. The example of 'how they do things at the Hall' could then well provide food for thought in the locality. As well as his tenants, the owner would probably be hoping to impress his friends. For this purpose, both the siting and architectural merit of the buildings could be important. Browick recommended a spot about a quarter of a mile distant from the house. 'If more remote the supply of provisions for the house will be inconvenient, and the afternoon stroll of visitors to the farm an effort; if nearer, the farm traffic will invade the privacy of the walks and drives'.[68]

The more famous of these home farms were centres for experimentation. That at Holkham was sent seeds and fertilisers and the results scientifically analysed. In a letter to the Duke of Bedford, Francis Blaikie, the agent at Holkham, was able to state that mangolds grown at Holkham contained 8% more sugar than turnips.[69] In 1876, the Duke of Bedford set up his own experimental farm at Woburn, working initially on the effects of manure and continuous cropping on yields.[70] However, it was not only the famous names who indulged in this type of activity; the agricultural society journals, both local and national, reported the experiments of many other landowners. Borwick acknowledged in 1862 that some home farms had proved of great use to the agricultural world. 'Who can tell how much agriculture owes to the stimulus imparted in former days by the Woburn or Holkham gatherings? Have not Tortworth, Althorp, and other places done much for the Shorthorn, Goodwood for the Southdown, and Kinnaird Castle for the Aberdeen Angus?'[71] Certainly it was as centres for pedigree stock that many were best known. Both the Model Farm at Holkham, designed in the 1850s by G. A. Dean for the Earl of Leicester, and Cronkhill Farm, Attingham, built for the fifth Lord Berwick (Figure 2) are examples of farmsteads specifically designed for livestock breeding.[72] Placed, as they often were, in the parkland around the great house, home farms contained a disproportionate amount of pasture to arable land and so they were particularly suited to livestock. The improvement of stock could be an expensive business, and one practical

FIGURE 2.
Loose boxes at Cronkhill, on the Attingham estate in Shropshire. This farmstead is located next to a fine villa built by the architect John Nash for Lord Berwick's agent, and after 1848 became a base for Lord Berwick's famous Hereford cattle. The interiors have thatch fitted under the roofs, a reflection of the then prevalent belief that animals would fatten best in heated conditions.

advantage for the tenantry was that the purchase or hiring of pedigree bulls and rams from the home farm was often encouraged. Coke's prize Southdown rams and Devon bulls were for sale or hire at the Holkham sheep shearings.[73]

Numbers, dates and distribution

This research has located around 800 planned and model farmsteads, either through documentary references, or through the identification of surviving examples. The selection listed in the county synopses at the end of this book, although ranging from the grandiose to the utilitarian, attest to landlords' level of involvement in agricultural matters and their belief that farming was a high-status activity to which they wished to draw attention. There is no doubt also that many have been demolished without any record surviving and others have simply not come to light. We know that by the 1880s there were about 1,400 owners of over 3,000 acres,[74] this being the smallest estate that was regarded as producing enough rent to allow for major capital expenditure on improvements and raising its owner into the 'greater gentry' class.[75] There were also by this period as many as 5,000 country houses, all of which would probably have had a home farm nearby.[76] This suggests that a good proportion of owners were interested enough in agricultural improvement to build model or planned farmsteads for themselves or their tenants in the period 1750–1880.

From the information collected it is possible to show where they were built and the main periods of activity. The figures show two main periods of building, one between 1790 and 1820, when records of 166 dated farmsteads have been identified, peaking at 44 new farmsteads between 1800 and 1810;

FIGURE 3.
Block diagram to show by decade the date of construction of model farmsteads to which references were found during the survey.
Not all the farmsteads located could be dated, and so this diagram does not include all those that have been documented. Whilst new building reached a peak in the period of 'high farming', *c.* 1840–1870, the rise was far from steady. There is a pause in building during the post-Napoleonic War depression of the 1820s following a period of heightened activity during the Napoleonic Wars (1796–1815). This can be compared with country house building, which peaked in 1790–1830 and 1850–1870.

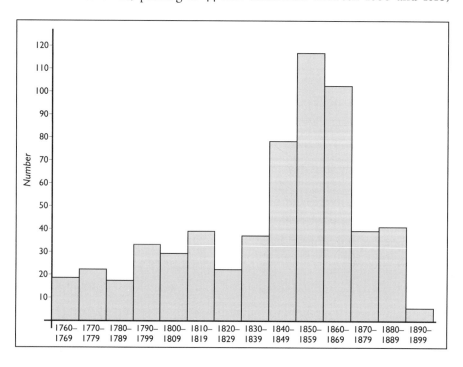

| | 1760–1769 | 1770–1779 | 1780–1789 | 1790–1799 | 1800–1809 | 1810–1819 | 1820–1829 | 1830–1839 | 1840–1849 | 1850–1859 | 1860–1869 | 1870–1879 | 1880–1889 | 1890–1899 |

FIGURE 4.
Graph to show the
level of wheat prices,
1770–1900.
The prosperity of
farming, especially in
the period before 1850,
was measured by
contemporaries in
terms of wheat prices.
Following a period of
gradual price rises up
to the 1790s, the
Napoleonic Wars saw
exceptionally high
grain prices, reaching
famine levels in some
years, encouraging a
shift into arable
farming on all but the
most inhospitable
soils. There followed a
short period of
depression before
prices rose again to a
level which remained
steady through the
middle years of the
century. This
prosperity was
maintained until the
1870s, when foreign
imports began to
depress prices and
grain production
ceased to be the most
prosperous branch of
farming. Instead it
was livestock farming,
and particularly
dairying, in which
profits were to be
made at the end of
the century. All this
affected both the type
and number of
farmsteads being built.

and a second between 1840 and 1870 with a total of 291, peaking at 104 in the 1850s (Figure 3). The earlier of these periods coincides with a peak in country house building between 1790 and 1830.[77] Each of these periods is characterised by a specific type of building to meet differing needs and they will be considered separately (Chapters 3 and 4). The first period covers the years of agricultural prosperity associated with the Napoleonic Wars, when cereal prices increased and rents rose by anything between 50 and 175% (Figures 4 and 5). There is no doubt that contemporaries believed that improvement, including the provision of good farm buildings to encourage intelligent, financially sound tenants, was both economically sensible and a patriotic duty. The second phase covered the thirty years after 1840 which was also a time of prosperity, based not only on steady grain prices, but the increasing value of livestock. Enclosure was rarely an option as nearly all open fields and most commons suited to arable farming had already been enclosed. If landlords wanted to increase the attractiveness and the value of their farms, they had to look to other means, and the provision of labour-saving industrial-style buildings suited to intensive cattle and manure production was one option.

The distribution of planned and model farmsteads across England is not even and is closely related to geology, soil types, settlement pattern and land ownership as well as changing farming prosperity. For the new agricultural practices to become widespread the remaining open fields had to be enclosed and fields and farms reorganised into individual units. This resulted in the creation in many areas, particularly down the eastern, potentially arable side of Britain, of a new agricultural landscape of straight roads, large regular fields and compact farmsteads isolated within their holdings. It is a consequence of such factors that these farmsteads are most heavily concentrated in the planned landscapes of central and north-eastern England, where they are set within the large square fields contrived in this period for efficient farming.

Sometimes, as on the newly drained lands of Thorney (Cambridgeshire),

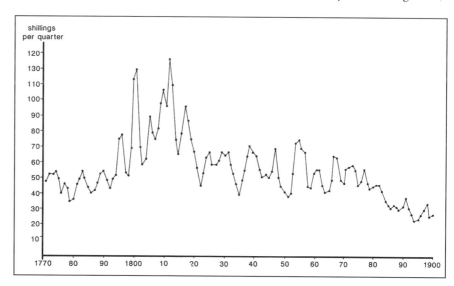

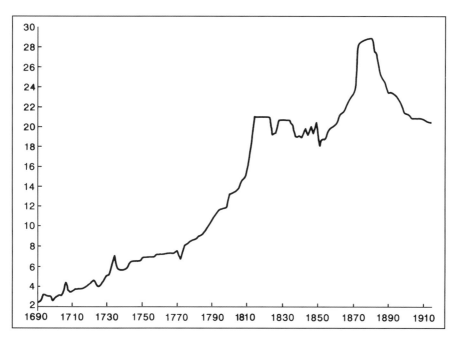

FIGURE 5.
Graph to show
movements in rents,
1690–1914.
Land values followed
very much the
changes in rents and
grain prices, except
that they often trailed
slightly behind,
following on rent
movements. Rents
would be set in leases
which in most arable
areas ran for anything
up to 21 years, and if
profits declined during
the lease, then the
tenant would have to
negotiate a rent
reduction, which
would inevitably lag
behind the price fall.
The building of
impressive planned
and model farmsteads
was concentrated in
the years of rising
values and landlord
optimism. In contrast,
periods of low prices
and declining values
were times when
estates spent money
on farm extensions
and repairs to keep
farms tenanted, rather
than complete new
steadings.

remodelled in the mid-nineteenth century for the Bedford estates, the farm-steads' regular distribution and architectural detailing help to give the region a distinctive unity and character. Only in the slightly higher area around Thorney Abbey does an early field layout remain (Figure 7). Planned and model farmsteads are very rarely found on those estate landscapes that, although distinctive by virtue of the shared architectural character of their farms and villages, have resulted from a gradual and subtle process of agricultural improvement rather than any wholesale transformation of the landscape. Only on rare occasions, indeed, are these farmsteads and their associated rectilinear field systems found in the midst of the irregular fields of an evolved countryside. Examples are the new 600 acre farm carved out of the small Cornish fields at Methleigh Barton by the Treweek family in the 1850s and John Morton's Example Farm built on Lord Ducie's estate at Tortworth, Gloucestershire. The farm of 250 acres was created out of old enclosed land and the original 46 irregular fields were reduced to 24. £3,500 was spent on drainage, tree and hedgerow clearance, new roads and buildings and 26 additional acres were gained by the removal of massively thick hedgerows. The result is still obvious in the landscape with the regular stone-walled fields of Example Farm con-trasting with the irregular fields and thickly wooded appearance of the surrounding area of Berkeley Vale (Figure 7).[78]

The scale of investment needed meant that steadings of this type were only suited to mixed farms of over about 200 acres. It was on the light chalk soils of Hampshire, Dorset and Berkshire as well as the coastal plains and moorland of Northumberland, that the largest farms were found by 1870, with over 10% of the farms in most of the other arable east coast counties being over 300 acres (Figure 6). Also important was the distribution of landed estates.

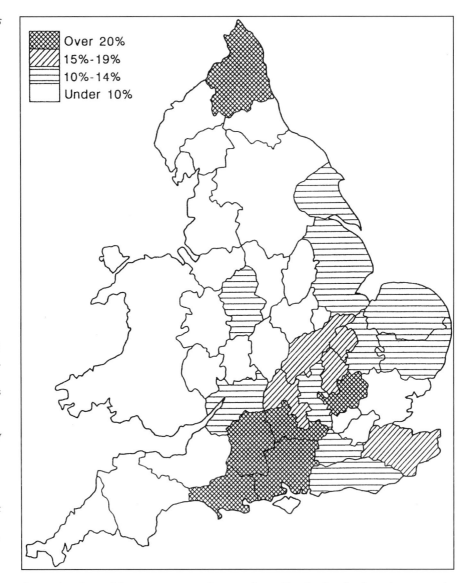

FIGURE 6.
Map showing the
percentage of farms
per county (pre-1974)
over 300 acres in 1851.
It can be seen that
nearly all the counties
with over 10% of
farms over 300 acres
contained light chalky
soils (the North and
South Downs, the
Wolds and the
Cotswolds), or were
on the dry arable east
of the country. The
pastoral farms of the
west were mostly
much smaller.

Legend:
- Over 20%
- 15%-19%
- 10%-14%
- Under 10%

Areas dominated by owner occupiers, such as Cumberland where 'property in land is divided into ... small parcels ... and those small properties ... universally occupied by the owners'[79] have fewer model farmsteads.

The distributions also differ between periods (Figure 8). Pre-1840 farmsteads are concentrated along the east coast on the great Northumberland, Yorkshire and Lincolnshire estates, as well as in Cumbria on the Greystoke and Lowther estates and on the Lilleshall and Trentham estates of the Marquis of Stafford. All of these were areas of newly enclosed and reclaimed lands, where old landscapes were being swept away to concentrate on grain production, whilst keeping livestock primarily for their manure. Arthur Young found much to praise on his *Northern Tour*, and described draining, liming, hedging and building roads as well as the erecting of buildings.[80] The distribution of

farmsteads built after 1840 is rather different. There was very little farmland left to reclaim, and only on Exmoor in the south-west, Thorney in the Cambridgeshire fens and Sunk Island in the north-east do we see a concentration of farms resulting from new enclosure. Emphasis was instead placed on the intensification of production, particularly livestock, on already existing land. Model farmsteads are scattered widely across wealthy estates, such as those of the Turnors in Lincolnshire, the Earls of Pembroke in Wiltshire and the Dukes of Bedford around Woburn and Tavistock. Building was likely to be particularly important in the dairying areas such as south Lancashire, Cheshire and Essex, where numbers of cows were increasing as railways were making the transport of liquid milk to the cities possible. Lancashire rents,

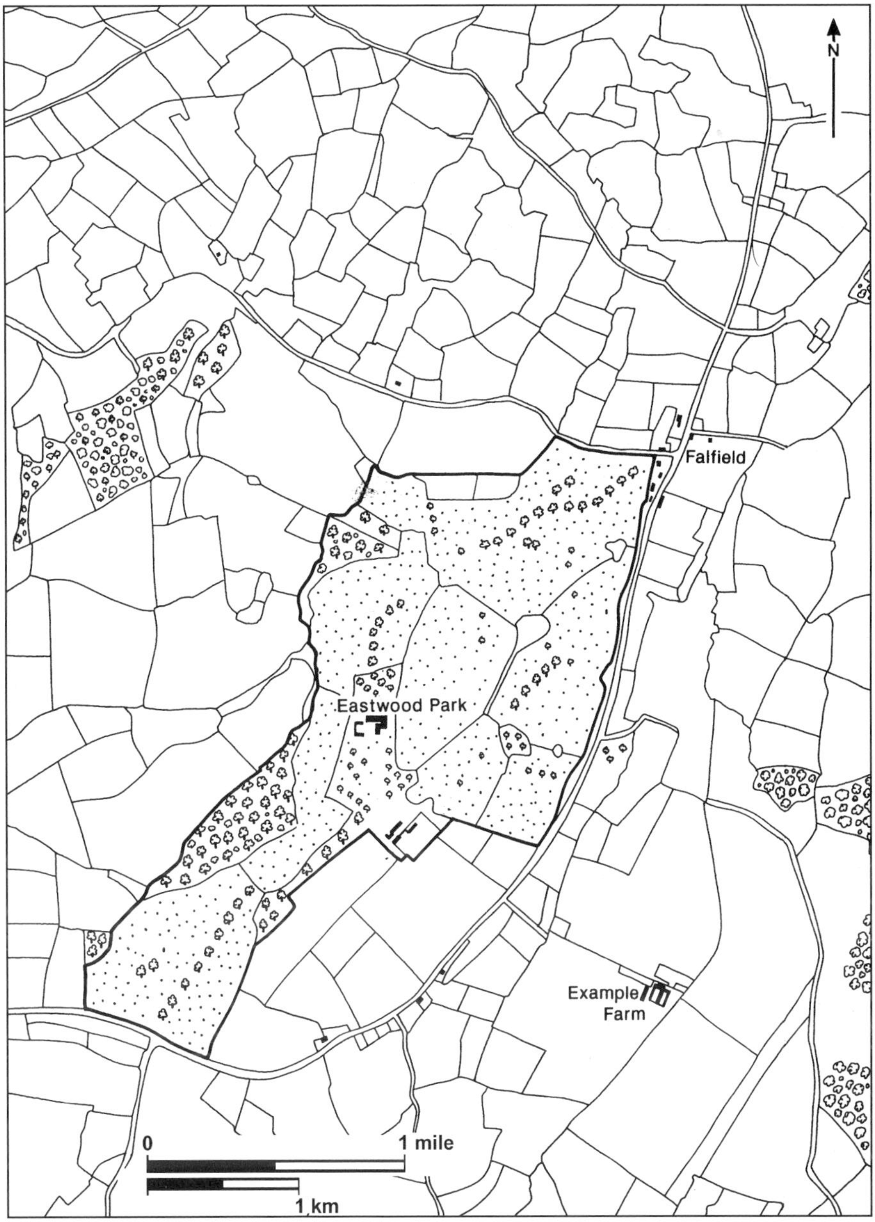

FIGURE 7
(*opposite and right*).
The farmsteads of
Thorney
(Cambridgeshire) are
associated with the
comprehensive
remodelling of its
landscape. The regular
and enlarged fields
around the planned
farmstead at Example
Farm at Cromhall
contrast with the
surrounding
landscapes of small
anciently enclosed
fields.

for example, for farms supplying the cotton towns with dairy products rose 18% between 1871 and 1896 (years conventionally associated with depression).[81] Thus, the shift in farming prosperity which is so obvious from the documentary sources is clearly shown in the pattern of new farm building.

Many reasons specific to particular landed families are also important. The estates of the Marquis of Stafford (Shropshire, Staffordshire and Sutherland), the Duke of Bedford (Tavistock, Thorney and Bedfordshire), the Duke of Westminster (Cheshire), and the Duke of Norfolk (Sussex) had capital coming from sources other than agriculture which their owners chose to invest, not only in home farms, but also in planned buildings for their tenants. Personal inclination was another factor. The Dukes of Marlborough, for instance, did little on their extensive Oxfordshire estates. When Young visited in 1809 he 'saw no truly well-contrived farmery'.[82]

Examination of other areas of the United Kingdom provides graphic evidence of these factors at work. Much of Wales is mountainous with the consequence that large agricultural estates are clustered along the coastal fringe and counties adjoining the English border.[83] Elsewhere the opportunities for developing arable or mixed farming along the lines being promoted by the improvers did not exist; both the soil and the terrain mitigated against it. As a consequence, model farmsteads were never an important building type in Wales, dominated as it was by small gentry and pastoral farms. Only five are

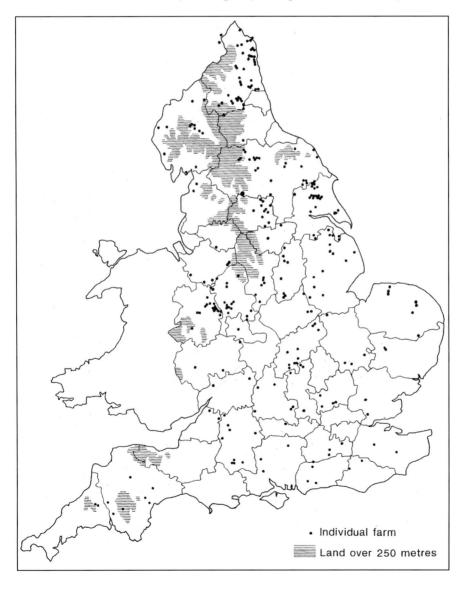

• Individual farm

▨ Land over 250 metres

listed by Robinson in his gazetteer of Georgian model farms.[84] Lord Penrhyn was responsible for drainage along the north Wales coast and new farmsteads were built to serve the reclaimed marsh as well as a home farm beside his stately home at Penrhyn Castle. Improved transport and the demand for food from the industrial centres of south Wales and Lancashire encouraged agricultural development and estate expenditure on farm building from the mid-nineteenth century. The most spectacular is the creation of John Naylor, a Liverpool banker who erected a huge home farm at Leighton, near Welshpool in the 1850s, including a monumental pair of circular pigsties.[85] By the end of the century, dairying for the cities of Liverpool and Manchester was becoming profitable and new cowhouses arranged around yards were being built in the north east of the Principality.

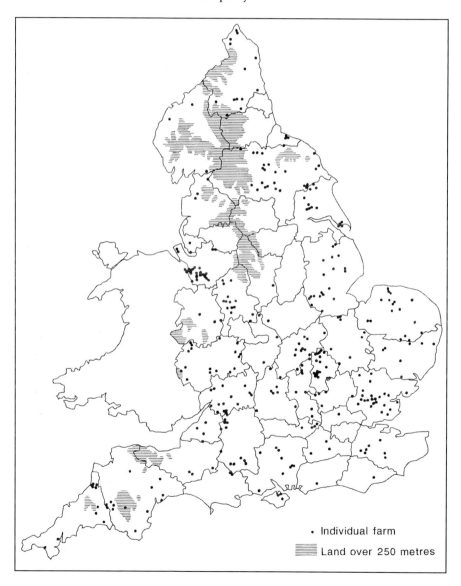

FIGURE 8
(*opposite and right*).
Distribution of located and dated farmsteads in England built before (*opposite*) and after 1840.

• Individual farm

▨ Land over 250 metres

Lowland Scotland, by contrast, was an area of development from the eighteenth century. With much land north of the border still unenclosed and in the hands of large landowners, change had begun by the late-seventeenth century with Lord Belhaven's *The Countryman's Rudiment* of 1699 being one of the earliest farming text books. The pace of improvement increased after the Act of Union (1707) and was later influenced by the Edinburgh School of economists led by Adam Smith. In 1723 the Society for the Improvement of Knowledge of Agriculture and Science was founded in Edinburgh. This, the oldest agricultural society in Europe, was followed in 1790 by the establishment of the first university chair of agriculture, again at Edinburgh. The chair was held be a series of influential men, the second of whom, David Low, wrote farming text books which continued to be standard works throughout the nineteenth century. Scottish farmers and landowners were amongst the best educated in Europe and many held important positions within British agriculture. Sir John Sinclair from Caithness was president of the Board of Agriculture set up during the Napoleonic Wars and another improving Scottish landowner. Lord Kames was an active member.

What makes the Scottish experience so different from the English, and thus worthy of a separate study, is that the eighteenth- or nineteenth-century replacement of traditional buildings, often by planned steadings, was almost complete. Very few earlier buildings survive, particularly in lowland Scotland, so here we are looking at a landscape and built environment often totally created by the improvers. Some of the grandest model farmsteads in Britain are found on Scottish estates. One of the earliest was planned for the third Duke of Argyll in 1729 when he started reclaiming land at Whim in Peeblesshire. Most of the buildings were replaced in the 1780s, although some drawings amongst the Saltoun papers have survived.[86] By 1780 fragmented farms had been replaced across much of south and east Scotland by enclosed holdings with centrally-sited steadings, and by 1840 the transformation was complete across the lowlands. Well-known architects such as Robert Adam were working on many of the more important estates from the 1760s, and the use of good stone as a building material has meant that the steadings have survived well. From the beginning the new farmsteads were powered by water, horse or steam, with extensive cattle courts often enclosed on four sides and entered through a central gateway with a dovecote over an archway. The Board of Agriculture County Reports attest to this wholesale process of rebuilding and, with the very important exception of the great north-east coast farms of Caithness and Sutherland estate, the contrast between the improved south and east and backward north and west is regularly reflected in them. About 200 Georgian model farms have been recorded in Scotland.[87] Change was slower in the Highlands, with most model farmsteads not being constructed here until the period between 1840 and 1880.

It has been argued that this period witnessed the birth of a truly British aristocracy, with interests that extended beyond former national and provincial borders.[88] Some English landowners, such as the Marquis of Stafford who worked through his Scottish agent James Loch, controlled extensive English and Scottish estates, whilst many Scots spent much time in the south and reported back to their stewards on improvements that they had seen and heard about in England. Architects such as Robert Adam worked both north and south of the border. In the eighteenth century Scottish owners were looking for tenants from the south to bring the new ideas north, by the nineteenth century English owners were looking north for progressive agents. One of the most famous was Francis Blaikie, who spent sixteen years working on the Holkham estate in Norfolk (see pp. 110–11).

Britain in Europe

There is considerable evidence that the planned and model farmstead was a uniquely British type, representative of a distinctive system of land ownership and management. The improvements of British agriculture were much admired and European noblemen sent their sons to study British methods.[89] George III's daughter, Charlotte, was married to Frederick, Duke of Wurtenburg and took an interest in the agriculture of the region. The Duke created for her a small farmstead 'quite in the English style',[90] but how much influence it had on the farming of the region is doubtful. In France, planned groups designed 'à l'Anglais' coincided with the return of exiles after the Restoration of the monarchy in 1815.[91] One example concerns a certain Father Antoine, abbot of a monastery near Nantes who imported Durham cattle and legume crops and opened a Catholic farm school.[92] Catherine the Great of Russia encouraged and supported students who visited Britain to study agriculture, amongst other things. Arthur Young tutored several groups of Russians who visited his farm in Suffolk, and those of Robert Bakewell, the famed livestock breeder, at Dishley, Leicestershire, and Robert Arbuthnot, a frequent contributor to Young's *Annals,* in Surrey.[93] Scottish architects worked on Russian country estates and Scottish builders were responsible for the introduction of earth building, or *pise* to Russia where they built the School of Practical Farming and Agriculture in 1798, very much on the Palladian lines currently fashionable for model farmsteads in Britain (Figure 9).[94] Interest in estate building was increasing with the westernisation of Russia. The eccentric Prince Bolkonski, in Tolstoy's *War and Peace,* shocked polite society by allowing his estate architect to dine at his table 'although the position of this insignificant individual was such as could certainly not have caused him to expect such an honour.'[95] William Halfpenny's book, *Twelve Beautiful Designs for Farmhouses* (1750), was known in Russia and the landowner and architect, L'vov, was familiar with the writings of Charles Middleton (*Picturesque and Architectural views of Cottages, Farm Houses and Country Villas,* 1793). After the completion of the School of Practical Farming L'vov decided to build a similar one on his estates at Nikolskoye and another near Moscow.[96]

Those members of the British aristocracy who were responsible for financing such buildings on their estates were probably the wealthiest in Europe. 'In no

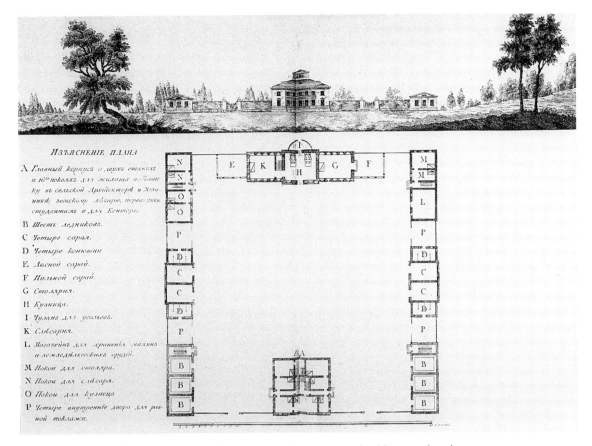

ИЗЪЯСНЕНІЕ ПЛАНА

A Главный корпусъ о двухъ этажахъ
  и 16ти покояхъ для жилища пробни-
  ку въ сельской Архитектурѣ и Механи-
  никѣ; земскому лѣкарю, переводчику
  студентамъ и для Конторы.

B Шесть ледниковъ.

C Четыре сарая.

D Четыре конюшни

E Лѣсной сарай.

F Пильной сарай.

G Столярня.

H Кузница.

I Чуланъ для угольевъ.

K Слѣсарня.

L Магазейнъ для храненія махинъ
  и земледѣльческихъ орудій.

M Покои для столяра.

N Покои для слѣсаря.

O Покои для кузнеца

P Четыре внутренніе дворы для раз-
  ной поклажи.

other country in Europe were wealth, status and power so highly correlated or so territorially underpinned'.[97] Only rarely, as in the river clay areas of the northern Netherlands were landlords responsible for building farmsteads for their tenants, and here the buildings were erected on traditional lines. Even where the house front was given a fashionable classical façade, to reflect the increasing prosperity of the tenantry, or formed part of a parkland view, as at Linschoten, near Utrecht, the cowhouse was integral with the house as was customary all along the North Sea region. In this region landlords from the seventeenth century had been responsible for drainage and buildings and farms were held on leases. Generally in Europe, however, the same dual role of landlord and tenant in agricultural change did not develop. Most estates in Western Europe were under 10,000 acres, whilst further east they were larger but included much poor land and were often mortgaged and highly indebted. Some English agents such as George Dean undertook work for European clients such as Hungarian princes,[98] and by the end of the nineteenth century landowners in the new nation states of Italy and Germany were showing an interest in farming matters. A new generation of landowners on the Russian estates after the emancipation of the serfs in 1861 were reading English books on agriculture and planning wholesale changes, and some of this enthusiasm found its way back into England. The Russian wife of the eleventh Earl of

FIGURE 9.
The School of Practical Farming and Agriculture, designed by the Scottish architect, Adam Menelaw, and the Russian Nicholas L'vov and built near Pavlovsk in 1798.

Pembroke, Catherine Woronzov, was responsible for the introduction of an Italianate style into the farm buildings of farms on the Wilton estate in the 1850s. However, except for a very few exceptions, it was the traditionally distinct roles of landlord and tenant capital which had established itself in Britain that allowed for a landlord-dominated programme of farm building to develop here in a way distinct from that on the Continent.

CHAPTER THREE

The Philosophy of 'Improvement', 1660–1790

Types and chronology of 'improvement'

The increase in landlord interest in improvements can be safely dated to the period after the Civil War, when many landowners, particularly on the royalist side, were left heavily in debt. This, according to one contemporary, John Houghton, forced many landowners to take an interest in improvement. 'The great improvement made of lands since our inhuman civil wars, when our gentry, who before hardly knew what it was to think ... fell to such industry and caused such improvement as England never knew before'. Writing between 1692 and 1703, his volumes, *A collection for the improvement of husbandry and trade,* can be seen as one of the earliest works advocating the general improvement of estates by their landlords.

After the crop failures of the 1690s, the first half of the eighteenth century was generally one of good harvests and low prices. Low cereal prices stimulated efforts to maximise profits through the increased output of easily transportable grains, rather than livestock. 'For those with an especial flair for farming, high profits were possible, given a fair share of good fortune, an enterprising disposition, and sound business acumen'.[1] After 1750, the growing demand of an increasingly urbanised and rising population led to price rises, the widening of the market and a climate favourable to innovation. Between 1751 and 1821 the population of England and Wales doubled, but imports of grain remained insignificant except in years of agricultural disaster. This was achieved by an increasingly professional and commercial farming community, prepared to intensify their farming methods on newly enclosed, marled and drained land. To keep the land fertile, more animals had to be kept and their manure conserved. These animals needed feeding during the winter and so more fodder crops, such as cultivated grasses, pulses and turnips were grown. These non-cereal, spring-sown crops could replace the traditional fallow year in traditional rotations. Land could be well-cleaned by ploughing before it was planted. When the seeds were drilled or dibbled in rows, the weeds could be kept down by constant hoeing. Thus the functions of the fallow year – to break the disease cycle created by uninterrupted growth of cereals, and to clean the land – could be achieved and a valuable crop grown at the same time. All these husbandry innovations were becoming understood and gradually being taken up in the years of both low and high prices after 1700.

The eighteenth century was generally marked by rising land prices and rental values. At the end of the seventeenth century land could be bought for as little as 16–18 times its annual rent, so that a purchaser could secure a financial return of 5–6% gross. By the 1730s 28–30 years' rental value was more typical, giving a yield on the investment of about 3.5%. By the 1770s it was well over 30 years' value.[2] Land in itself was therefore not a good investment (except for the social return and political influence that a larger estate would bring). However, if the landlord then undertook improvements, his monetary return could be far greater. Nathaniel Kent reckoned in 1775 that improvements could be expected to yield three or four times the return to be obtained from simply buying land.[3]

The initial impetus towards improvement was, therefore, financial. Enclosed land, arranged in well laid-out fields approached by good roads, would command a higher rent than a farm consisting of strips scattered across the open fields. The most profitable forms of improvement were those which brought uncultivated land into cultivation, and included large-scale projects such as the drainage of fenland as well as many less ambitious reclamation schemes. However, these undertakings could be highly capital intensive and sometimes, as was the case with the many inundations of the fens, failures. Safer was the enclosure of open fields and commons, and it was on this that the early text books on 'improvement' concentrated.

Approximately 45% of the land area of England had been enclosed by 1500. The rate of enclosure increased in speed after the Restoration, and by 1700 the figure had risen to 71%.[4] Although these figures can be open to interpretation, they do show that piecemeal enclosure had greatly reduced the percentage of farmland in open fields by 1700 and that large areas of the country were already enclosed by the time parliamentary enclosure began in earnest around 1760.[5] This was particularly true of the pastoral areas of the south and west and also those midland counties such as Leicestershire and Nottinghamshire which had been most affected by static and falling prices for grain after 1650, when landowners were putting land down to grass. If a landowner managed to buy up most of a parish, there was little opportunity for opposition and enclosure would be the result of agreement with the few other freeholders. Even after the beginning of parliamentary enclosure, enclosure by agreement still continued, and because this often goes unrecorded, actual rates of enclosure are difficult to determine. Parliamentary acts were sometimes used to tidy up and give a legal status to earlier changes, so actual changes on the ground and to farming practice may have been minimal. It is probable that less than a quarter and possible as little as a fifth of England was affected by enclosure between 1750 and 1840, and some parts of anciently-enclosed England would hardly have been affected at all (Figure 10).

To the landowner, the arguments for enclosure were persuasive. Not only was the removal of the unbounded and archaic landscape of open fields, particularly where they were visible from his house and park, aesthetically pleasing to the man of taste, but also eighteenth-century commentators reckoned that rents could be doubled on enclosed fields. In fact a figure of 30% may be more accurate.[6] Increases in productivity probably did not justify this rise, as during the eighteenth century rents were rising faster than farmers' profits and farmers were consequently laying out a greater percentage of their income in rent. This represents an increase in landlord's power in the farming system, but at the same time the independence of farmers was also increasing as they were free from the constraints of a communal system. This freedom, which allowed them to experiment, innovate and benefit from specialisation and the new market economy, was worth paying for in increased rents.[7]

Once the foundations were in place, in the form of estates held mostly freehold, within which the landowner could act unfettered by restraints imposed by customary rights, he could let farms could be let on his own terms and for a limited time. Detailed, legally binding leases first appear in significant numbers from the 1660s and increased greatly in the eighteenth century. As the profits to be gained from improvement were proven, interest in estate management increased. The conditions were right in some cases from the 1660s, increasing slowly through the next fifty or so years and more rapidly with the rise in farm prices which began in the 1740s, and accelerated still further from the 1780s and until the end of the Napoleonic Wars.

Husbandry clauses in leases were easier to enforce on enclosed than open land, enabling further improvement such as marling, liming and draining, and the eighteenth century witnessed their increasing formalisation. Because the tenant had to provide the working capital, it was all the more important for the landlord to attract farmers with enough credit to stock and seed the farms as well as pay their rent, thus providing further encouragement for the landlord to fulfil his side of the bargain. By the 1770s, when the agricultural commentator, Arthur Young, was writing his regional *Tours*, there were examples in

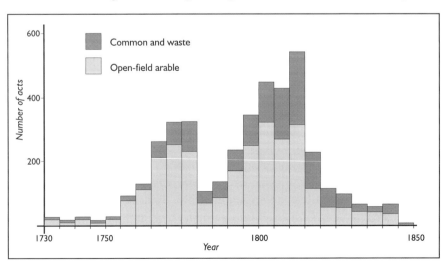

FIGURE 10.
Block diagram to show the number of parliamentary enclosure acts passed for each five-year period, 1650–1850. The two main phases of parliamentary enclosure were 1765–80 and 1790–1820, with the enclosure of commons being more important in the second period. However, it is important to remember that much enclosure, particularly on the all-powerful estates, did not require an act of parliament and so these figures are an underestimation of the real extent of change.

36

most counties of landlords who had enclosed and laid out new farmsteads as well as providing the roads necessary for the new commercial farming.

Farming books and farmstead layouts

There is little evidence that seventeenth-century interest in agricultural improvement manifested itself in formal layouts with improved buildings. Farming text books began appearing in English in the sixteenth century, but it was not until Gervase Markham's *English Husbandman,* first published in 1613 and which contains a plate of a 'husbandman's house', that anything was written on buildings. Markham recommended a courtyard layout to the west of the house, with a horse pond to the west and on the north side stables, an ox-house, cowhouse, and 'swine coates' (pig sties), all with doors facing south. Hay and corn barns, poultry houses and malting kilns were sited to the south, flanked by 'hovels to carie your Pease ... under which you shall place, when they are not in use your Carts, Waynes, Tumbrells, Ploughes, Harrowes'.[8] The use of the word 'hovel' by Markham, to describe an open-sided building for storage of implements below and corn above, suggests a Midland origin for his writings.[9] This use of vernacular names for the buildings and implements of the farm was typical of the farming books which increased significantly through the seventeenth century, and which were rooted in the observation of local farming practice. Many of these regional terms were still evident when the Board of Agriculture county surveys were produced during the Napoleonic Wars, and some have survived to the present day.[10]

Practical observations, rooted in sound understanding of local traditions, characterised the writing of Roger North of Rougham in Norfolk, another late-seventeenth-century gentleman who interested himself in architecture. A lawyer by training, he became interested in architecture after the Fire of London. Not only did he design the gateway leading from the Temple into Fleet Street, but he also observed the current methods of erecting farm buildings. His book, *A Treatise on Building,* first published in 1698 has comments on regional differences in barn design, but nothing on the farmstead as a unit. He noted that barns in East Anglia, where 'farms are great and croppes bulky and there they know nothing willingly but clapping into the barne', were larger than those to the north and west, where 'the thrift of landlords' had 'not afforded barns, so the people have found out ways of making their stacks with tolerable security'.[11]

The evidence of estate maps suggests that rebuilding was often well arranged in the orderly manner of a medieval base court, but still rooted in vernacular building traditions. Two East Anglian plans, one of Channons Hall, Norfolk, and another of Cranley Hall, near Eye, Suffolk, dated 1626, show the buildings for the demesne farmstead consisting of stables, barn and granary arranged in a 'U'-shaped plan. At Cranley, most of the buildings and the associated moated manor house still stand, comprising a fine example of a carefully planned manorial farm layout typical of seventeenth-century Suffolk timber-framed

construction (Figure 11). Another seventeenth-century planned group survives
at Taynton (Gloucestershire) where three substantial two-storey buildings with
stone slate roofs form a 'U'-shaped plan behind the house. One is a stable,
or ox-house, the central one opposite the house is a barn, and the third,
matching the stable across the yard, has most recently been used as a store
and cider house, with a cellar. The buildings are embellished with the family's
coats of arms, and comprise early examples of brick construction in the Vale
of Gloucester (Plate 4).

The activities of Sir Thomas Parkyns of Bunny (Nottinghamshire), demonstrate the interests of a middle-ranking landowner with an interest in
architecture. He inherited his estate in 1680, his monument in the parish
church describing him as having built 'most of the farm houses in Bunny and
Brademore'. All of these were robustly constructed in brick, newly introduced
to the area, the barns being either detached from the farmhouse or in-line
under the same roof. There were at least five farmsteads built along the street
in Bradmore, intended to serve the parish's open-field farms (Figure 12).
No enclosure act exists for Bradmore, but the last open fields in Bunny
disappeared in 1793. The fields were then enclosed and divided between farms
of 150 to 200 acres, the farmsteads remaining in the villages. Other than barns,
there are no surviving farm buildings in the parishes of Bunny and Bradmore
which can be dated to the late-seventeenth or early-eighteenth century.[12]

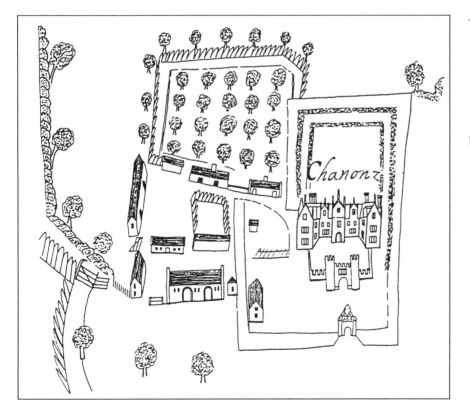

FIGURE 11
(*left and opposite*).
Seventeenth-century
farmsteads from map
evidence.

The manorial complex
at Channons Hall, at
Tibbenham in
Norfolk, is arranged
around a yard. The
impressive threshing
barn with two sets of
double doors is sited
below a possible cattle
shed surrounded by a
temporary fenced
enclosure. The
building of these
temporary 'par yards'
is described in
eighteenth-century
Norfolk diaries.

The plan of Cranley
Hall, near Eye in
Suffolk, dated 1626,
shows an early
example of a
courtyard group sited
close to a fine
seventeenth-century
manor house.

Further north, in the Lake District, another landowner was investing in specialised farm buildings. Daniel Fleming of Rydal Hall built himself a large bank barn with space for 44 beasts to be tied below and a threshing barn above. Both the accounts for the building and the barn itself (Low Park Barn) survive and we know the work was carried out in 1659. A second bank barn was built by Fleming at Coniston Hall in 1688.[13] Both these buildings are early examples of a type of multi-purpose building, ideally suited to the hillsides of the Lake District, which was to become widespread both in this region and other upland areas of Britain in the nineteenth century (Figure 13). It is a distinctive regional type, owing nothing to the influence of pattern books or fashionable architects, that as will be seen later played a key role in some of the most advanced farmstead layouts.

Lord Belhaven's book *The Countryman's Rudiment,* written in 1699, is the first to include a section on the layout of farm buildings. He repeated Markham's advice that the buildings should be placed around a courtyard

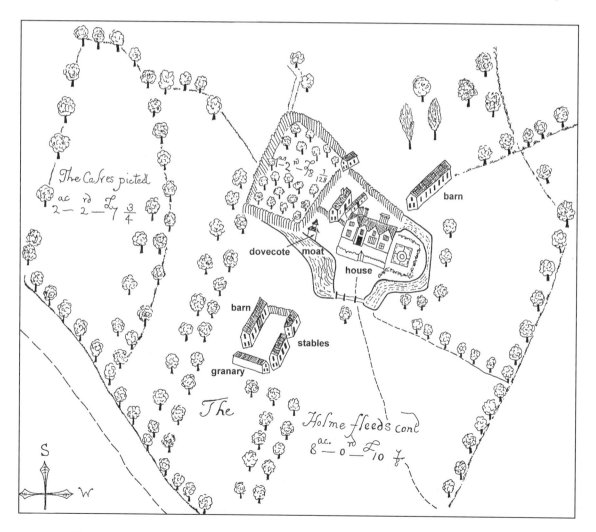

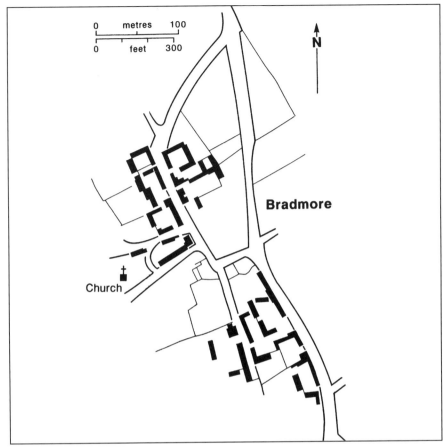

FIGURE 12.
Sir Thomas Parkyn's new farmsteads with their long barns were all built along the village streets, as is shown on this plan of Bradmore. The surviving buildings behind the barns, creating some courtyard layouts, are all of a later date, but they may be on the site of earlier buildings.

FIGURE 13.
The bank barn at
Townend Farm,
Troutbeck, was built
in 1666 for the
Browne family. It
stands opposite their
farmhouse, the central
ramp leading up to
the first-floor
threshing barn.

while the house should be on the north side facing south and the barn aligned
north-south to the west with the rickyard behind it. Opposing barn doors to
the west and east would allow the most to be made of the prevailing wind
when creating a draft through them for winnowing. To the south were the
stables and byres and to the east a straw barn. Entrances should be into the
yard so that all could be surveyed from the house.[14] Belhaven's advice
anticipated the Hanoverian courtyard plan, but most landlords continued to
build in styles strongly rooted in local traditions, albeit in an orderly manner.

The eighteenth-century courtyard farm

The earliest known English design for a complete farmstead was drawn in
about 1650 as an architectural exercise by a student of Inigo Jones, John Webb.
Taking its inspiration from the villas of the Venetian hinterland, it is a
courtyard design with identical classical façades and a fine five-bay house along
the front.[15] Unlike all previous farm building, the origins of this building type
are to be found not in vernacular farm building traditions or manorial layouts
around a base court, but in the villa-farm architecture of Andreo Palladio
(1508–80), developed for private estates around Venice. These had been bought
by wealthy merchants in the sixteenth century and drained and developed by
them as small farms. As in Britain, land improvement was seen as a moral
duty, the reclamation of uncultivated land being described by the Paduan

noble and architectural expert Alvise Cornaro as 'holy agriculture'. Both old established families and newcomers were busy with improvements. Once built these farmsteads were intended to provide an income, and practicality and functionality were the basis of villa-farm design. Palladio was the most influential of the Italian Renaissance architects who revived the symmetrical planning of classical Roman architecture, and its strict adherence to the laws of proportion. His *Quattro Libri dell'Architectura* (1570), which first appeared in English with new illustrations in 1720, allowed his work to be fully appreciated here. Copies were to be found in the libraries of most of the great houses.

A fervent admirer of Palladio was the prominent Whig and influential amateur architect, Richard Boyle, third Earl of Burlington (1694–1753), who gathered around him a group of intellectual friends and architectural theorists who shared his ideas and relied on his patronage. As new books such as James Stuart and Nicholas Revett's *Antiquities of Athens,* published in 1762, showed

FIGURE 14. Palladio's illustration of Villa Dicani from his *Quattro Libri* shows a 'villa-farm' with its house and farm buildings surrounding it.

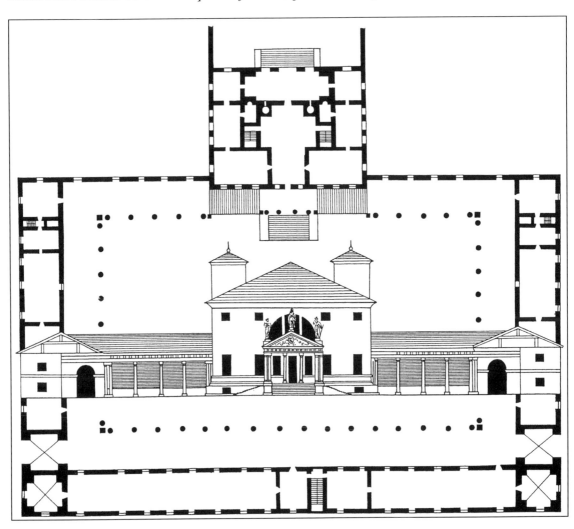

that the architecture of the ancient world was far richer and more varied than had previously been thought, Palladio's strict rules of proportion and symmetry began to go out of fashion in country house architecture. However, Palladio's villa-farms, which included stables, cattle sheds, barns and implement stores contained in quadrant wings enclosing courtyards (as at La Badoera, *c.* 1550–60), were layouts easily adapted to the British situation (Figure 14). Most landowners could relate with ease to Palladio's observations on the appropriate harmony of form and function: 'An edifice may be esteemed commodious, when every part or member stands in its due place and fit situation, neither above or below its dignity and use ...'.[16]

The courtyard plan can thus be traced to the medieval base court and to the Palladian villa-farm. It also happened to be the most suitable for the new farming systems of the agricultural revolution. These allowed for the production of more winter feed in the form of turnips and hay made from the improved grass crops. Increased yields could only be sustained by the spreading of large quantities of manure which was produced by cattle fed and sheltered in yards where they trod down the straw left after the corn was threshed out. The most important building was the threshing barn, characterised by at least one set of double opposing doors, one into the stack yard and the other into the cattle yard, also known as the stockyard or foldyard. It was placed to the north of the yard providing warmth and shelter to the south. On the east and west sides of the yard were cattle sheds and stables. The house was placed on the south side, its front typically facing away from the yard (Figure 15). Most eighteenth-century model farmsteads were based on this plan and, although there were regional variations, it was widely followed in the nationally available pattern books. For instance, the type of housing provided for cattle varied across the country, influenced by the methods traditional in the area. In upland and dairying areas where straw was less plentiful and the weather more inclement, they tended to be stalled in sheds down one side of the yard, with stables down the other. In the centre of the yard was a manure pit into which the sweepings from the stables and stalls would be piled ready for spreading on the fields. In lowland, arable, and more temperate regions, cattle were kept loose in yards with shelter sheds around the sides. The yard was open and undivided, although temporary hurdles could be put across it to divide up stock if necessary. Stock were primarily valued for their manure, and thus for their role in maintaining the fertility of the soil and increasing yields of the more profitable grain. Whilst grain prices were rising slowly in the second half of the eighteenth century, and then steeply rising during the Napoleonic Wars at the turn of the century, livestock could be more difficult to sell. By 1750, Smithfield was the dominant market where prices were high enough to justify the walking of cattle for several days to get there. However, it was a risky trade with profits fluctuating wildly depending on supply. Many farmers claimed that if it were not for the necessity of collecting and preserving manure they would not keep cattle.[17] The open courtyard, or double-courtyard plan dominated by the barn, and including a house on one side, thus remained the basis of farmstead design throughout the eighteenth century.

The integral role of the farmhouse suggests that these planned tenant farms were not for gentlemen farmers who turned their back on the real business of farming. These men, whose houses faced park-like pastures to the front, looked straight onto their livelihood at the back, with, as at Sledmere, only a narrow passageway dividing the house from the yard (see Figure 41). Some houses, such as those on the Hornby Castle estate (see pp. 49–51), were designed as parkland features, rather than convenient houses for tenants, whilst those at Holkham estate, such as Kempstone Lodge or Leicester Square, were specifically designed a 'better class of tenantry'.[18] Even at Leicester Square the rear of the house still looked out onto the yard, if from a slightly greater distance (see Figure 54). Although the reasons for the close proximity of the farmer to his yard was always said to be so that he could keep a close eye on his livestock and his workers, it is possible that security was also a subsidiary motive. During the troubled years of the Napoleonic Wars and its immediate

FIGURE 15.
An early model plan was that drawn by W. Pitt and published in *The Annals of Agriculture* in 1788. The barn (f) opens into both cattle yards for the easy distribution of straw, although the waggon lodge (c) is rather inconveniently placed within them.

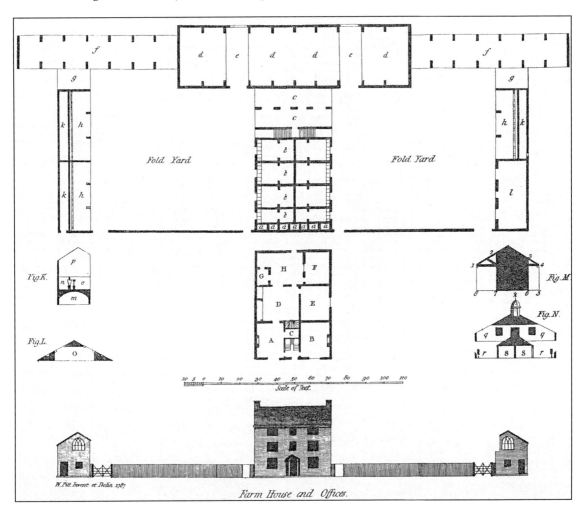

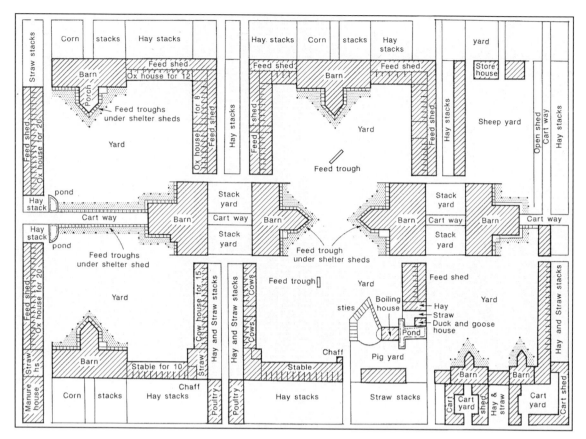

FIGURE 16.
Arthur Young's plan of a farmyard, published in 1770. The stables were sited near supplies of hay, chaff and straw, with the hay taken directly from the hay stack to the loft above the stable. Similarly there was spacious cover for cabbages, carrots and turnips for the cattle near their sheds and room for slicing and cleaning the fodder. Straw was fed from troughs in lean-tos around the barn. The stack yards for unthreshed straw were adjacent to the barn at the rear.

aftermath, riots, incendiarism and cattle maiming were never far from farmers' thoughts. A Norfolk witness to a Select Committee on Agriculture in 1833, replied to the question, 'Is there the same good feeling between farmers and labourers that there was formerly?', replied, 'Nothing like there was before the fires'.[19] In more idealistic terms, the farmhouse beside its farm showed 'a union and proportional connexion between the different classes of society ... [and] ... the air of general and friendly intercourse, which, when properly conducted, is the true spirit of social life at a British residence'.[20]

Although enclosure, followed by draining, marling, and laying out new farms with regular fields within a ring-fence, formed the basis of improvement for which the landlord was responsible, few eighteenth-century writers on the topic devoted much space to the provision of the farm buildings themselves. Only Arthur Young, in his *Farmer's Guide to the Hiring and Stocking of Farms*, published in 1770, provided plans[21] for ideal farmyards, one for a 'considerable' farmstead with two yards, and a scaled-down version. Although they are difficult to interpret, contrasting greatly with polished architects' plans, they include practical details which indicate that they are the work of a farmer. These include innovative features that did not find their way into accepted farm architecture until much later. Young's buildings were designed to reduce the cartage of raw materials. Feed rooms were built along the back of the

45

FIGURE 17.
Arthur Young's
feeding system allowed
feed to be delivered to
cattle and pigs via
hatches, chutes and
feeding tubes.

cattle sheds, from which they were parted by a wooden partition in which sliding wooden shutters allowed food to be passed to the mangers. Hay was stored above and there were chutes for pushing it down into hay racks. Sliding windows linked the storage for chopped straw (or chaff) to the barn. The straw stacks were placed around the barns ready to be thrown down straight onto the threshing floors through pitching holes (Figure 16). The system of providing feed to the pigsties (Figure 17) was more complicated with 'boarded tubes' running from the granaries to the coppers and cisterns where the feed was prepared, and then to the hog troughs; thus 'a prodigious deal of labour, inconvenience and expense is saved'.[22] No evidence has been found that these ideas were taken up at the time, although they may well have influenced the designs of William Strutt at Belper, some thirty years later (see pp. 94–100).

Architects and estates

Some of the earliest examples of planned and model farmsteads are to be found in the north of England. Here was unenclosed moor and wold waiting to be reclaimed and enclosed, funded by the new money from industry, commerce and particularly mining which was beginning to find its way into landowners' pockets. This was a trend which was to increase in importance after 1790 and will be further considered in the next chapter. The north-country association with early developments in planned farm building is further demonstrated by the publication in 1747 of the first book of British farm building designs by the London-trained architect, Daniel Garrett.[23] From 1720 Garrett had worked as a clerk of works for Lord Burlington, and had an extensive practice by the 1740s working on country houses and smaller projects,

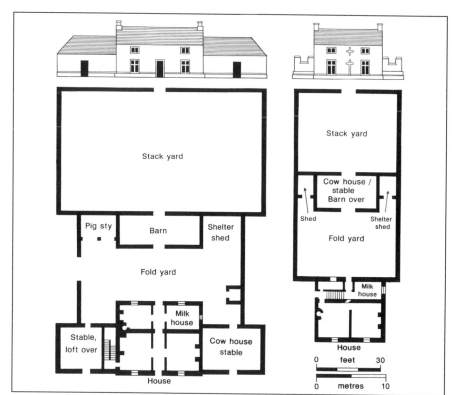

FIGURE 18.
Daniel Garrett's farm plans are among the earliest published examples of architect designs.

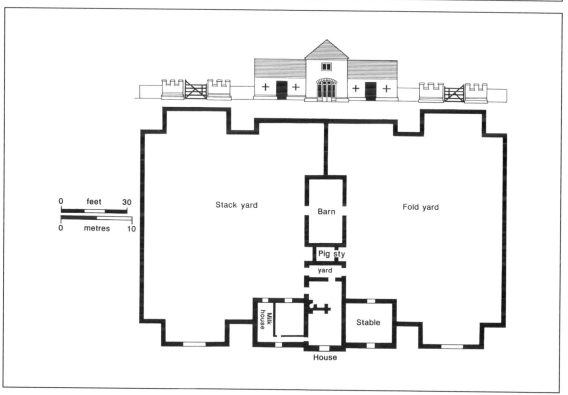

mostly in the north of England. His style was not original, but rather 'straight forward Palladian'.[24] The book contained ten plans for farms of various sizes, built in 'as regular, cheap and convenient a manner as possible'. They were all neat, symmetrical and utilitarian designs. He realised that the reclamation of much of the upland areas of northern England had created the need for the building of new farmsteads, and his plans were all for tenants rather than the more pretentious home farms. Although most commentators thought that building planned farmsteads to serve small acreages was not worth the investment, Garrett included some designs for farms under 100 acres. In the smallest a two-storey house with no more than a kitchen, parlour and dairy downstairs, formed the front of a walled yard. Opposite the house, across the yard, was a barn flanked by a narrow shed on one side and a hovel (an open-sided shed) on the other. The stack yard was situated behind the barn. The larger versions included a byre, a stable and a pigsty, but still the main elements were two walled areas enclosing the cattle yard and stack yard, on either side of the barn, and few other buildings. Unusual features are the recesses in the yard walls, possibly to provide wind shelters for stock. No accommodation is provided for animals except for a few cows, and any shelters would have been temporary ones erected in the yard. This complete lack of livestock shelter is surprising, particularly in farmsteads designed for the north of England where the climate is harsher and cattle could be housed for over 26 weeks over the winter.[25] It is possible that the plans were only intended as an outline into which individuals could fit buildings ancillary to the barn, and possibly the recessed areas were to allow for more accommodation being inserted. Nearly all the plans include a small enclosed area between the house and buildings labelled as a 'yard', perhaps intended for milking (Figure 18). The popularity of Garrett's book is shown by the fact that two more editions were published, one in 1759 and another in 1772.

Garrett's book was followed, three years later, by its southern equivalent, William Halfpenny's *Twelve Beautiful Designs for Farm Houses*. These simple, symmetrical courtyard layouts in a restrained mixture of classical styles, expressed in pediments, blank arches and lunettes, and a few Gothic crenellations and cross arrow-slits, make little attempt to disguise the functions of any of the buildings. Although no surviving farm buildings can be firmly attributed to either Garrett or Halfpenny, we know that Garrett was working on the Wallington estates (Northumberland) for Sir William Blackett in the 1740s, remodelling the front of Wallington House and designing the model village to house estate workers at Cambo. However, all these buildings have been greatly altered since their original creation. Sir William Blackett was the prototype of the new Northumberland industrialist/landowner who owned the manor of Winlaton and its collieries, was the lessee of lead mines on Alston Moor and had shares in collieries at Newburn, Brunton, Fallowfield and Acomb.[26] He could well afford not only to re-arrange the countryside around Wallington, but also to employ a leading north-country architect. Amongst his plans at Wallington are some for un-named farms. Typically for the period, the house is shown in the centre of the south façade. Two yards, a stack yard to the west and cattle yard to the east, were divided by a barn. Except for a small shelter shed in the cattle yard, there are no other buildings. This simple plan was an eminently practical one, one that addressed the farmstead's principal purpose of providing a barn with easy access from a stack yard and to a yard where stock could be kept and manure collected in the winter. There are similar double-yard plans in Garrett's book. One in the Wallington archives designed for Berwick Farm, Onstead, was either not built or does not survive. Again, only rarely are other buildings such as small stables, byres, or shelter sheds shown on the plans. It is possible that the landowner only provided the major buildings and yard outline and it was up to the tenant to put up less permanent minor buildings within this framework.

Although few surviving farms can be linked to Garrett's plans, his plain classical styles strongly influenced the attitudes of landowners and the work of their architects. One of these was James Paine, who in the 1750s had taken over Garrett's practice and whose work in the Palladian style was applied to houses and farmsteads alike, most notably at the Home Farm of 1767 at Weston Park (Staffordshire). Another was the York-based architect, John Carr. Like other architects of his generation, Carr was self-taught, having begun life as a stone mason. He had not travelled abroad, but had worked on many architect-designed houses, including Kirby Hall designed by Lord Burlington, before starting out on his own. Twice serving as Lord Mayor of York, and well connected within Whig circles, Carr's practice was predominantly based on the patronage of Yorkshire gentry and businessmen, many of whom were busy enclosing land and 'improving' their estates.[27] His style was basically a Palladian one, with the wings of his houses and farm buildings treated as subservient pavilions, but he could equally well work in a severe classical style or an ornate Gothic one if that was what his clients preferred. The farmsteads on the Hornby Castle estate (North Yorkshire) of the Dukes of Holderness were created as eye-catchers to be viewed either from the park or, in the case of Street House Farm, from the Great North Road (the modern A1). As Cobbett wrote: 'Against a great road, things are made for show'.[28] They were designed in 1766 for the 4th Duke of Holderness, who had already enclosed his estate and laid out good roads. On three of the four farms, the house has an octagonal central block, with on either side a screen wall connected to matching farm buildings similar to those in Garrett's books. The barn was positioned along one side of the courtyard with a matching block opposite, probably originally a stable with a granary above. In one case the yard is open towards the park and opposite the house, whilst at Arbour Hill the house faces north across the park. Only at the home farm is the house a simple rectangular plan, with the barn opposite across the yard. All these farmsteads are solid and well-built with good architectural detailing, but their landscape value was considered to be of greater importance than the domestic convenience of the farmers (Figure 19, Plate 5).

At Constable Burton, in North Yorkshire, Carr had designed a villa for Sir

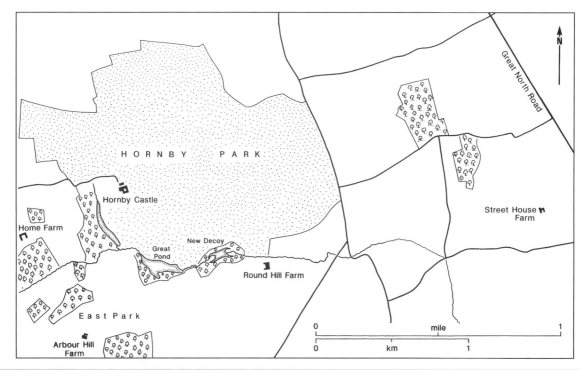

FIGURE 19.
(opposite and above)
The Hornby estate.
Two of Carr's stable
ranges, at Street
House and Hornby
Home Farms.

Marmaduke Wyvill in 1767, and probably an L-plan farm group at nearby Foal Park Farm with a castellated screen fronting stables and loose boxes, with a barn and cowhouse in the other wing (Figure 20). Carr was also responsible for a similar Gothic range at Plompton High Grange, also in North Yorkshire. Jeffrey's survey of the North Riding, made in 1771, just before 'improvements' took place, shows the Foal Park within a fenced area and not yet cultivated. The main period of estate expansion and purchase of farms began after 1774, when the estate was inherited by the Reverend Christopher Wyvill, who died in 1822. By 1851 it covered 3,600 acres in Constable Burton, Spenithorne, Harworthy, Hunton and Bellerby.

At Raby Castle (County Durham), where Paine had designed the Home Farm in the 1750s,[29] the Park Farm was designed by 'his Lordship [the Earl of Darlington] himself', with the cattle yard divided in two and a walkway around the edge, in which the cattle were foddered in the winter and the manure conserved. In a period when the fertility of the soil, and therefore crop yields, were entirely governed by the amount and quality of farmyard manure available, buildings that enabled the efficient collection of manure were all-important. The most usual method at this date was to make it in strawed pens and yards and store it in manure heaps or middens for spreading when it was fully rotted. At Raby the liquid in the yards was drained off into a reservoir. The barn, 90 feet (30m) long and with two threshing floors, stands at one end of the cattle yard, with the stack yard behind, and as well as this

FIGURE 20.
Foal Park Farm,
Constable Burton
(North Yorkshire),
showing how
conventional farm
buildings were placed
behind the castellated
façade.

yard there were pigsties with hen houses above, stables and stable yard, a sheep yard, cartsheds and granaries. Young commented on the practical arrangement of the buildings: 'I cannot but admire the ingenuity of the contrivance [in which] his lordship ... has so well adapted each part to its respective use and so well connected those that mutually depend on each other ... His management respecting manure is much more masterly than that of his northern neighbours and principally by means of his excellently contrived farm yard.' Here we have one of the earliest agricultural, as distinct from architectural, comments on a planned farm design. However, Young did not limit his comments to the purely practical. The Gothic screen along the front was built

Figure 21.
The Gothic screen
wall at Raby Castle
(North Yorkshire),
designed by James
Paine in 1755.

to the designs of James Paine in about 1755 and is illustrated 'to shew how much beauty and utility maybe united' (Figure 21).[30]

From the 1780s the momentum of pattern book publishing increased dramatically. 'Nowhere in the world was such a wide range of rural architectural projects discussed, illustrated, and published in such numbers.'[31] Their authors were obviously responding to a proven demand and hoping to attract potential clients. It is clear from both the books and specific examples discussed here that a particular layout is typical of this first generation of planned farmstead. They were usually on a courtyard plan with the house on the south side. Behind was an undivided yard, although in some of Garrett's plans for large farmsteads, the yard was divided into two by the barn. The barn was usually on the north side with a stack yard behind. Other buildings around the yard included the stable and perhaps a byre or shelter shed. Granaries and feed stores were to be found in some designs in corner pavilions around the yard. The obsession with all things Italian and classical is shown in the way most designs were based on a classical symmetry, with even the Gothic extravaganzas having an orderly layout behind the façade. Many of the surviving examples from this pre-1790 period were built for tenant rather than home farms, after wholesale programmes of reclamation as in the Yorkshire Wolds.

James Paine, John Carr and Daniel Garrett were by no means the only architects who turned their hand to designing farmsteads in the period before 1790, for nearly all those with a country house practice designed estate farmsteads as part of their work. Although all these men worked in both classical and Gothic styles, it was the austere symmetry basic to classical ideals which was more suited to the accommodation of farmstead design and where most progress was made in unifying the twin considerations of form and function. Robert Adam and Sir John Soane provide two examples of well-known figures in the profession who produced many drawings for farmsteads, most of which were never built in their complete form.

Robert Adam came from a family of architects founded by his father, John, with extensive contacts in both Scotland and England. By far the most important of Robert Adam's early English commissions was for Nathaniel Curzon (created 1st Baron Scarsdale in 1761) who inherited the Kedleston estate (Derbyshire) in 1758. Adam started work there in 1760, on his return from Italy. One of his first commissions was to provide designs for two farmsteads, Servant's Farm and the Home Farm, their elevations being kept, in Adam's words, 'as plain as I could'.[32] The Kedleston farmsteads were designed at a time when there was little practical advice on farm layout available in print for the aspiring architect (Young's *Farmers' Guide* was not published until 1770 and his *Tours* until 1771). Their innovative and experimental layouts were undoubtedly influenced by the inclusion by Adam of Lord Scarsdale's tenant, John Sherwin, in the drafting of the design specifications. The advantage of having a central barn was that the straw from threshing was then equally available for use in the livestock sheds and stables around the barn, and was a layout developed particularly, as we shall see, by Samuel Wyatt. Nevertheless, there were practical problems with the design of Servant's Farm, which consisted of a quadrangle of farm buildings with a central barn. The barn would have shaded the yard with its stables and cowsheds to the south. The troughs for the stalls had to be approached through the stalls as there was no feeding passage and there was no manure pit in the yard (Figure 22).

At the same time Adam began work on the designs for the Home Farm at Ireton. The first plan, dated 1764, was rectangular with domed two-storey pavilions at each corner. The dominant central building in the north range, a granary over an open-fronted cartshed, was a design which was developed later by Samuel Wyatt at Shugborough as part of a mechanised yard. Adam's choice of location, however, was not practical as farmers usually preferred their cartsheds to face outwards onto a roadway and not the potential quagmire of the farmyard. However, it did present an imposing façade and was a design which was developed later by Samuel Wyatt at Shugborough as part of a mechanised yard. Adam was then asked to work on alternative designs: his most innovative was drawn in 1764 and shows a circular layout with the four main blocks of barn, house, stables and dairy, linked by a colonnade (Figure 23). This impressive plan was never executed, and a second, more innovative plan – with four rectangular blocks linked by colonnaded arcs housing livestock – was produced later the same year. However, this plan was not executed either and instead a third design was produced: this comprised a courtyard plan with a central entrance flanked by stables and cow byres, and pavilion type workshops in the corners.[33] Whether this was built in its entirety is not clear, since only an L-plan range remains. Another plan, with semi-circular ends and straight sides was produced, but never executed, for the Wonersh estate in Surrey. The semi-circular ends contained stables and the straight sides, barns on one side and coach houses on the other.[34] This preoccupation with pure geometry made for novel architectural layouts, but they lack the practical advantages of, for instance, the Raby design, and it is perhaps partly for this reason that they were rejected by his clients. Adam was more successful in his native Scotland where the most complete example of his work, a complex plan based on a broken saltire cross, was built for the Earls of Cassilis at Culzean Castle in Ayr (Figure 24).[35] The two barns project from the central square of the cattle yard into the rick yards with only the cattle sheds, stables

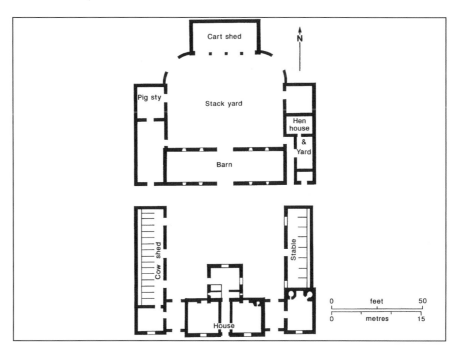

FIGURE 22.
Robert Adam's designs
for Lord Scarsdale at
Kedleston
(Derbyshire) in the
1760s included a
conventional layout
around two yards
divided by a barn.
It would have been
more practical to have
the pigs and hens
nearer the house and
the dairy, because they
relied on whey and
household scraps for
their feed.

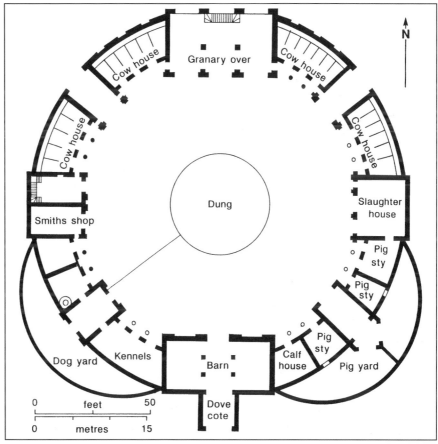

FIGURE 23.
The first layout
proposed by Robert
Adam for the Home
Farm at Kedleston
(Derbyshire) was
circular in plan.
A final more
conventional design
was probably never
executed in its entirety.

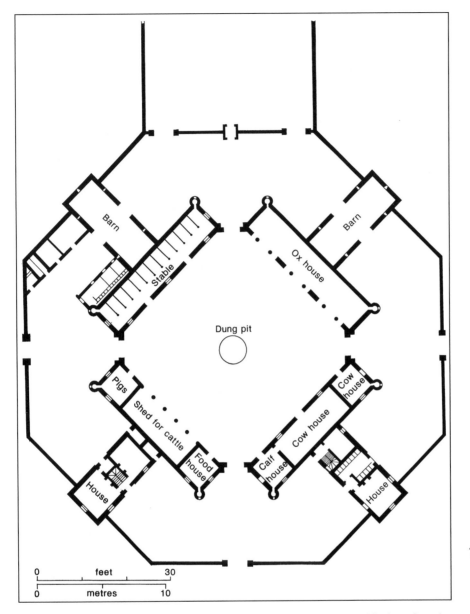

Barn

Stable

Ox house

Barn

Dung pit

Pigs

Shed for cattle

Cow house

Cow house

Calf house

Food house

House

House

| 0 | feet | 30 |
| 0 | metres | 10 |

FIGURE 24.
The complex design at
Culzean Castle in
Ayrshire shows Adam
at his most inventive.

and shelter sheds facing inwards. The unthreshed corn could therefore be
easily moved into the barn and threshed. However, there is no easy way from
the barns to the yards and sheds where the straw would be needed. A second
shortcoming in practical terms is the inward facing cartshed which would have
been difficult for vehicles to access from across the cattle yards.

Many of Sir John Soane's commissions comprised dairy buildings at the
more picturesque end of the market. The most famous of these are his designs
for Philip Yorke at Hamels (Hertfordshire). Here Soane was able to pursue
his interest in the 'primitive', as promoted by Rousseau and developed under
the Picturesque movement. In 1787 he produced a series of drawings, the

thatched roofs and overhanging eaves also being highly practical methods of controlling the temperature in the building. The primitive look was accentuated by baseless columns made out of tree trunks with the bark left on, which supported the Doric porticos. Soane's library contained books on agricultural buildings including a copy of volume I of *Communications to the Board of Agriculture*, devoted entirely to farm buildings and cottages. One of the contributors, Sir Henry Holland, for whom Soane was Clerk of Works, persuaded Soane to submit cottage designs to Sir John Sinclair at the Board. However, *Communications* was not published until 1797, and little practical advice was available before then. Presumably it was up to the client to stipulate his requirements from an agricultural point of view, and the architect to transform them into a building. Soane's earliest farm design while working with Henry Holland was for Cadland Farm (Figure 25). It is now demolished, but the plan shows a yard on either side of a central road. Poultry, pigsties with 'green yards' in front and nag stables were on one side of the road and the barn, cart horse stables and cowhouses on the other. A covered way, allowing the oxen and cows to be fed from a feeding passage, comprised a practical innovation which would have been welcomed by the farmer.[36] Soane was also interested in semi-circular plans, with two such cowhouses being built, one at Marlesford, Suffolk, in 1783 and another (which still stands) at Burn Hall, Durham.[37] He was proud enough of his design to exhibit it in the Royal Academy show of 1784. Of his complete farmstead plans, the buildings at Wimpole are the only ones to survive. Here there is a very traditional courtyard layout with a barn on one side originally designed with a house opposite and stables and cow byres down the sides. Soane's interest in rural simplicity is shown in the use of traditional building materials such as thatch and weatherboard on a brick plinth, although the constructional form of the barn was probably based on Swiss precedent.[38] There are many more plans drawn by Soane for farmsteads which were never built, most of them showing conventional and practical layouts around one or two yards.

The idea of planned farmsteads was, therefore, still a new one, and as yet there was little practical agricultural advice in print. Although we have seen that Adam had the advice of a practical farmer, and that many of the farming text books current at the time were in the library at Kedleston, as a trained architect he clearly understood the rules of classical architecture far more than the needs of agriculture.

In contrast, Samuel Wyatt (1737–1807)[39] was the first architect of note to give thought to innovative and practical solutions to agricultural problems. Working almost entirely in the neo-classical style and producing designs of considerable architectural quality, he was interested in experimentation with both layout and building materials, particularly slate which he used for the base of the stall divisions. The wooden mangers were protected by plating them with iron and edging with tin.[40] His interest in slate, which also included its use for window sills, damp proofing and water troughs, was linked to his brother who was an agent for the Penrhyn estate with its extensive slate quarries, and that in iron with his many connections with Birmingham iron masters. His design for Wimmington poultry house incorporated iron columns and was built between 1782 and 1785 – an exceptionally early date for such a technique. In 1800 he produced designs for the new Albion Mill in London with an independent, internal load bearing structure. It was one of the most advanced multi-storey iron structures in the world, although his plans were never executed as the London Flour Company, for whom it was designed, folded in 1802.[41] Wyatt was also interested in mechanisation and his links with Matthew Boulton led him to recommend steam engines to some of his clients, including the Duke of Bedford at Woburn. His design for the Whitebarn at Shugborough Home Farm (Staffordshire), not built until 1805, includes a barn with a threshing machine worked by a water wheel (see pp. 221).

Unlike many other architects of his generation, his background was an agricultural one, with relatives who were land agents and farmers as well as architects. This informed a sound understanding of the functional requirements of farm buildings in their own right. His friends and associates tended to be engineers, scientists, industrialists and inventors rather than artists and architects (see p. 14). He did not visit Italy, and had to rely on experience gained firstly in his father's architectural practice in Litchfield and subsequently his management of the carpentry contract for Adam's work at Kedleston, quickly followed by his appointment as clerk of the works. Here he was able to avail himself of the extensive library at Kedleston, reading widely from the architectural and agricultural books there. He was gradually given increased responsibility for the design of estate buildings, learning much from discussion with both Adam and the practical farmer, John Sherwin, whose daughter he later married. His own farming knowledge was no doubt important, and he

FIGURE 25.
Cadland Farm was Sir John Soane's earliest farm design, produced in 1777.

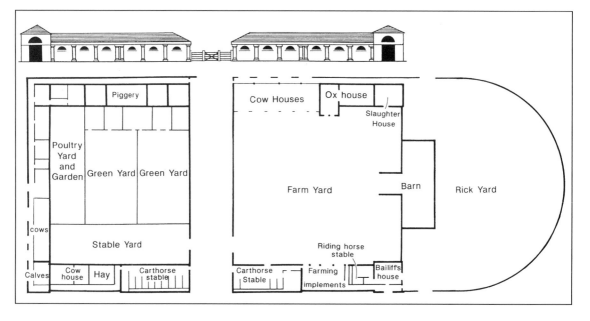

was able to act as an intermediary between Lord Scarsdale and Adam. Burley Farm, undertaken in 1765 for Lord Scarsdale and derived from Adam's first plan for the Home Farm, was his first farmstead design (Figure 26). This was a tenanted farm on the estate, built to a rectangular plan around a central manure pit. The barn was located in the centre of the north side, which thus provided shelter for the yard; the carts were placed in the shade on the south side of the yard so that their paintwork was protected from the sun. In the corners were octagonal corner pavilions.

From Kedleston Wyatt went on to practise independently. His first commission, at Sandon (Staffordshire) for Nathaniel Ryder, was the result of Lord Scarsdale's recommendation: such personal contacts were always important to architects working in the small world of the aristocracy and landed gentry, and much work followed from the Kedleston connection. The resulting farmstead (Figure 27) was praised by Nathaniel's son Dudley, the second Earl of Harrowby, for its practicality. 'I do not know of any set of farm buildings better adapted to the purpose, or where the mean is more justly taken between too much and too little architecture.' [42] The farmstead was built between 1779 and 1783, after Nathaniel had had an opportunity to familiarise himself with the farming suited to his newly-purchased estate. His journals record both his interest in details of the design, such as the ventilation of the dairy, and his discussions on agricultural methods with Wyatt, such as the merits of various ways of feeding sheep. Wyatt's plans demonstrate his use of regular geometry in the production of a very workable farmstead layout. It is divided into two yards, with open shelter sheds for cattle served by a feeding passage behind similar to those at John Soane's buildings at Cadland. Unusually, the dairy forms one side of the yard and the pigsties, where the whey would be used as feed, were on the other. There is no indication that the smells from the farmyard created any undue problems for cream production. The carthorse stable divided the cattle yard from the lower yard, the barn forming one side. Once the buildings on his home farm were completed, Nathaniel was able to pursue his agricultural interests and experiments, as recorded in his journals, from a convenient and suitably architectural set of buildings. [43]

By the end of the century Wyatt was working at Holkham as well as on Coke of Holkham's son-in-law's estate at Shugborough (Staffordshire) – yet another example of the importance of family connections in the operation of patronage (see p. 219). A layout developed uniquely by Samuel Wyatt from the 1770s, but harking back again to Adam's designs, consisted of using the barn as a central element with cattle sheds and stables around. This was first used at Hatch Farm (Essex) for Lord Petre in 1777 (Figure 28) and then at Holkham (Norfolk) (see Plate 11) and the Demesne Farm at Doddington (Cheshire) in the 1790s. It is possible that Jeremy Bentham's idea of a central controlling focal point, advanced in his *Panopticon* design of 1791 and enthusiastically taken up by the Utilitarian movement for schools and workhouses, may have influenced Wyatt's thinking. As we have seen, however, the advantages of this layout were mixed. A central barn meant that the straw could

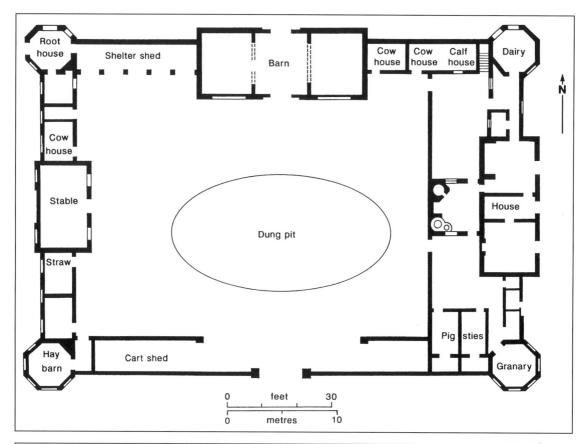

Root house

Shelter shed

Barn

Cow house

Cow house

Calf house

Dairy

N

Cow house

Stable

House

Straw

Dung pit

Hay barn

Cart shed

Pig sties

Granary

0   feet   30

0   metres   10

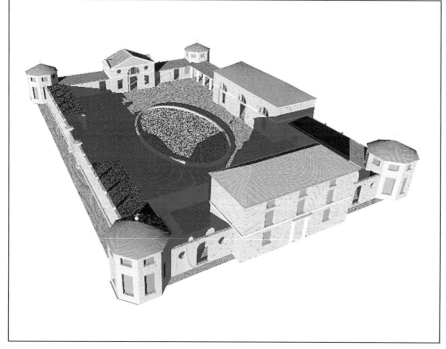

FIGURE 26.
A plan and perspective reconstruction of Burley Farm (Derbyshire).

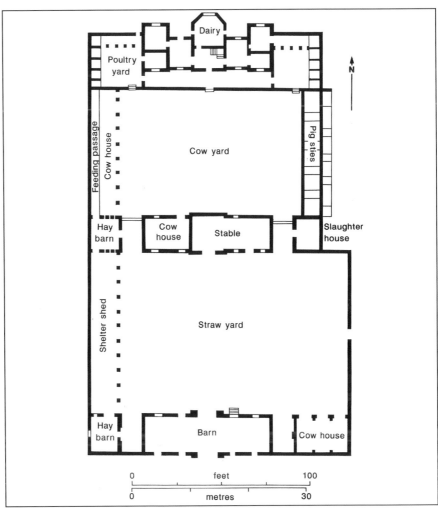

Dairy

Poultry
yard

Feeding passage

Cow house

Cow yard

Pig sties

Hay
barn

Cow
house

Stable

Slaughter
house

Shelter shed

Straw yard

Hay
barn

Barn

Cow house

0   feet   100

0   metres   30

N

FIGURE 27.
The Home Farm at
Sandon (Staffordshire)
was designed by
Samuel Wyatt and
built between 1779
and 1783 for Nathaniel
Ryder. The
perspective
reconstruction shows
the house with its
central projecting
dairy in the
foreground.

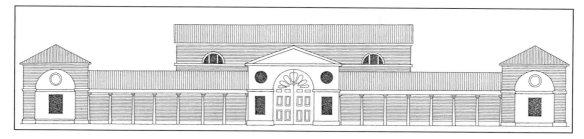

easily be distributed amongst the cattle yards and stables, but the unthreshed crop had to be brought in from a more distant stack yard.

FIGURE 28.
Hatch Farm,
Thorndon, Essex
(1777). A central barn
enabled the easy
distribution of straw
to the livestock sheds,
but the stacks had to
be brought in across
the yards to the barn.
The redrawing of the
barn façade is from an
architectural drawing
in Essex Record
Office and the bird's
eye view is
reconstructed from an
aerial photograph.

The home farm and the landscape

A diversity of motives influenced those landowners who envisaged the creation of planned and model farmsteads as part of a wholesale redesign of the landscape, including land reclamation, enclosure and park creation. The home farm's position in the landscape reflected changing fashions in the layout of parks in the second half of the eighteenth century. The great geometric gardens laid out from the late-seventeenth century and illustrated by Kip and Knyff in their *Britannia Illustrata* of 1709 were divorced from the surrounding working countryside, farmsteads being very rarely shown. By contrast Horace Walpole saw William Kent as the obliterator of the boundaries between gardens and nature. Kent's extensive designs, popularised by his work at Stowe in the 1730s, allowed for the creation of framed pictures or views containing buildings. In keeping with the philosophy of 'beauty and utility', the line between 'aesthetic' park and 'functional' farmland was becoming blurred. Sometimes, as in William Southcote's park at Woburn (near Weybridge in Surrey), this view contained a farm. Southcote is credited with the introduction to England of the concept of the French *ferme ornée* (the most famous example of which was Marie Antionette's Petit Trianon). Southcote's estate consisted of about 150 acres, thirty-five of which comprised ornamental gardens; of the rest, two thirds were pasture and one third arable. Around the farmstead was an ornamental walkway from which there were views across the fields, there being no attempt to create 'model' farm buildings in the accepted sense of the phrase.[44] However, the landscape designer, Humphrey Repton, expressed a widely-held view that farms and gardens could not be mixed in his *Observations on the Theory and Practice of Landscape Gardening,* published in 1803: 'They [*ferme ornées*] are so totally incongruous as not to admit any union but at the expense of beauty or profit'.[45]

Some mid-eighteenth-century working home farms expressed this incongruity of function in being separated from the garden and hidden behind picturesque façades. Lightoler's *Gentleman's and Farmer's Architect* (1762) includes many classical and Gothic designs, including a triangular castellated sheepcote designed for a hillside position, which could be constructed either complete or as a 'ruin' with fencing in the gaps of the collapsed masonry, so

FIGURE 29. Lightholer's *Gentleman's and Farmer's Architect* (1762) included a variety of farm buildings, some castellated, and others of a simpler classical design. Farmsteads usually included a barn, cowhouse and stable around a yard with the house on one side. The castellated sheep cote was designed as a parkland eye-catcher.

that 'when seen from a genteel home [it] forms an agreeable object' (Figure 29). At Rousham (Oxfordshire) a castellated cowhouse forms part of the garden designed by William Kent between 1738 and 1740. Kent's naturalistic landscape broke away from the geometric garden layouts of his predecessors. His walkways were serpentine rather than straight, enabling objects in the landscape to be viewed as chance encounters rather than as part of a regulated 'Baroque' layout. The cowhouse, just outside the gardens, was thus one of these 'encounters' and illustrates clearly the narrow, but important divide between landscape gardens and agricultural pursuits. The fact that this building opens away from the formal gardens into the fields demonstrates that agricultural pursuits were not, as in the *ferme ornée,* envisaged to be part of the garden. Rather it should be viewed from it. Thomas Wright designed several castellated barns at Badminton (Gloucestershire), part of a series of park buildings and follies. The most grandiose of these is Castle Barn with battlements, flanking turrets and the end of the barn disguised as a gatehouse. Another Castle Farm was designed by the Duchess of Norfolk at Worksop (Nottinghamshire). Stables, hog sties and poultry houses occupied three sides of a huge courtyard, with an open shelter shed in one corner. Castellated barns on the fourth side were placed either side of the house, 'in the back part of which her Grace has a room fitted in the Gothic taste for drinking tea'.[46]

The eleventh Duke of Norfolk's activities at Greystoke (Cumbria), which

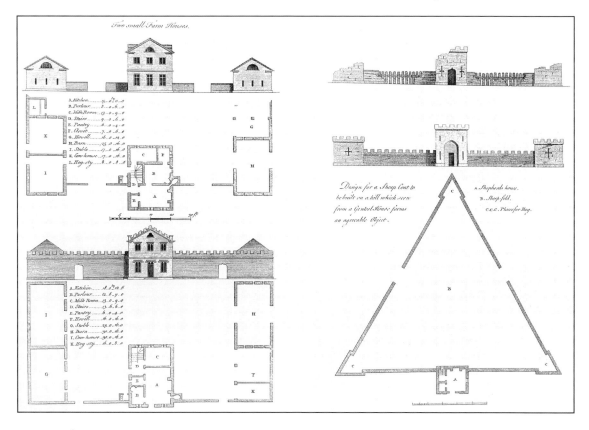

had been transformed in the eighteenth century as a park was created, new
fields were laid out, farms built and a straight road cut through from Penrith,
exemplified this duality at its most extreme. The eleventh Duke was an amateur
architect, ardent Whig and supporter of the Americans in the War of
Independence. In this he was at odds with his Tory neighbour Lord Lonsdale
whom he sought to aggravate by vaunting his pro-American sympathies in his
buildings.[47] With the help of the eminent architect, Francis Hiorne, who was
working on the Duke's Arundel estates at the time, he built castellated
farmsteads visible from the road, which he named after famous battles in the
American War of Independence. Fort Putman is the most elaborate, with the
farmhouse and buildings enclosed by mock fortifications (Plate 6). The outside
wall of the cowhouse is faced with a row of blank Gothic arches separated
by six semi-circular piers rising, chimney-like, above the eaves, each ringed by
coronets of stiff stone petals from which rise cones surmounted by balls.
Bunkers Hill is less extravagant in design, although a castellated curtain wall
and Gothic arches enclose a small conventional yard. Barn, stables and byres,
shrouded from view behind their picturesque Gothic screens, were designed
as eye-catchers in the surrounding agricultural landscape (Figure 30). A planned
courtyard arrangement of buildings is adhered to, but the buildings are seen
embellishing the approach to Greystoke Park. They emphasise the Enlightenment belief that beauty and utility could be combined in a useful and
productive landscape. This message, along with the political overtones, would
have been understood by the Duke's educated guests approaching Greystoke,
as they turned off the Great North Road at Penrith.

Dairies, the most elaborate and highly decorated of model farm buildings,
most obviously expressed the philosophical pastoral ideal. Traditionally, the
dairy was the responsibility of the lady of the house, and by the late-eighteenth
century milk had gained romantic associations with rural purity and goodness.
But the design of dairies had to be based on practical principles. They were
often octagonal buildings, tiled for coolness and ease of cleaning, with few
windows, more often on the north side, and plenty of ventilation through
latticed or slatted openings filled by wire mesh or gauze. Some had fountains
to help keep them cool. The jugs and settling bowls needed to be highly
glazed for cleanliness and were often very decorative. Wedgewood soon
dominated the market for both pottery and tiles. Many dairies contained
collections of oriental porcelain as at Alnwick and Woburn where the Chinese
dairy was especially designed as a setting for the Duke's collection.[48] Most
dairies were placed near the house and away from the farm buildings to prevent
the cream being tainted by farmyard smells, but as we have seen that at Sandon
(Staffordshire) was at the centre of the model farm itself, designed to make
an elegant focal point in the view along the valley (see Figure 27).[49] Dairies
continued to be a popular and necessary part of farm design with some of the
most elaborate, such as Queen Victoria's at Frogmore, being built after 1850.

The relationship between farmsteads and the 'improved' landscape was,
however, already absorbed in a broader political debate. The link between

FIGURE 30.
The house at Bunkers
Hill, Greystoke
(*above*) with the stable
and first-floor granary
building to the rear
(*below*).

parkland and farming, the aesthetic and the practical, was at the heart of eighteenth-century 'improvement', a word indicative of the ordering of the natural order and which embraced both land improvement schemes, agricultural innovation and the creation of landscaped parks. One view envisaged the happy juxtaposition of a productive landscape and objects of beauty and interest as being symbolic of a nation at ease with itself, a counter to the social fragmentation and instability heralded by industrialisation.[50] Thus a visitor to Harewood in West Yorkshire in 1777 described how 'the whole country forms a theatre of ornamented farms'.[51] Ruggles, in concluding his lengthy correspondence to the *Annals of Agriculture* on 'Picturesque Farms', wrote that whilst cottages and possibly eye-catchers such as field barns could be placed for picturesque effect, farm buildings must be practical: 'neatness and propriety of form ... will ... catch the observing eye of taste'. The whole group could be surrounded by a plantation and contain a clock tower with a weather vane, 'no useless ornament to the industrious'. 'The whole suite of buildings thus surrounded and thus ornamented with a turret bosomed high in towering trees, will captivate the eye with the appearance of a rural village, the residence of honest industry, and its companions, health and cheerfulness'.[52] On the other hand, the landscape gardeners Humphrey Repton stated that 'objects of mere convenience' such as stables and barns should be removed altogether if they could not be made more ornamental.[53] At Holkham, however, Samuel Wyatt's Great Barn (see Plate 11, Figure 49) could be seen from the Hall and equally importantly, the Hall was visible to the visitors who attended the sheep shearings at the barn. In 1801, John Lawrence urged that parks should, together with the home farm, be used as 'a theatre for the display of all the notable varieties of experimental husbandry'.[54] Whaley, in his *Observations on Modern Gardening* written in 1770, wrote that gardening 'was no longer confined to the spots from which it borrows its name, but also the disposition and embellishments of a park, a farm, or a riding'.[55] John Curwen commented upon the mixture of lawn and cultivation as it existed at Holkham in 1809, where he noted 'What can be more beautiful than the diversified scenery which there presents itself. The effects of order and industry, combined with abundance, must be gratifying to every spectator'.[56] Similarly, as at Life Hill Farm on the Sledmere estate (see pp. 85–9), tree planting could spill out of the park onto the tenanted farms. Some of this was specifically designed as game cover, a potential source of friction between those tenants who resented the damage by game birds to their crops and landlords who valued their sport. This duality could extend beyond the park and woods to the water. Ornamental lakes formed an integral part of water systems powering machinery, as at the Reverend Benyon's home farm at Culford (Suffolk) and the home farm at Letheringsett (Norfolk), as well as collecting points for water meadows as at West Lexham (Norfolk). Rowland Hunt, the author of an essay for the Board of Agriculture, expressed the philosophy of embellishment at its most extreme: 'The desperate schemes invented by professed surveyors, of raising mounds, sinking holes, boring through banks ... tend only to increase expense and to cast a gloom of magnificent solitude around a mansion. Whereas a judicious, but not a forced introduction of the farm and its accompaniments, adds cheerfulness and business to the scene itself'.[57]

Just over forty planned and model farmsteads built before 1790 have been identified, comprising a very small but highly significant percentage of all those known to have been built. Far more important, however, as a practical influence on farm design than the many books on decorative farm buildings already published was the first volume of *Communications to the Board of Agriculture*, produced in 1797. In this for the first time we find a serious discussion on designs for farm buildings, in a book primarily of agricultural rather than architectural interest. As such, it marks a turning point in the literature and is a product of the period of patriotic improvement ushered in by the Napoleonic Wars, which is the subject of the next chapter.

CHAPTER FOUR

Patriotic Improvement, 1790–1840

Patriotism and the king

The 1790s began with a boost to the cause of agricultural improvement from the most influential quarter. In 1790 George III took on the management of Windsor Great Park and employed the well-established land agent and author of *Hints to Gentlemen of Landed Property*, Nathaniel Kent of Kent, Claridge and Co. to supervise its development. The park at that time consisted of large tracts of barren land which were either low-lying and boggy, or upland heath. Kent realised the importance of this commission, not only to his own career, but more generally to the cause of improvement if 'men of distinction' were seen to be setting an example. 'Agriculture is unquestionably one of the most rational and laudable employments that can engage the attention of Men – It is productive of numberless blessings to Society and is the source that gives birth to all Manufactures and Commerce'.[1] Here we see the patriotic duty of increasing agricultural output being emphasised yet again. His plan included the reduction of the number of deer and replacing them with cattle and sheep, the draining of land, removing rushes, flattening ant hills, a limited amount of breaking up and reseeding of pasture and making plantations. On this improved land two new farmsteads were to be built. One was for a light arable farm to be managed on the 'Norfolk system' and to be called Norfolk Farm. Kent had worked extensively for Norfolk landlords, including Thomas Coke of Holkham Hall (see pp. 107–11). He was, therefore, familiar both with the land improvements undertaken in the area involving enclosure, drainage and marling, and with the systems of crop rotations later known as the 'Norfolk four-course'. These were designed to end the need for the fallow year and increase fodder available for the expanding livestock numbers. The other farm, on heavier clay, was to be managed as a dairy farm on a West Country system and called Gloucester Farm (the name was later changed to Flemish Farm), with a rotation of crops alternately for feeding man and beast. 'A farm of the kind here described, situate so near the capital, would excite attention, challenge imitation and be productive of great good to society.'[2] The king's motives were said to be three-fold: to create useful labour, to engage in experimentation in agriculture and 'to excite imitation where success might encourage it'.[3]

Kent, who in his *Hints* had advised against expensive, showy buildings,[4] intended to avoid unnecessary expenditure, even on this prestigious site. Consequently, when the two farmsteads were laid out in 1791–92 no architect was employed and recycled materials were used. He wrote in his journal in July 1791: 'Examined several of the buildings standing near the (Cumberland) Lodge to inform myself which of them would answer removal to the intended Norfolk Farm'. A week later he measured and staked out all the proposed buildings at Norfolk Farm, ready for inspection by George III. Stables, ox-stalls, cart house and pigsties were moved to their new site at the very reasonable cost of £300.[5] In May the following year he marked out the foundations for the barn at Norfolk Farm which was completed and thatched by August. Similarly, many of the buildings at Flemish Farm were moved from elsewhere in the park. Although Flemish Farm was rebuilt by Prince Albert and Norfolk Farm has since been radically altered, Kent's plans and elevations survive (Figure 31). Both show very traditional layouts with barns, stables and ox-stalls arranged around a yard, with a stack yard behind the barn. The elevations suggest a symmetrical classical façade with blind arches and lunette first-floor openings reminiscent of Wyatt's agricultural buildings. It is difficult to match the elevations with the plans, which suggests that one or other was modified before building. As little of either of these farmsteads remains, it is impossible to know which of these are more accurate. Some minor concessions to fashionable architecture were made and Kent recorded in his *Journal* the painting of the local red Berkshire tiles grey so that they looked like slate, to achieve an acceptable 'country house' style. Conventional drawings for ox-stalls and stables are included in the *Journal,* as well as a more original design for a cart house and granary for Norfolk Farm (Figure 32), with two high side aisles 'to hold occasionally at each end a Loaded Wagon'.[6] None of these buildings survive.

FIGURE 31 (*overleaf*). Kent's plans for Norfolk Farm and Flemish Farm, built within Windsor Great Park in 1791–94. Both are simple conventional groups with the house forming part of one side of a courtyard plan. Differences between them stem from the fact that Norfolk Farm was primarily an arable one, with a larger barn and extensive ranges of stabling, and Flemish Farm a livestock one.

Patriotism, war and its aftermath

During the 1790s and following the example of George III, interest in land improvement and farm buildings increased, accelerating under the impetus of greatly inflated grain prices during the Napoleonic Wars. The patriotic duty to expand agricultural output was stressed by the improving landowner of Caithness and initiator of the Scottish *Statistical Account,* Sir John Sinclair, when arguing for the setting up with government funds of the Board of Agriculture (of which he subsequently became the first president). 'No nation could be happy and powerful', he argued in echo of Kent's sentiments, 'that did not unite a judicious system of agriculture to the benefits of ... industry and ... commerce.' The Board was to act as a central office for information and exchange of ideas between farmers, both at home and abroad. Its purpose was also to conduct agricultural surveys and encourage improvement.[7] Its final establishment in 1793 is an indication of the importance ascribed to farming as war threatened and finally broke out in 1796.

27th 28th & 29th July 1791

Had the Honor to attend His Majesty to the Norfolk Farm, and explained the Situation, of all the intended Buildings.

PLAN of the said Buildings & Farm Yard.

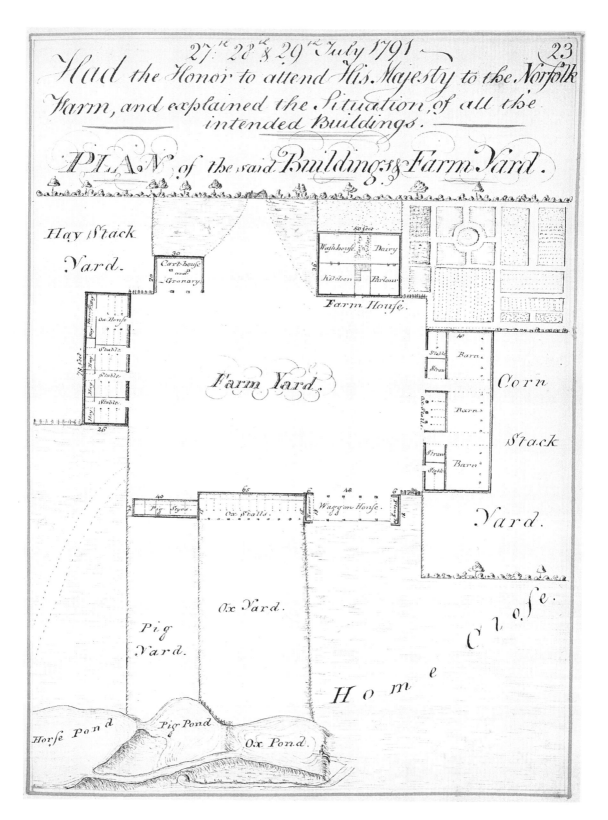

Hay Stack Yard.

Cart-house and Granary.

Washhouse — Dairy
Kitchen — Parlour
Farm House.

Farm Yard.

Ox House
Stable
Stable

Corn

Stable — Barn
Straw
Barns
Straw
Stable — Barn

Stack

Yard.

Pig Styes. Ox Stalls. Waggon House.

Pig Yard.

Ox Yard.

Home

Close.

Horse Pond. Pig Pond. Ox Pond.

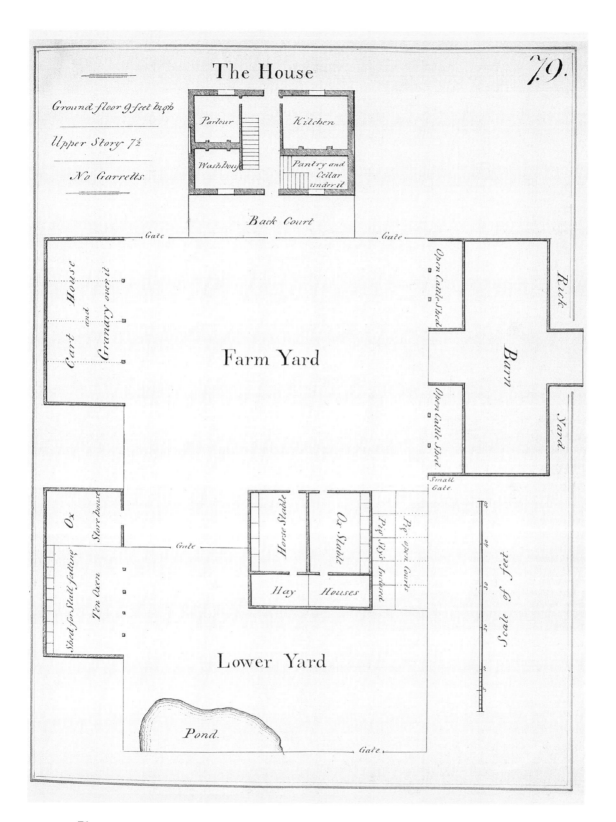

The House

79.

Ground floor 9 feet high

Upper Story 7½

No Garretts

Parlour

Kitchen

Washhouse

Pantry and Cellar under it

Back Court

Gate

Gate

Cart House and Granary over it

Open Cattle Shed

Rick

Farm Yard

Barn

Open Cattle Shed

Yard

Small Gate

Ox Storehouse

Horse Stable

Ox Stable

Pig Styes Inclosed

Pig Styes open Courts

Gate

Shed for Stall fatting

Ten Oxen

Hay

Houses

Scale of 50 feet

Lower Yard

Pond.

Gate

71

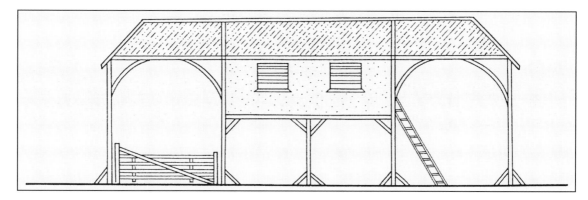

Soon after war was declared grain prices immediately rose by 50 shillings to the artificially high price of over 80 shillings a quarter, and in 1801 and 1811 to the famine levels of over 120 shillings. Rents followed profits up, although the degree of rise varied greatly from estate to estate (see Figure 5). High prices and rents, reinforced by the Board of Agriculture's belief that increasing productivity was a patriotic duty, provided ample incentives to landlords in the improvement and planning of new farmsteads in order to attract tenants with capital. This activity was at its greatest during the Napoleonic Wars (1796–1815), and an indication of this interest is the number of enclosure acts passed by parliament (see Figure 10). These reached a peak of 349 acts between 1810 and 1814 (26% of all those between 1730 and 1840).[8] This surge of activity is mirrored in farm building activity. The planned and model farmsteads erected during the Napoleonic Wars (1796–1815) account for fully two-thirds of those recorded between 1760 and 1840 (see Figure 3).

The Board of Agriculture was responsible for commissioning the county by county *General Views of Agriculture* and for publishing *Communications to the Board*, the first volume of which appeared in 1797. Part of it was devoted to farm buildings and cottages with the section on farm buildings written by Robert Beatson, a Scotsman and ex-soldier turned writer who also wrote several Scottish volumes of the *General Views*. That the Board should turn its attention to buildings so early in its existence served to emphasise the key role it considered that good cottages and farmsteads played in improvement. The plans produced for farmsteads are of two types. Firstly, there are the familiar courtyard or double-courtyard designs with the barn in the middle. By 1797, the first threshing machines were beginning to find their way onto farms. One design incorporates a water wheel to provide power to the barn, although there is no sign of where the water supply would come from or how the wheel would be protected from animals in the yard (Figure 33). The house was still an integral part of the yard, in this case abutting the central barn. A second group of plans shows a curved arrangement of freestanding barns and stables linked by walls across a yard behind the house. The buildings are all plain with little architectural embellishment, but the layouts are on the whole impractical. No surviving examples have been located. As we have already seen, Robert Adam, Sir John Soane and Samuel Wyatt all produced farm

FIGURE 32. Kent's design for a carthouse and granary to be erected at Flemish Farm was described by Kent as intended 'to hold occasionally at each end a Loaded Waggon – the middle part for carts with gates to each – over which a granary.'

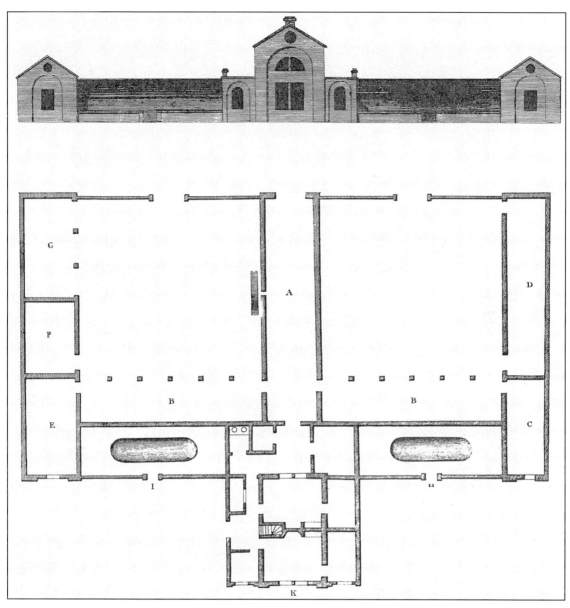

FIGURE 33.
A plan for a farmstead with a water-powered barn (marked A), from *Communications to the Board of Agriculture* (1797).

plans making use of a circular or semi-circular layout. The agricultural writer, William Marshall, had some sympathy for this architectural model and was an advocate of an octagonal layout, to avoid the corners of a rectangular plan. In 1791, he became agent to Lord Heathfield on his West Country estate at Buckland. Here he built 'a suite of farm yards and buildings on a large scale'. The yard was in a 'semi-octagonal form, inclosed on one side with cattle sheds, on the other by a line of stables and farm offices'.[9] In 1825 Loudon illustrated an octagonal farmstead said to have been built by Marshall (Figure 34).[10] The house is on the south side with an entrance gate and granaries opposite. The remaining six sides are occupied by stables and shelter sheds

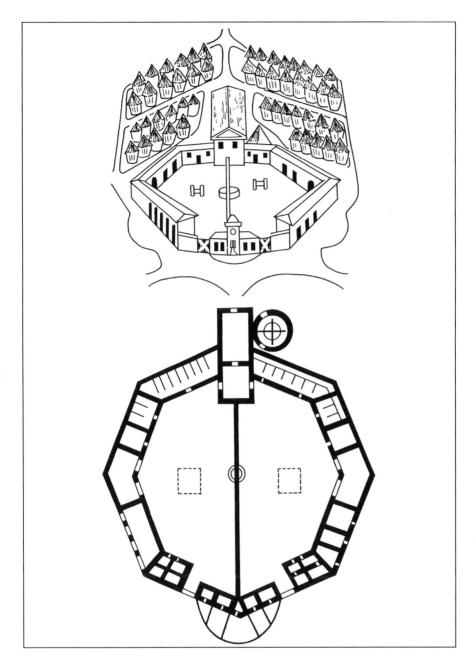

FIGURE 34.
Loudon's plan of an
octagonal farmstead
was said to have been
built by Marshall, an
enthusiast for the
polygonal plan where
there were no
awkward corners for
cleaning out or for
animals to get into.

whilst a barn with steam-powered threshing equipment extends into a stack yard to the rear. A more elaborate drawing of a similar design appears in a later edition of Loudon's *Encyclopedia*, in 1831.[11] None of these buildings survive in England although several curved and semi-circular examples still exist in Scotland, particularly on the Duke of Argyll's estates.[12] The rather irregular example at Schoose (see Figure 48), may have been influenced by Marshall's arguments. Surviving examples of either the curved or nuclear layouts with the barn in the centre are rare, and usually the work of established architects.

By the early-nineteenth century these various experimental forms had largely been dropped in favour of the well-tried and eminently adaptable courtyard arrangement. The end of the war, moreover, had brought an immediate collapse of grain prices to their pre-war price-levels, and with it an agricultural depression that removed the incentive for such extravagant schemes. A land-owner-dominated parliament passed the Corn Laws to restrict imports, but farming confidence remained low and farms were difficult to let, particularly during the banking crisis of the early 1820s, when even the best-run estates were suffering from high levels of rent arrears. At Holkham, the amount collected dropped from £31,678 in 1821 to £30,950 in 1824. This was the only instance of a decline in revenue on this estate before the depression years of the 1880s.[13] In spite of this collapse of farming confidence, new farmsteads continued to be built, if at a slower rate and with practical rather than architectural considerations coming to the fore. These changes can be followed through the literature of the period. There was a rush of publications in the first thirty years of the nineteenth century, many of which were of little practical use, but the most valuable was that of Charles Waistell, chairman of the Committee on Agriculture of the Royal Society of Arts. *Designs for Agricultural Buildings* was published posthumously by his nephew in 1827. In the preface, his nephew stated that Waistell had been designing buildings for fifty years, many of which had been built. With good buildings 'Even a moderate farm will not only be enhanced in value, but will also command a choice of desirable tenants'.[14]

As Waistell's nephew also remarked: 'When farmers cannot live, money cannot be spared to make improvements'.[15] Gradually, however, conditions improved and there was a change in plan form to provide for changing farming conditions. Although grain prices did not reach the famine levels of the Napoleonic Wars, they soon recovered from the immediate post-war depression (see Figure 4). An increasing population and a steady and ensured market provided the incentive for farmers to increase their output which, in the absence of artificial fertilisers, meant that even more stock needed to be kept and their manure conserved. New designs, therefore, sought to provide more cattle accommodation in larger yards, divided by blocks of shelter sheds. More yard-fed stock was kept and more accommodation was needed for them. This led to the development of the double-courtyard 'E'-shaped plan. Some of the Greenwich Hospital and Alnwick farmsteads in Northumberland (see Figure 39) have as many as five yards divided by shelter sheds. The range of specific building types continued to increase, with granaries over shelter sheds some-times replacing and sometimes built alongside the barn on the north side of the yard. Root stores and other feed stores were required to supply the increased numbers of cattle accommodated on the farmstead during the winter months.

Mechanised threshing and the flow of corn and straw through the barns to the cattle and the granaries, and then of the manure out to the fields, was also perceived to be of prime importance. The barn was often placed at right-angles to the yard complex and out into the stack yard to allow for a

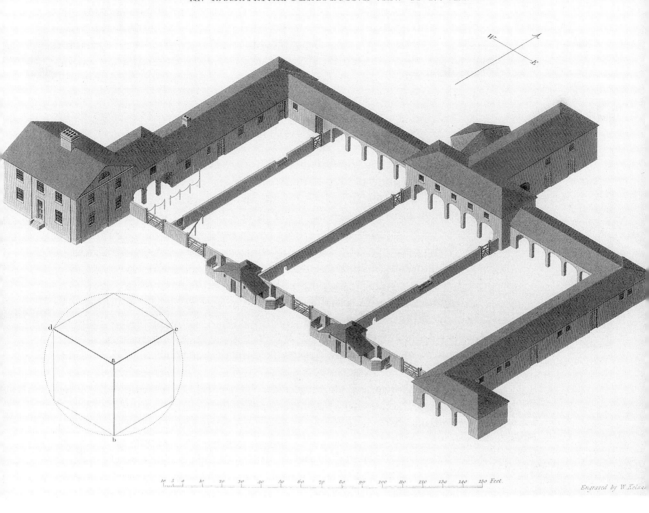

Engraved by W. Kelsal

power source such as a water wheel, horse-engine house or steam-engine house to be built or a portable engine to be pulled up beside it (Figure 35). Practical considerations were all-important, and Waistell published plans showing how he had adapted his old buildings in Caterham to suit modern farming.[16] He wrote that 'Farm buildings being intended solely for the purpose of utility, should be simple in their form and perfectly plain ... to utility alone everything in agriculture must be subordinate'.[17]

1833 saw the publication of another important book in the chronology: J. C. Loudon's *Cottage, Farm and Villa Architecture*. This was followed by his *Encyclopedia of Agriculture* which went through many editions. The general principle that farm buildings should be regular, preferably around one or more courtyards, and have an architectural character that paid attention to the site, purpose and scale of the farm was now generally accepted, and he was critical of the more fanciful designs to be found in many pattern books. Moreover,

FIGURE 35.
A perspective from Charles Waistell's book, *Designs for Agricultural Buildings* (1827). As a result of the prosperous war years and farmers' increased social status, farmhouses were generally being built at a short distance from the yard.

76

many were designed as prominent features in the landscape, standing as an indication of the landowner's interest in agriculture and buildings associated with it. That change was slow, particularly during the years of depression, is indicated by the fact that Loudon could republish the Board of Agriculture designs in the fifth edition of 1844, nearly fifty years after their original publication. The major period of change was not to come until the following decade with the spread of 'high farming'.

Mechanisation and regional variations

As interest in the building of planned and model farmsteads increased with the rising rents and agricultural profits of the war years, the threshing machine began to make its appearance on the farm. Although there had been several attempts to construct an alternative to hand flailing, the first effective machine was invented by George Mieckle and built at Kilbogie in Clackmannanshire in 1786. By 1800 it had been refined to such an extent that its basic design changed little over the next fifty years. Although smaller versions were developed, it was generally a huge machine, which could occupy two floors of a barn. The original machine was horse-powered, which remained the most usual source of power until the 1850s in view of the erratic availability and expense of wind and water power and the fact that, as the original low-pressure boilers were so wasteful of fuel, steam was only economical close to coal fields. All these power sources could be so arranged as to work machines for feed preparation such as chaff cutters, barley hummelers and turnip slicers, but generally these did not find their way onto farms before the 1830s.

The earliest horse engines (gin-gangs) consisted of a large wooden crown wheel with wooden gearing and shafts that required protecting from the weather, and so needed an entirely new sort of farm building in the form of a round house on the side of the barn. They spread rapidly across Northumberland, Durham, and Yorkshire as well as the south west peninsula and east lowland Scotland – all areas which had seen a shift from being low-wage areas in the mid-eighteenth century, to being high-wage ones with the development of industry at the end of the century. Wages in Northumberland and much of Yorkshire and Lancashire could be as high as 11 shillings in the 1790s, whilst in parts of the Midlands they were as low as six shillings and eight pence. The south remained on average a low-wage area throughout the period under discussion, but with pockets of much higher levels near the tin and copper mines.[18] These wage differentials emphasise the patchy nature of industrialisation up to the middle of the nineteenth century. The evidence of the Board of Agriculture reports, although inconsistent and subjective, suggests that it was in these areas of high-wage levels that threshing machines were 'in general use' by the early 1800s: this is supported by Keith Hutton's map of surviving wheel houses in the British Isles.[19]

Threshing machines were more likely to be economical on large farms, such as the home farms of estates or the newly laid out enclosure farms of

Northumberland and the Wolds: 'It is impossible to erect a good substantial four-horse mill, with every appendage for less than from £250 to £300'.[20] In addition, they were unlikely to be worthwhile if there was a surplus of labour as was the case over much of southern England up to the 1840s. One of the complaints of the Swing rioters in 1830 was the introduction of threshing machines, and they frequently demanded their destruction. In this, they were occasionally supported by the magistrates. Those for North Walsham (Norfolk) printed a notice urging farmers to dismantle threshing machines and increase wages.[21] Here, employing fewer men simply meant rising poor rates as the number of unemployed increased. After 1840, as labour surpluses declined and farmers began to complain about increasing wage bills, mechanisation began to make economic sense.[22] Even so, stationary engines remained confined to larger farms and were still most likely to be found in the north of the country. Even where threshing machines were installed, some of the crop could still be hand-flailed. Barley for malting, for example, was said to be damaged by machines. In general, therefore, barns continued to have double threshing doors but were built out from the farmyards so that a power source could be built beside them.

It is thus clear that the distinction between the mechanised north and hand-powered south continued throughout the first half of the century, even on otherwise innovative layouts. Different agricultural regions had also developed distinct traditions of building types which were incorporated into the standard courtyard plan. The bank barn – a building type developed on gentry estates in late-seventeenth-century Cumbria[23] and spreading from there throughout western Britain, is to be found as part of the layout of many planned and model farmsteads within these regions. It made ideal use of the fall of the land and could be incorporated into a larger, planned layout. Here, on a south-facing slope, a two-storey building would be built into the hillside with a lower floor of cattle stalls opening south, and a threshing barn above (see Figures 13 and 80). The barn typically had wide double doors to the north and an opposing winnowing door to the south, at first-floor level. The larger planned and model farmsteads included a courtyard of buildings to the south of the barn, while on smaller holdings, this multi-purpose building could be arranged to include all the needs of the farm. Because of its position on sloping ground on a valley side, water power could frequently be diverted for use in the barn. Trebartha Barton Farm, built between 1820 and 1830 as a planned home farm for the Rodd family in east Cornwall, combines these features and local building traditions, such as slate-hanging, with a courtyard layout and water power (Plate 7).[24] A variation of this plan form, found in Cornwall and along the north Somerset coast, was not built into a bank, but free-standing corn sheaves having to be loaded up into the threshing barn at first floor level. Worgan's *General View of Cornwall*, written in 1811, illustrated several farm-steads, including one unusual design for a central barn/fodder house and wool loft/granary above, all under one roof. 'I do not think so many conveniences can be procured anywhere, on a cheaper plan'.[25] Cornwall is not an area of great estates, but there was wealth to be made from the mines where some of the latest steam technology was introduced for pumping out flood water. It is no coincidence that one of the earliest steam engines for agricultural purposes was built and installed in 1811 at the Home Farm, Trewithen House, Probus, by Richard Trevithick the noted mining engineer and steam engine designer, for the industrialist Sir Christopher Hawkins.[26] Linhays (hay lofts, open along one side above cow byres) were a traditional west country solution to the problem of providing hay storage. The most elaborate survival in a formal home farm layout is that designed by Anthony Keck (1726–1797) and built at Moccas (Herefordshire) in 1783–4, where wide arches support the roofs of hay lofts on two sides of a huge courtyard. Keck's work was mostly confined to the West Midlands and included jails and work houses as well as country houses, often described by contemporaries as 'neat brick edifices'.[27] On the north Somerset Acland estates the farmstead at Holt Ball includes both a linhay and bank barn, whilst at Trebartha Barton the openings of an original linhay have since been filled in.

New landscapes: north of England estates, 1790–1840

As we have already seen, it was in the north of England that some of the greatest landscape changes of the eighteenth and early-nineteenth century took place. Here large areas of open land were waiting to be developed. Up to the end of the seventeenth century, the influential East Yorkshire landowners had been concentrated on the low-lying clay lands, but in the eighteenth century newcomers such as the Sykes and the Middletons were buying the cheaper uplands which they saw as good investments, ripe for development.[28] Henry Strickland, author of the *General View,* wrote in 1812: 'Formerly, a clay soil was alone thought desirable for cultivation, and a low rich one for residence.' However, the cheapness of the unenclosed wold lands and the attractiveness of the landscape for the creation of parks had changed this pattern, and this change was repeated elsewhere throughout the north.

Northumberland, as we have seen, was a county where agricultural improvement, involving enclosure of commons and wastes, draining and liming of land had been going on from before the 1760s. The Union of Scotland and England had increased security in the area and allowed landowners to develop their estates and improve agriculture. There had been a decline in the fortunes of many Northumberland landowners in the late-seventeenth century which had resulted in land sales, and many of the new landowners were improvers. The lack of freeholders generally gave owners a free hand to enclose and reorganise. Village settlements were abandoned and replaced by new farmsteads and cottages.[29] J. Hodgson, writing in 1827 in his *History of Northumberland,* stated: 'Many villages in Northumberland have entirely gone down, but farm houses and cottages have risen up in their place in more convenient situations, a mode better adapted to the growth of good principles and usefulness than the village systems'.[30]

Over a forty-year period up to 1805, the value of some farms had increased threefold.[31] The county was dominated by huge estates and large farmsteads. Over 20% of farms were over 300 acres and over half of the county was owned in holdings of over 10,000 acres; many of the owners, such as the Leylands of Haggerston (17,644 acres), Earl Grey of Bilton (17,599 acres), and Lord Tankerville of Chillingham (28,930 acres), were resident.[32] Because of the sparse population and the dominance of large estates, few parliamentary acts were needed for enclosure, but those there were covered extensive areas. For instance, the enclosure of Hexham and Allendale in 1800 covered 42,000 acres, and resulted in the creation of 650 allotments divided between 280 individuals, most of whom would need new sets of farm buildings.[33]

The proximity of hill grazing and lower lying light lands suitable for root crops meant that a mixed farming system of cereals could develop, relying for its productivity on the manure from turnip-fed sheep and yard-fed cattle. The Northumberland farmer, George Culley, author of *Observations on Livestock*, was responsible with his brother, Matthew, for improving both cattle and the Cheviot breed of sheep. Less suited to arable were the clay lands of the coast, and even as late as the mid-nineteenth century Caird commented on the backwardness of farming there.[34]

Vital to the economic development of the area was coal mining. This not only provided mass employment, which meant there was a shortage of labour for the farms, but it also put immense profits into the hands of the landowners, of whom the Duke of Northumberland at Alnwick was the most important. The coal of Northumberland had long been exploited, but the eighteenth-century population increase and industrial demand resulted in a massive explosion of output. The increased demand for food resulted in 'a colonisation of waste land on a grand scale not seen since the thirteenth century'.[35] As we have already noted (see p. 48), the Blacketts reinvested their industrial wealth in the area around Wallington. In 1787, Lord Swinburne returned to his Glendale estate in North Tyneside and created a model estate on some of the poorest soils in the county, whilst Greenwich Hospital was to develop its farms with money made in its smelt mill, opened near Langley Castle in 1767.[36]

Towards the end of the eighteenth century the exhaustion of the more accessible coal around Newcastle and a great improvement in mining techniques led to the development of deeper mines between Newcastle and the coast. The port of Blyth began to develop with the opening of the pits at Plessey.[37] All this promoted a ready market for farm produce in the growing towns and mining communities, whilst the increasing employment opportunities created a shortage of farm labour. The region's farms were also enormous by national standards, ranging from 300–400 acres to as much as 1,000–1,200 acres. As a result of these factors, many farmsteads provided early examples of the adoption of stationary engines and mechanical threshing. Cobbett, writing in 1832 noted that in this 'country without people' the threshing was done by machinery and horses. The farmsteads between Morpeth

FIGURE 36.
The long row of farm
workers' cottages
below East House
Farm, Chiswick
(Northumberland),
built for the
Haggerston estate.

and Hexham were enormous. On one he saw a hundred stacks of wheat in the yard 'and not another house within a mile or two'.[38] This lack of housing contributed to one of the characteristic features of the region: the existence of rows of small cottages beside its large steadings. These could be designed as a terrace set slightly apart from the farmstead, or sometimes the cottages formed one side of the farm courtyard (Figure 36).

In such areas where agricultural wealth was often supplemented by huge coal mining profits, new building could continue through the leaner years of the 1820s. Good buildings were still needed to attract men with capital. John Grey, the influential agent to the extensive Greenwich Hospital estates, thought that nearly all the farmsteads on farms of over 200 acres in Northumberland had been rebuilt in the 80 years previous to 1840. 'They commonly form three sides of a square open to the south; the highest buildings being on the north side ... with the stack yard to the north of the square and the barn, containing the threshing machine projects into it at right angles ... To reduce distances to be carried granaries were divided either side of the barn'. The granaries were usually positioned over shelter sheds opening into the yard, with stables and byres running down the two sides.[39] In spite of their size, the general principles of layout remained the same. Cattle were kept in the open yards, with feed stores along the south wall and access both from the outside and into the yards. Shelter sheds with granaries above occupied the north side. A barn with an engine house on the side extended north from the north side into the stack yards, with a long wagon lodge connected to it. The house was separated from the farmyard by a wall and roadway. This type of farmstead, which was already appearing on the Alnwick estates by 1805, continued to be built for at least another twenty years. The house was not now part of the courtyard, but stood slightly separate, leaving a U-plan open to the south, often with the barn opening both into the granaries and shelter sheds so that grain and straw could easily be moved to its destination. To the north was the stack yard, from which the raw material for threshing was transported to the barn, which by the 1820s was likely to be provided with some form of motive power.

By far the most wealthy and influential amongst Northumberland land-owners were the Dukes of Northumberland, based at Alnwick Castle. It was the second Duke who was responsible for a programme of improvement in the early-nineteenth century, and in 1805 he appointed the Newcastle architect, David Stephenson (1757–1819), as the official estate architect. He had no country house commissions to his name, and so may seem a surprising appointment if it were not for the fact that he was a protegé of the Ridley family at Blagdon, just north of Newcastle.[40] Here again we see the operation of local connections in the relationships between architect and patron. The terms of his employment stated that in the case of improvements at the time of the renewal of a lease, expenditure should not exceed five years' increase of rent on the new lease. In the case of yearly-let farms, requests by tenants for new buildings should be referred to the Duke personally. If the expenditure was to exceed a quarter of the year's rent, then the farm would need to be revalued. As we have seen, the tenant was often involved in the discussions about new buildings and all building plans had to be approved by the Duke.[41]

In 1806, Stephenson compiled a book of about fifty plans entitled *Northumberland Farm Buildings*.[42] The houses, built of grey ashlar, are all exactly the same with simple double-fronted classical façades with central doors under an arch containing the Percy coat of arms. The farms themselves vary in size from extensive layouts, such as the buildings set around four yards at Chalton costing £510, to smaller schemes costing £200. The more expensive schemes included a barn in a central position in the north range, jutting out at right-angles into the stack yard in order to allow for a horse or steam engine to be built alongside it. This design, which we have seen was advocated by Charles Waistell in the 1820s (see pp. 75–6), was advanced for this date. None of these drawings shows any type of engine house and all the barns have

FIGURE 37.
The square
horse-engine house
with a granary above,
dating from the
mid-nineteenth
century, at Longdyke
rarm, Shilbottle
(Northumberland),
one of Stephenson's
farms.

opposing threshing doors for hand threshing. All the buildings are simple, practical designs with little in the way of ornament.

Another Northumberland architect, John Green, also worked for the second Duke. He was known for his severe and economical styles: Park Farm, built in 1827, is a fine example of his work (Figure 37). The original layout was totally symmetrical with four matching corner pavilions and an impressive north front. The U-plan was open to the south towards the house, with the barn extending out from the centre of the east side (Plate 8). East Brizlee, also within the park, is a similar symmetrical farmstead but on a smaller scale, with each side of the U containing central two-storey blocks linked by lower wings (Figure 38).

Almost as important as the Alnwick estates in terms of influence were those of Greenwich Hospital, managed by John Grey for much of the first half of the nineteenth century. Plans of about fifty of its farmsteads survive, showing that thirty have a planned layout of a U- or E-plan, or even occasionally a

double-'E'shape.[43] Grey published plans of some of them. One at Outchester, near Bamburgh, for a farm of just over 500 acres, provided five south-facing yards. The straw barn formed the central block on the north side, with open shelters and granaries above on either side. The barn itself, worked by steam power, was at right-angles to the strawbarn at the back of the buildings (Figure 39). Similar buildings at Throckley were powered by a horse engine.[44] The 'E'-shaped layout shown on the early plans still survives at the solid, stone-built farmstead of Thornborough High Barns, although the wheel house for the horse engine has gone. The stable block is positioned along one side, the cattle sheds being originally set around the second yard. Mr Colbeck wrote in 1848 that the buildings 'erected by the Commission of Greenwich Hospital under the direction of John Grey of Dilston contain every convenience a farmer could desire'.[45]

Further south, reclamation and improvement was continuing in Yorkshire. Two-thirds of the East Yorkshire wolds were enclosed by parliamentary acts after 1730, with the 1770s being the peak decade when fifty acts were passed. Two hundred and fifty townships and 206,000 acres were reorganised, either as a result of parliamentary acts or private agreements. Enclosure was accompanied by a conversion of old pasture to a new arable system, based by the 1780s on the folding of sheep on turnips.[46] An improved method of building dew ponds was perfected by Robert Gardener of Kilham in about 1775.[47] These ponds, dug into the chalk but lined with clay, allowed these dry lands to be used for both arable and livestock. As a result, a great many farmsteads were created at a distance from old settlements. Strickland, writing in *The General View* in 1812 said, 'where new erections are required, more convenient plans for the buildings are adopted and more eligible situations fixed on'.[48] He described as typical a courtyard layout open to the south with a barn and stable to the north, shelter sheds to the east and the house to the west with a high brick wall broken by a tall, boarded gate to the south.

The East Yorkshire estate which was most prominently associated with this activity was that of the Sykes family of Sledmere. Sir Christopher was directly involved in the enclosure of Sledmere and Croome in the 1770s, his principal motive being the enlargement of the park (Figure 40).[49] Here, again, we see beauty and utility going hand in hand. This duality can clearly be seen at Castle Farm, in the home park, which was designed by John Carr as an eye-catcher with only a very modest set of buildings behind the embattled façade. In the 1790s Sykes was buying property in Garton-on-the-Wold where he reorganised farms, created plantations and built new farmsteads, agricultural improvement being again less important than his stated aim to make a 'ride towards Beverley six miles through my own grounds'.[50] Approximately fourteen estate farmsteads near Sledmere were designed by Sir Christopher, and elevations showing the farmhouses with flanking yard walls and pavilions survive amongst the estate papers. These comprise one of the earliest documented groups of planned farmsteads.[51] However, the drawings are only of classical-style front elevations, similar to those in the pattern books of the time, which were intended for view from the roads that passed through the estate and the park. Typically, the buildings are grouped around a single yard with the house on the south side, divided from the yard by a wall and a narrow passageway (Figure 41). The buildings are usually symmetrical, executed in a subdued

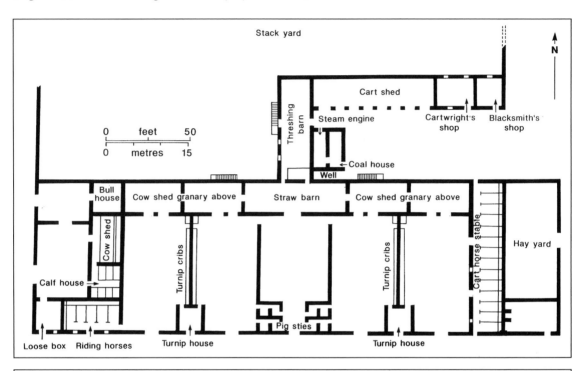

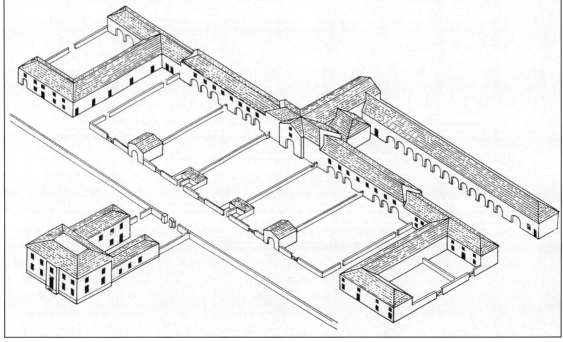

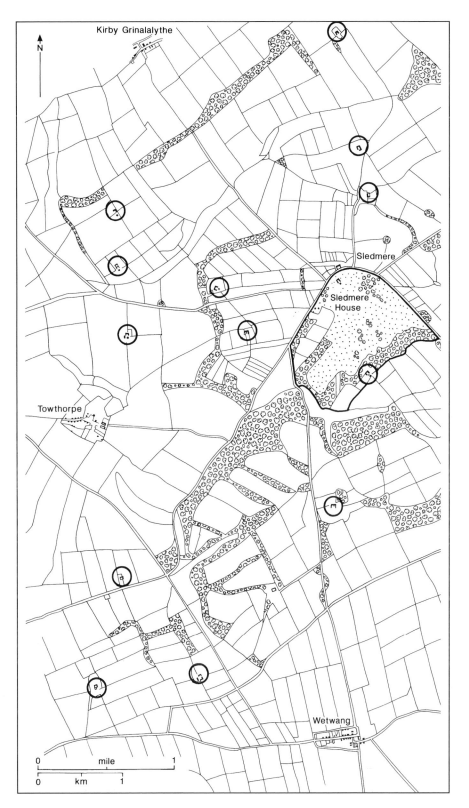

FIGURE 39 (*opposite*). Much of the extensive building undertaken by the Greenwich Hospital estates in Northumberland was the work of John Grey. Outchester Farm, near Bamburgh, was illustrated by Loudon shortly after it was built in 1837.

FIGURE 40. The newly enclosed landscape around Sledmere Park. The newly-created farms are circled.

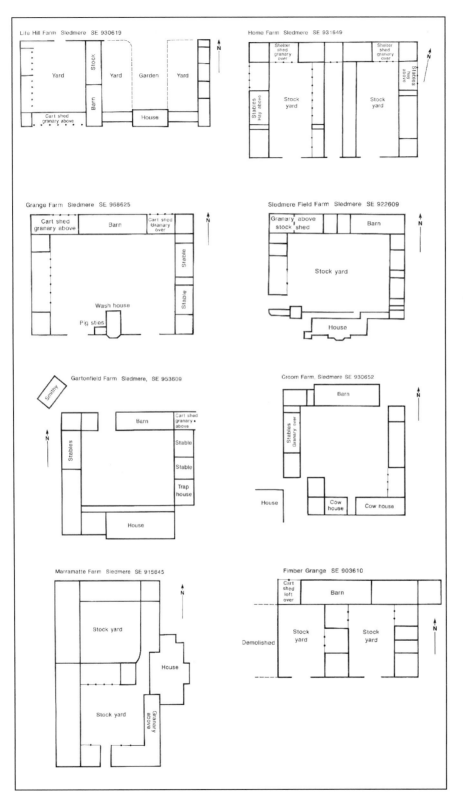

FIGURE 42 (*opposite*). Sykes's design for Maramatte Farm, Sledmere. The photograph shows the long multifunctional rear building which incorporates a granary with hay and straw lofts above fodder and mixing rooms.

FIGURE 41. These block plans of the Sledmere farmsteads show their simple courtyard layouts, with the house only divided from the yard by the narrowest of passageways.

88

classical style, sometimes with a three-storey corner or central pavilion for modest display (Plate 9). The walls facing the house or the roadway are frequently faced with stone, but the backs are of less prestigious brick. In spite of the imposing façades, the fact that the farmhouses backed right onto the cattle yards placed them firmly at the centre of the working farm; a reminder that these early planned farmsteads were built for tenants who were practical rather than gentlemen farmers (Figure 42).

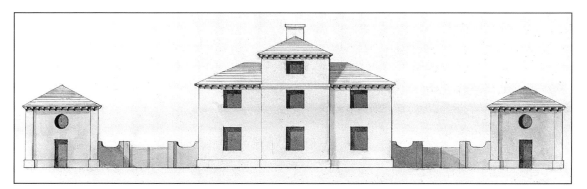

Other large estate owners were also at work, with the Legards of Ganton and the Willoughbys at Birdsall two of the most important. The enclosure of the Birdsall estate did not begin until the 1790s, when thorn hedgerows and shelter belts – often following ancient boundaries – were planted to protect new farmsteads in exposed positions. Over twenty new farms were created in the parishes of Birdsall, North Grimston, Wharram Percy and Warram-le-Street, many of them for farms of over 600 acres. Ten of them were true 'Wold' farms, created on new sites out in the newly enclosed fields, while the others continued to form part of nucleated settlements. Most of the farmsteads, both here and at Sledmere, originally consisted of a farmhouse with barns, implement sheds and stables around a single cattle yard. They conformed very much to the plan published in Isaac Leatham's *General View*. An essential part of every farmstead was the dew pond where animals could be watered. Many of the farmsteads went through a second phase of improvement in the 1860s when cattle yards were divided to provide for greater specialisation in stock rearing methods, and steam engines inserted which make the original buildings sometimes difficult to interpret. The most impressive rebuild was at the home farm at Birdsall in 1868 where covered yards replaced the old cattle yard and a steam engine was installed to provide power.[52]

A factor that has had an important regional influence on the farming landscape and buildings of the north of England is that the income of many landowners was derived from outside agriculture. Whilst in previous centuries profits of law and government office as well as judicious marriage had been common to landowners in all parts of England, by the eighteenth century there was a regional divide associated with the industries of the north. The Duke of Northumberland's wealth was founded on coal and the Ridleys of Blagdon (near Newcastle) owned both collieries and a family bank. The Curwens owned much of the port of Workington. Of the ten largest land-owners in East Yorkshire in the eighteenth century, the Thompsons (later barons Wenlock) were York merchants who had become rich importing goods (particularly wine) from the contintent, the Sykes family were merchants in the Baltic trade operating out of Hull, the Broadleys were also Hull merchants and bankers and the Willoughbys (Baron Middleton) had profited from Nottinghamshire coal.[53] This was likely to influence the amount of money available for improvement and it also meant that they might bring ideas to farm building from the world of industry. The ready availability of capital meant that such landowners could well afford to continue improving after the boom of the Napoleonic War period had ended.

The improvements to the Shropshire and Staffordshire estates of the Marquis of Stafford would not have been possible without a considerable income from coal and iron, in addition to the enormously profitable Bridgwater Canal. The work carried out by the second Marquis and master-minded by his agent, James Loch, from 1812, were amongst the most famous in the United Kingdom. Land was enclosed, marsh drained and sometimes as many as five farms amalgamated. Thirty seven sets of new premises were built on his English

FIGURE 43.
Illustration from Loch's *An Account of the Improvements on the Estates of the Marquis of Stafford.* Day House Farm, built between 1812 and 1813, was one of two farmsteads with a steam engine and a paved walkway between the central yard and its associated livestock sheds. This well-arranged farmstead has outward facing turnip houses on the east side, into which carts could unload from the fields. Doorways in the back wall of the cowhouse facilitate the easy feeding of livestock.

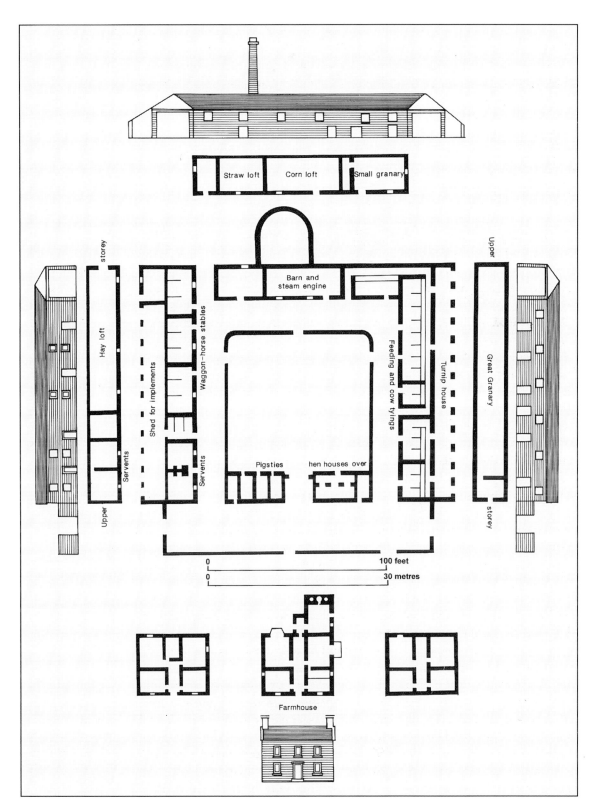

Straw loft Corn loft Small granary

storey

Upper

Hay loft

Shed for implements

Waggon-horse stables

Servents

Servents

Barn and
steam engine

Feeding and cow tyings

Turnip house

Great Granary

Upper

storey

Pigsties

hen houses over

Upper

0   100 feet

0   30 metres

Farmhouse

91

estates and eight more considerably enlarged. Loch, as the estate's manager, took an intense interest in every detail of the work, both on the Marquis's English estates and on the million or so acres which his employer had acquired, through marriage, in Sutherland. 'Without him [Loch] no man shall lift up his hand or foot in all his Lordship's domains'.[54] Although an estate architect, John Smith, was employed at Trentham from 1805 until his death in 1817 Loch, as manager, concerned himself with the details of every farm improvement, and sent long letters to the architect often criticising unnecessary expense or the use of faulty materials. In order to justify the social upheavals involved, particularly in Scotland where his policies resulted in the clearance of people from many of the Sutherland strathes, and to explain his philosophy of improvement, Loch wrote in 1820 *An Account of the Improvements on the Estates of the Marquis of Stafford.* Here plans and descriptions of many of the farmsteads were published. What shines through his writings more than anything else is his supreme confidence in what he was doing. It was the duty of the great landowners to 'improve' for the national good at almost any human cost. Loch had studied law at Edinburgh University in the 1790s and was a member of the group of economists supporting the ideas of Adam Smith. As agent for one of the largest aristocratic estates in Britain, he was able to put his economic theories into practice. In 1816 he wrote the 'property of a great English nobleman must be managed on the same principles as a little kingdom, not like the affairs of a little merchant.' Similarly, to one of his sub-agents he wrote, 'You must look forward fifty years so that you may make the most of the present'.[55] This freedom to lay long-term plans would no doubt have been the envy of many less well-off landowners, but his sentiments are ones with which they would have had sympathy.

The unique collection of published farm plans in Loch's book (Figure 43) allows for an analysis of farm layout on these model farms built, mostly between 1813 and 1820, to serve holdings of between 100 and 300 acres. They were expensive, at about £1,500 each to build, and were mostly of a simple U-plan layout, open to the south and flanked on the other sides by cowhouses, stables and barns. Only one steading was built with a steam engine house, whilst another was water-powered and a third had a horse walk. They are of a simple, practical design – typical of the early period of improvement – with large open yards and little provision for mechanisation (Figure 44). Built of brick with tiled roofs they are well-laid out and proportioned, but with little in the way of architectural pretension. Loch described them as being of a 'common country style,' 'uniting as many advantages with as few faults, as any buildings of the sort, and will supply useful hints to others'.[56] In the main, therefore, we see the practical land agent prevailing over architectural extravagance. However, even these functional buildings were not without their critics. The drastic changes in land management being carried out aroused great enmity and criticism in print. Loch's autocratic methods of reorganisation and farm amalgamations led to the dispossession of families whose leases, held for three generations, were coming to an end in the early 1800s. They caused

FIGURE 44. Block plans of a selection of the Marquis of Stafford's farmsteads in Shropshire and Staffordshire. The house was never part of these farmyards, but built a short distance away. The arrangements at Tearn Farm, Ercall Magna, were more elaborate, with central cattle yards surrounded by a walkway. On most farmsteads there was no mechanisation, only Day House Farm and Tearn Farm having steam engines.

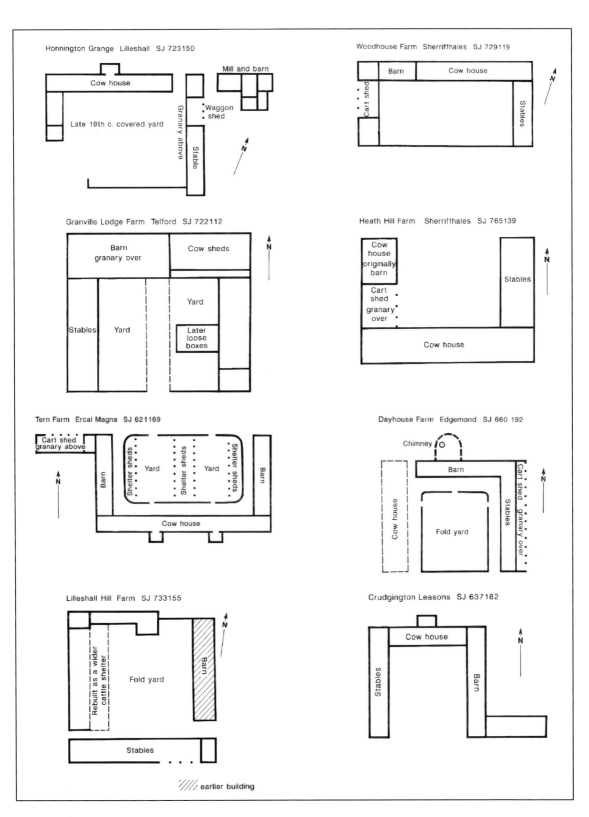

Honnington Grange Lilleshall SJ 723150

Cow house

Mill and barn

Granary above

Waggon shed

Late 19th c. covered yard

Stable

N

Woodhouse Farm Sherriffhales SJ 729119

Barn

Cow house

Cart shed

Stables

N

Granville Lodge Farm Telford SJ 722112

Barn granary over

Cow sheds

N

Stables

Yard

Yard

Later loose boxes

Heath Hill Farm   Sherriffhales SJ 765139

Cow house originally barn

Cart shed granary over

Stables

Cow house

N

Tern Farm Ercal Magna SJ 621169

Cart shed granary above

Shelter sheds

Yard

Shelter sheds

Yard

Shelter sheds

Barn

Barn

Cow house

N

Dayhouse Farm Edgemond SJ 660 192

Chimney

Barn

Cow house

Fold yard

Cart shed granary over

Stables

N

Lilleshall Hill Farm SJ 733155

Rebuilt as a wider cattle shelter

Fold yard

Barn

Stables

N

Crudgington Leasons SJ 637182

Cow house

Stables

Barn

N

////. earlier building

93

great social dislocation and certainly made him enemies. Consequently, the buildings came in for criticism along with everything else. They were described as inconvenient and improper and 'should be taken down'. After the amalgamations the new farms were taken on by 'opulent people, for none else could venture upon them'. 'It appears to be the rage of the day with great landed proprietors to build elegant houses and farm offices upon their estates, so as to allure people of independent property into farming speculations.'[57] However, the evidence both of the published plans and the buildings which still stand would suggest that they were robust in construction and well-suited to the new large farms they were built to serve (Figure 45).

If the planned farmsteads of this Staffordshire industrial magnate conform to the plans current at the time, those of the Derbyshire industrialist, William Strutt of Belper, do not. William Strutt was responsible for building and running spinning factories in Milford, Belper and Derby within one of the heartlands of the industrial revolution in the Derwent valley (Plate 10). The Strutts' involvement in Belper began in 1787 when Jedediah Strutt built a

FIGURE 45
(*above and opposite*). Tearn Farm was built around three sides of a court with central cattle yards and a long cartshed/granary range along the back. The stall divisions for cattle are still in place (*above*). The wide doorways into the byres are typical of the Stafford estates and the doors with vertical slits may well be an original design (*opposite*).

cotton spinning mill in the town, taking advantage of the fast-flowing River Derwent. Business expanded and in 1796 a second mill was built in which were used the innovative building methods which were later introduced to farm buildings. The factories were iron-framed with floors tiled for fire protection. Ventilation to the different floors was provided through hollow earthenware pipes set within the walls and vents. Unlike most industrialists who moved away from the source of their wealth when they came to buy a country estate, the Strutts continued to reside within their mill towns with family homes in Milford and Derby. Land was purchased either side of the River Derwent for both agricultural and industrial use and more land was obtained with the enclosure award of 1791. After Jedediah's death in 1791 his policy of expansion was continued by his sons, George and William. By 1826, 1,419 acres was owned in and around Belper, including at least four farms, each over 150 acres.[58] The motive behind this expansion was not simply the establishment of a landed estate, but also to ensure control over the river and the water power it provided for the mills, as well as providing food for the

factory workers, particularly a supply of fresh milk. All the farmsteads were
equipped with ample cattle sheds, cheese rooms and dairies. The estate policy
towards its farms was one of consolidation. The buildings on the smaller farms
were variously described in 1823 as ranging from 'very indifferent' to 'in ruins',
whilst on those of over 150 acres they were 'in good repair'.[59] Unfortunately,
few early-nineteenth-century surveys or plans of the buildings survive. The
name, Moscow Farm, suggests a late-Napoleonic War creation, and a map of
Belper dated 1809 shows that the buildings there had not been erected by
then.[60] Certainly, the early-nineteenth century was the time of the major
expansion of the Strutts' business, farm accounts showing that they were taking
a great interest in the produce of the in-hand farms. The only surviving plans
are for the mid-nineteenth century. They show that the core of most of the
farmsteads existed by 1844, whilst additions took place up to 1856, by which
time most of the buildings which now survive had been built.[61]

The layout of these farmsteads owed less to conventional pattern books
than an understanding of the work flows of factories, reminiscent of those
recommended by Young in 1770 (see Figure 17). By taking advantage of the
fall of the land, for example, raw materials could be transferred from one stage
of the agricultural process to the next. The most impressive surviving examples
are Moscow Farm (now converted into houses), Cross Roads Farm, Wyver
Farm and Dalley Farm. They all contain the same innovative features which
so interested the Strutts in their factory design – ventilation ducts, iron framing,
stone floors and vaulting for fire proofing. Several took advantage of the steep
valley sides of the Derwent Valley to create split-level buildings, making use
of the slopes with inclined walkways and chutes to allow for the efficient
movement of raw materials from the higher storage areas to the lower livestock
sheds. This lack of symmetrical formal layout does not detract from the
'planned' nature of the farms, but rather increases the interest of these
innovative designs. Indeed, Cross Roads Farm which originated as a public
house called 'Owl Inn' had changed its name to Model Farm by 1857. Although
it incorporated pre-existing buildings its layout was extremely efficient. At the
centre was the corn mill and mixing house. From the mill, threshed corn
could be easily transferred to the granary, flour to the bakehouse, and straw
and chopped or ground food to the animals. Labour-saving devices included
a flour chute in the bakehouse and a trap door in the entrance arch which
enabled carts to be loaded from the granary above. Use was made of the
sloping site. For example there was first-floor access to the barn/corn mill
from the western yard. A drain was used to convey whey from the dairy to
the pigsties at a lower level. The slope of the land also allowed liquid manure
to be drained from the yards to tanks which were sited below, close to the
fields where it would be used. Although there is no surviving provision for
powered machinery on the farms, there was a steam engine at Cross Roads
in the 1850s, replaced by a horse engine in 1861,[62] and a horse walk to work
a chaff cutter is shown on the 1858 plan of Dalley Farm.

Equally, Wyver Farm, Belper is a good example of a farmstead designed to

FIGURE 46.
The buildings at
Wyver Farm were
built in the first half
of the nineteenth
century into the
sloping valley sides of
the River Derwent,
and take advantage of
the different levels for
the efficient
movement of feed and
manure. This also
involved terracing and
the building of
massive walls to hold
back the earth. The
cattle yard is at the
higher level behind to
the right of the
storeyed range (1),
which has chutes (2)
providing fodder to
vaulted cowhouses
beneath.

make the best use of the sloping valley sides. Part of the farmstead consists of an L-plan group of two storeys with cow stalls below (Figure 46) on the downhill side, allowing for hay and feed to be stored above the stalls, and loaded in directly from the uphill side. Feeding chutes in the stone-flag floor of the store enabled feeding of the cattle stalled below, the ceilings of the byres being vaulted. There is a similar arrangement over the stables. A feature of this farm, and on a larger scale at the neighbouring Dalley Farm, is the range of bins for holding wet grain from local breweries, which again could be tipped in at one level and shovelled out into the cow stalls at another. The arrangements at Dalley are more complicated than those at Wyver, with inclined walkways for barrowing feed, and a mixing room below a feed store with cylindrical chutes through the floor to deliver food to mixing troughs (Figure 47). Here the roofs are supported by iron trusses and the ceilings between floors are vaulted. All the buildings on both farms are well ventilated, using cast-iron ventilation grills. In some buildings there are wall vents inside

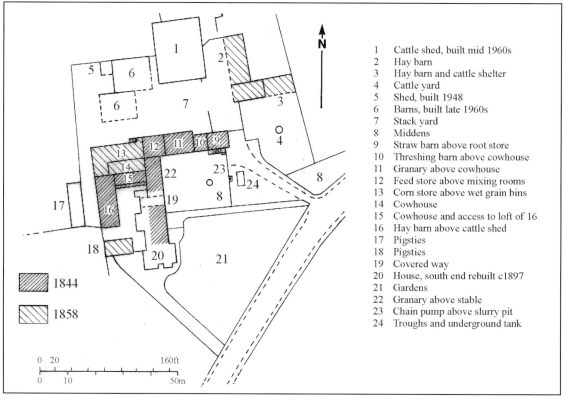

1   Cattle shed, built mid 1960s
2   Hay barn
3   Hay barn and cattle shelter
4   Cattle yard
5   Shed, built 1948
6   Barns, built late 1960s
7   Stack yard
8   Middens
9   Straw barn above root store
10 Threshing barn above cowhouse
11 Granary above cowhouse
12 Feed store above mixing rooms
13 Corn store above wet grain bins
14 Cowhouse
15 Cowhouse and access to loft of 16
16 Hay barn above cattle shed
17 Pigsties
18 Pigsties
19 Covered way
20 House, south end rebuilt c1897
21 Gardens
22 Granary above stable
23 Chain pump above slurry pit
24 Troughs and underground tank

1844

1858

0   20   160ft

0   10   50m

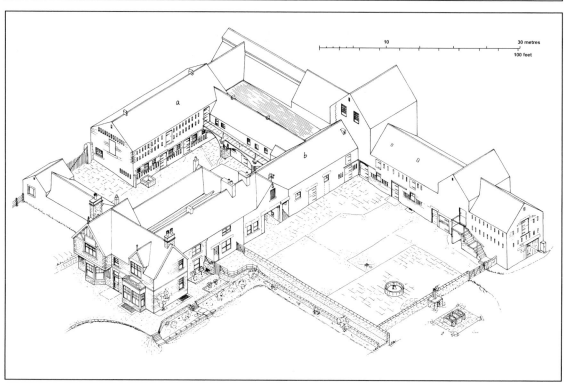

10   30 metres

100 feet

FIGURE 47.
Dalley Farm was one
of the Strutt's
farmsteads in Belper,
and was probably built
in the 1830s. Its plan
does not conform to
any layouts popular at
the time, yet it
incorporated advanced
ideas on the flow of
processes round the
buildings. The block
plan shows the
evolution of the
buildings, based on
maps of 1844 and 1858.
The threshing barn
was at first-floor level
with feed stores on
one side and a straw
barn on the other.
Feed for mixing was
dropped through the
floor into the mixing
room beside the cow
house. A wet grain
store with hatches to
an outer roadway
could be emptied from
an internal passage
leading to these and
other cowhouses. A
large hay barn (a)
above a cowhouse
range stood at the
back of the group and
a high-level walkway

led to the feed stores above the front range of cow houses (b). The iron frame is bolted through to the outside wall
with iron rods, and cruciform cast-iron columns support the roof purlins. The photographs show one of the roof
ventilators, with a row of cast-iron ventilation panels below, in the hay and straw barn, and the interior with its
cast-iron columns and stone flag floor. The buildings are of brick, with the public sides of stone.

the wall and up onto the roofs. These complex and fascinating buildings are early examples of the transfer of industrial building design into farm buildings, pre-dating the 'high farming' period. There is no record of an architect being involved.

All the farms concentrated on dairy farming rather than cereal production, with by far the majority of their land being under grass at the time of the tithe survey. Of the 188 acres at Wyver, about 55 were arable in 1844. Sixty six acres of Dalley Farm were within Belper parish and all but two were meadow or pasture. The substantial buildings on the Strutt farmsteads stored both winter fodder such as turnips and industrial by-products such as spent grain from breweries. At Cross Roads Farm a long roadside building had hatches opening onto the road through which the grain could be unloaded from wagons. On the other side the building opened into cattle yards so that the grain could be easily delivered to the stock. Water pipes brought clean water to the farms and drains led to liquid manure tanks, from which the contents could be pumped up for dispersal around the fields. At nearby Shottlegate Farm (also on the Strutt estates) pipes led from the dairy to storage tanks near the pigsties, where the whey was stored until it was needed for the pigs.[63] All the farms were well provided with dairies and 'workrooms' for butter and cheese making. Despite these innovations, the Strutt farms received little publicity and their innovatory features were not taken up by their neighbours.

Another owner who derived his fortune from outside agriculture was the eccentric John Curwen of Schoose Farm, Workington (Cumbria), who owned both collieries and the local docks. In the early 1800s, he followed the patriotic trend and turned his attention to agricultural improvement. On enquiry he found that his own farm was run at a loss and so he set himself the task, with the help of his devoted and efficient steward, Charles Udall, of putting the farm into good condition. This involved draining and cleaning the land. He was an enthusiastic experimenter who believed that it was more efficient to cut grass and take it to stalled cows than to feed them in fields or yards. This novel and extremely labour-intensive method was unlikely to gain popularity. In 1805, he established the Workington Agricultural Society with an annual show at Schoose, the first of its kind in the region. This presumably prompted Curwen to build an imposing set of buildings there. Plans published in 1809 show the buildings very much as they survive (Figure 48). They conform to an irregular octagon, possibly influenced by Marshall's ideas already discussed (see p. 73), and consisting of a castellated Gothic arched 'gatehouse' with flanking 'curtain walls' behind which were cowhouses. The gatehouse served as an eyecatcher in the uphill view from Workington Hall. Behind was an enclosed yard, with a barn in one corner served by a horse engine for working barn machinery. By 1808 this had been replaced by a windmill, just outside the yard, which worked a threshing machine, chaff, turnip and carrot cutters and a machine for bruising oats – unusually early examples of machines for feed preparation. The Gothic appearance of these buildings is reminiscent of the farmsteads on the Greystoke estate, on which they may have been

FIGURE 48.
This view of Schoose Farm, near Workington, Cumbria, was published in 1809. The plan shows an irregular layout with a two-storied bank barn built into a slope, with the windmill beside it. To the north of the barn is a pentangular yard with a 'gate house' facing Workington Hall. A large stable block housed both farm and colliery horses and a long livestock shed with a dairy in a cellar below housed Curwen's cows which he chose to feed indoors all year round. This group can hardly be described as a planned farmstead, yet it was the site of Curwen's agricultural shows and he regarded it as a showpiece.

modelled. To the north were stable yards and to the south an immense stack yard surrounded by arched openings (identified as 'stacks' on a contemporary plan) [64] the purpose of which can only be guessed at. To the east was a vaulted dairy block under a storage area, next to a water mill for feed preparation. The buildings follow no recognised plan and their bizarre appearance probably reflects the nature of their creator rather than any rational thinking on farm

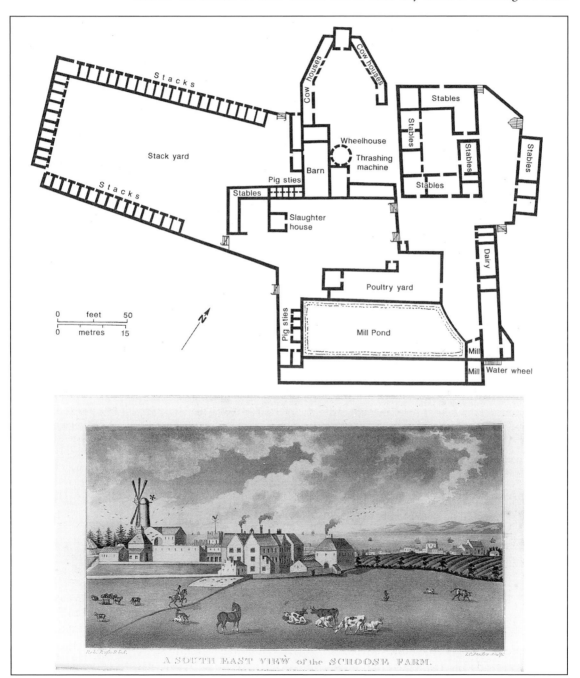

A SOUTH EAST VIEW of the SCHOOSE FARM.

building design. Curwen admitted that his belief in the advantages of keeping livestock indoors all the year round meant that he needed more buildings than 'is the usual mode' and the fact that he provided horses for use in his mines accounts for the extent of the stables.

In 1808 Curwen published *Hints on the Economy of Feeding Stock and Bettering the condition of the Poor,* in which he promoted his labour intensive ideas on cattle and horse feeding. His book, *Hints to Gentlemen Farmers,* was published in 1809 and gave advice on farm buildings. These, he said, should combine simplicity with utility. 'I must declare my decided hostility against the introduction of taste into farm buildings at the expense of convenience. I recollect one instance where a threshing machine was erected and the horses made to work in a cellar under the machine because the architect could not contrive any ornamental building for doing the work outside the barn … Simplicity and utility are the first objects in farm buildings; to have these constructed at the least possible expense, is a proof of ability in the architect and good judgment in the proprietor'.[65] If the castellations at Schoose are anything to go by, Curwen did not always follow his own advice. His agricultural shows continued for several years, but his farming activities were a failure in the long run. Instead, as an MP. he turned his attention to parliamentary corruption and the abolition of rotten boroughs.

FIGURE 49
(*below and opposite*).
The farmsteads
(circled) of Woburn
Park (Bedfordshire)
and Holkham Park
(Norfolk) and their
surrounding landscapes.

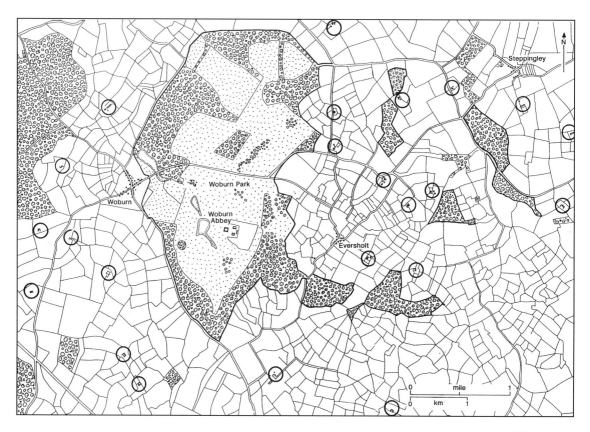

102

Modified landscapes: south of England estates, 1790–1840

The two great estates in southern England which received most publicity, and which were almost vying with each other for the pre-eminent position in farming circles, were those of the Cokes based at Holkham and the Dukes of

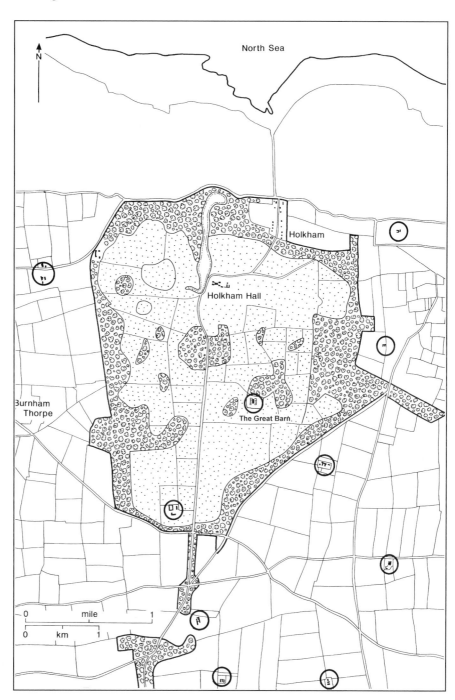

Bedford at Woburn. Throughout the Napoleonic Wars both men ran public sheep shearings on their home farms, where sheep were shown and sheared so that their conformation and the quality of their wool could be judged. Prizes for both essays and examples of improved farming were given and speeches made. These fashionable gatherings provided an opportunity to inspect the buildings at the home farms and other tenant farms in the vicinity, and brought gentry and aristocracy from Britain and beyond to Norfolk and Bedfordshire.

There are always exceptions to any generalisations that can be drawn between

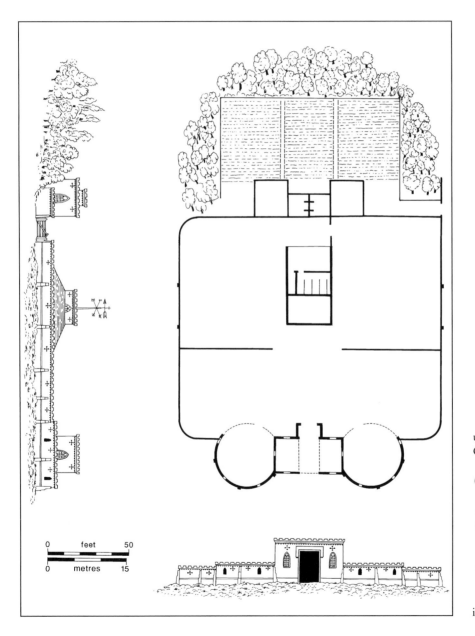

FIGURE 50.
Robert Salmon's
unusual and
unexecuted design for
Crawley Heath Farm,
Woburn
(Bedfordshire), where
two horse gins,
disguised in circular
castellated structures,
were to work
machinery. Behind,
within a yard, was a
livestock shed. The
rick yard was rather
inconveniently placed.

regions. Nevertheless, there are various factors which contributed to the different agricultural, landscape and building histories of the north and the south of England. Most significant is the strongly regional nature of industrialisation. As noted previously, this resulted in a lack of incentives for mechanisation in the predominately rural south, where population was rising but there was a decline in traditional rural industries such as spinning and weaving, compared to the increasingly urbanised and industrialised north, with its associated labour shortages. Secondly, more of the southern counties were gradually being drawn into the expanding London and Midland markets. Despite, a heightened demand for agricultural products estates did not dominate the countryside as they did further north. Many tended to be smaller because of the increased land values of the lowlands, and were less wealthy because they relied on agriculture for their income. Motives for improvement were likely to be more directly influenced by a desire to increase rents. Thirdly, as we have seen, so much of the region had been enclosed by the eighteenth century that landowners did not have a clean slate on which to work. The result is that whilst Coke of Holkham was able to create a new landscape, with most farmsteads set centrally within their fields, over much of the light land of north Norfolk, the Duke of Bedford had to work within an already existing field pattern around Woburn. Some farmsteads such as Steppingley were built in newly laid-out fields, while the fields around the village core at Eversholt were left unaltered. The resulting contrasts are obvious from the maps and in the landscape today (Figure 49).

The fifth Duke of Bedford took over his extensive estates in 1787, and immediately embarked on a programme of improvements, many of them conducted under the guidance of Robert Salmon. Salmon had come to the estate as clerk of works in 1790 and was promoted to 'architect and mechanist' in 1794, and agent in 1806, after the sixth Duke inherited. He was an early example of the new profession of estate architect, an enthusiastic draftsman and inventor whose designs for his machines and gadgets survive in the Woburn records. Amongst his unexecuted building designs are a horse-powered mill for the estate farm and some castellated buildings for Crawley Heath Farm, with two round towers containing horse engines (Figure 50). He also experimented in the use of new building materials such as *pise* (a form of unbaked clay built up between shuttering). Although some fine examples of his octagonal farmhouses built of *pise* survive, none of the farm buildings remain. In fact, a report of 1851 criticises the estate building of this period as being of the 'cheapest materials' which proved not to be durable.[66] Salmon's major surviving work is Park Farm which he equipped with up-to-date machinery, some of his own invention, and which he opened up to inspection at the annual sheep shearings which began the year Park Farm was completed, in 1797. The original buildings consisted of three ranges with yards behind and two-storey pedimented blocks in the middle of each range (Figure 51). The mill was originally timber-framed and worked by a water wheel. The buildings have been altered several times since 1800 but the elegant group, built very much

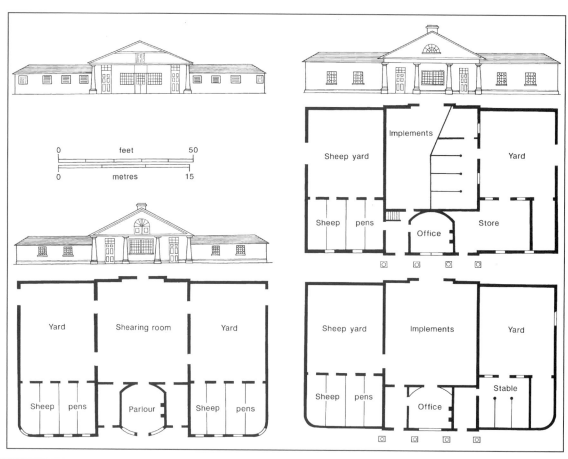

as a backcloth to the sheep shearings, is still discernible. The sheep shearing house with its pedimented front now functions as an estate office. The fifth Duke died in 1805 and was succeeded by his brother, also an agriculturalist of some renown in his early years. However, by 1813 he was beginning to lose interest and the sheep shearings ended that year. In 1821 he resigned from the Smithfield Club 'declaring that there was nothing further to be done in animal husbandry'[67] and lost interest in work on his estates. Except at Park Farm little survives of this early phase of development on the estate.

The fifth Duke's work at Woburn can be paralleled by the activities of his contemporary, Thomas William Coke of Holkham. Unlike the Duke of Bedford who was able to draw on wealth from his London property and his copper mines around Tavistock, Coke had to rely almost entirely on his agricultural estate for his income. Norfolk had long been seen as the home of agricultural improvements and certainly crop rotations including turnips and artificial grasses had been introduced by the end of the seventeenth century. 'Turnip' Townshend of the neighbouring Raynham estate had gained his nickname within his own lifetime[68] and by the late-eighteenth century the improvements on the light soils in the north-west of the county were regarded as the epitome of the agricultural revolution. Coke inherited his 40,000 acre estate in north-west Norfolk in 1776 and continued the policy of improvement inherited from his immediate predecessors. His political activities as a prominent parliamentary Whig ensured publicity for his agricultural activities. Enclosure, marling and encouragement of new farming methods through husbandry clauses in farm leases were not new, nor restricted within Norfolk to the Holkham estate, but their progress there was enthusiastically reported upon by Arthur Young and others. Coke realised the value of educated progressive tenants with capital to invest in farming and knew that long secure leases and good farm buildings were the ways to attract such men.[69]

Unlike the Duke of Bedford Coke did not employ an estate architect. He instead engaged the services of Samuel Wyatt (see pp. 58–62), who had worked on lodges and cottages at Holkham in the 1790s as well as on some of the farms. On the huge granaries over cart lodges on the Home Farm at Longlands are the overhanging eaves so much admired by the 'primitive' rustic architects. Like Salmon, Wyatt experimented in new building materials, not only using slates for roofs but also window sills and feed troughs. He also clad some of his farm buildings and houses, such as those at Longlands and the house at Leicester Square, South Creake, with mathematical 'tiles' (in reality facing bricks), a fashionable method of covering framed buildings in imitation brickwork. As we have seen, he also experimented with plan forms. The Great Barn at Holkham was built as the centrepiece for the Holkham sheep shearings and originally stood in the middle of its yard with cattle yards around and stables in lean-tos. His typically neo-classical love of curves is shown in the lunette windows in the gables and in the semi-circular wall around the horse pond (Figure 52, Plate 11). This theme is repeated in the crescent-shaped walls with their pyramidal-roofed pavilions in the field barn for Wheycurd Farm,

FIGURE 51.
Robert Salmon's Park Farm at Woburn (Bedfordshire) provided the backdrop to the annual sheep shearings. The sheep house with various schemes for its alteration into farm offices is shown on the drawings. The sheep were penned up or kept loose in the yard until they were taken into the large shearing room and then let out, shorn, to the rear. Visitors could sit in the parlour and ante-rooms and watch the shearing through the doors.

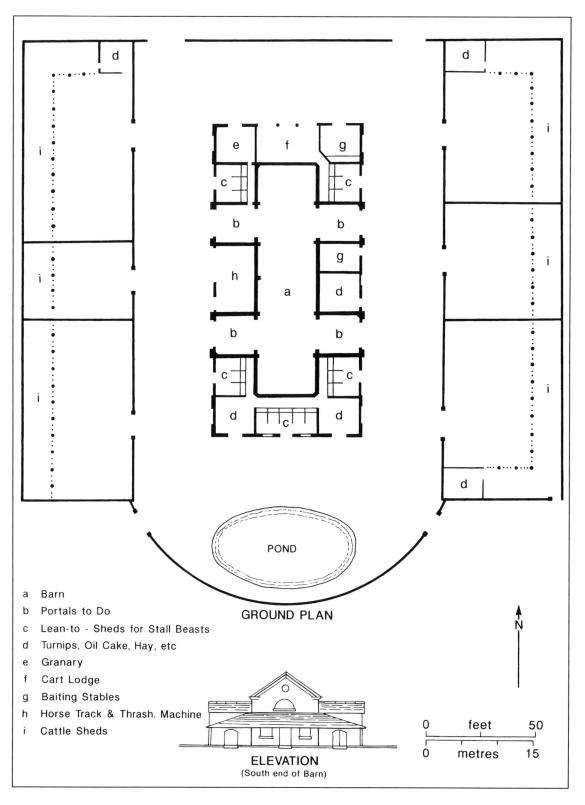

a Barn
b Portals to Do
c Lean-to - Sheds for Stall Beasts
d Turnips, Oil Cake, Hay, etc
e Granary
f Cart Lodge
g Baiting Stables
h Horse Track & Thrash. Machine
i Cattle Sheds

POND

GROUND PLAN

N

0   feet   50
0   metres   15

ELEVATION
(South end of Barn)

FIGURE 53 (*above*).
Field barns were
important on the
huge Holkham farms
where the outlying
fields could be a long
way from the main
farmstead. This field
barn at Wheycurd
Farm was designed by
Samuel Wyatt and
built in the early 1800s.

FIGURE 52 (*opposite*).
The Great Barn at
Holkham (Norfolk)
was the centrepiece
for the Holkham
sheep shearings. It was
designed by Samuel
Wyatt in the 1790s,
and included a horse
engine in one of the
lean-tos, to work barn
machinery (Plate 11).

Wighton (Figure 53). At Leicester Square Farm, South Creake curved walls connected the back of the house to the farmyard (Figure 54). A further development of farm plan is also seen here. The house, a fine double-fronted building, is distanced from the yard, not only by the curving domestic outbuildings, but by a wall. Here we see the beginning of a tendency to separate the house from the yard which was to increase during the nineteenth century as many farmers became more prosperous.

Other than Wyatt, there is no evidence of any architects working on farm buildings at Holkham during this period. Huge sums were spent by Coke on buildings and improvements, amounting to about £213,000 between 1790 and 1840, usually making up between 10% and 20% of rent,[70] but little of this found its way into architect-designed farmsteads. Instead it was buildings of a traditional Norfolk type which were being erected. Young commented on the 'new-built farm houses with barns and offices substantially of brick and tile'. 'There is no article that ornaments a country more than this: nor did Mr ['Capability'] Brown ever plan an approach to a great mansion that marks so much real splendour equally pleasing to the eye and heart, as well built farms and cottages'. He described the farm buildings at Waterden as 'so perfectly well arranged as to answer the great object to prevent waste and save manure'.[71] Built of local brick they consisted of a huge L-plan barn with cattle yards and stables. Three threshing floors emphasised the importance of hand

threshing in this low-wage area of surplus labour. By contrast, in 1804 he
wrote more critically of Wyatt's buildings at Leicester Square as being 'in a
style of expense rarely met with'. The filling of the huge barn was labour
intensive, 'a great expense at a time of year when labour is valuable'.[72]

When the Scotsman, Francis Blaikie became agent in 1816 one of his main
aims was to reduce what he regarded as extravagant expenditure on farm
buildings. That this expenditure had not resulted in planned estate farmsteads
can be attributed to the fact that much of the initiative for building seems to
have come from the tenants who had then been reimbursed by the estate. 'Mr
Coke's tenants', he wrote, 'are much in the habit of erecting unnecessary
buildings ... such buildings are not only attended with uncalled for expense
to the landlord in the first instance, but entail a lasting encumbrance on the
estate. For every particle of building not absolutely wanted is an encumbrance
to the estate and a deterioration of the property. These remarks apply more
immediately to Mr Coke's estates than to any other in the kingdom'.[73] Here
we see views typical of the land agent rather than the architect. Architect-
designed model farms were still regarded by practical managers as an unnecessary

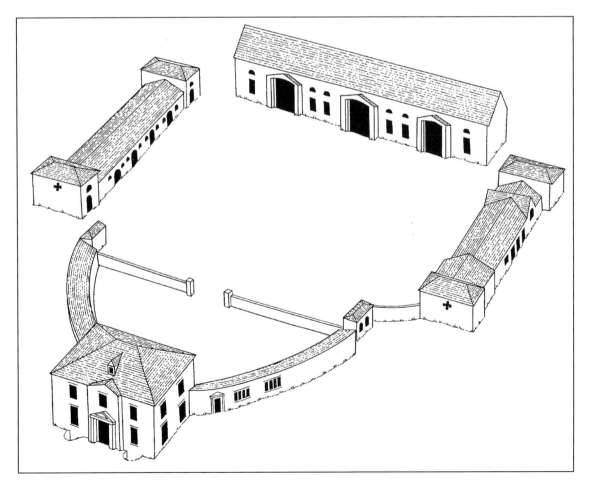

indulgence, less concerned with improved farming than accommodating the whim of the *dilettante* owner-farmer. The Wyatt-designed farmsteads at Holkham were built before Blaikie was appointed in 1816 and during the period when Coke was very much his own manager. New farm building continued on ordered layouts, but following simple estate designs using local red bricks and pantiles. Nine of the seventy or so farmsteads were entirely rebuilt between 1816 and 1840.[74]

Conclusion: the fulfilment of a patriotic duty?

It can be seen that in this first major period of activity planned and model farmsteads were erected for a variety of reasons and in a variety of forms. A small but significant proportion were designed by the great architects of the day, but generally owners were discouraged from this type of building by their agents. As with country houses, all but the grandest projects were designed by local architects, who were often builders as well.[75] Although some of the most famous improving estates such as the Duke of Bedford at Woburn, the Duke of Northumberland at Alnwick and the Marquis of Stafford at Trentham employed their own estate architects, others relied on their agents or indeed were amateur architects themselves. Gradually we see a change in the type of plan advocated, with the house being moved to a short distance from the yard, the number of stock yards increasing to allow for the keeping of more cattle, and the barn stretching from the stock yard into the rickyard to allow for some sort of engine beside it. Alongside the architectural influence, there was the industrial ideal of spatial efficiency, most strongly seen at Belper, and it was this aspect of farmstead design which was to increase during the Victorian era.

Patriotic duty was stressed in the contemporary literature. No doubt many would have agreed with Curwen when he wrote: 'When we see ill cultivated ground, dilapidated farms, wretched and dirty cottages, what are the ideas such objects normally excite? ... either the proprietor has been ruined by his improvements, or is possessed of such ignorance and blindness as neither to feel for himself or others'.[76] A useful countryside was more likely to produce good rents than a wild and barren one. The patriotic duty to produce more food for the nation conveniently coincided with the economic advantages of a rising rent roll. But even on the most extensive and wealthy estates, where much of the money for building was generated outside agriculture, their agents were cautioning against spending on extravagant building schemes which would only prove a burden in years to come. With a few very obvious exceptions, most planned farm buildings were therefore utilitarian and functional in design and reflected the solid prosperity based on the landlord-dominated, labour-intensive, hand-powered, mixed farming of this phase of the agricultural revolution.

FIGURE 54.
Leicester Square Farm, South Creake, was an outlying tenant farm on the Holkham estate, which was picked out for special treatment and a fine Samuel Wyatt farmstead was built there in the 1790s, costing about £3,500 to build. Arthur Young was critical of the huge barn, provided with three threshing floors, which he thought was too extravagant a building.

111

CHAPTER FIVE

'Practice with Science',
1840–1875

I am reading *Agricultural Chemistry* [by Sir Humphrey
Davy] because I am going to take one of my farms into
my own hands and see if something cannot be done in
setting a good pattern of farming among my tenants'.
Sir James Chattam, *Middlemarch, 1871*

Farm building activities picked up after the low ebb of the 1830s, as farming
fortunes began to recover. As we shall see, the beginning of change can be
dated to the late–1840s and the Royal Agricultural Society's Farm Prize
Competition of 1849–50. In many respects, this period coincided with that of
the High Victorian period of 1850 to 1870, encompassing the Great Exhibition
of 1851 (itself a showcase for British agriculture and technology), and the high
point of Britain's importance as an industrial power. This manifested itself in
flamboyant industrial buildings, from pumping works to railway stations, that
unified form and function in a diversity of styles.[1] It also witnessed the triumph
of industrial ideas in the field of farm building design, where the efficient flow
of raw materials through the building and the provision of a suitable power
source to work machinery were of paramount importance. Foundries such as
'Musgroves of London and Belfast' advertised regularly in the *Journal of the
Royal Agricultural Society of England*, their stall divisions and feeding troughs
replacing the work of local carpenters on farmsteads across the British Isles.

It is the farm buildings erected in the twenty years after 1850 which are of
greatest value from the point of view of the agricultural, as distinct from the
architectural historian. At no other time was the provision of the appropriate
buildings necessary for the adoption of new methods more important, and it
was the landlord's responsibility to provide this essential infrastructure. Farm
building developments closely reflected changing farming practice and the
degree to which changes recommended in farming text books were actually
taken up on the ground. Farm buildings were now regarded as industrial
buildings, with the needs of mechanisation placed at the forefront of design
(Figure 55). Not only was the threshing of grain carried out by machine, but
so was much of the fodder preparation. A feed preparation room adjacent to
the power source was now part of all well-planned farmsteads. Cake crushers

and grinders as well as chaff cutters, turnip slicers and grain bruisers were belt-powered from an engine. The threshing barn was usually located either above or beside the feed processing room, with a straw barn between it and the yards. Steam power began to be more generally used on many farms, particularly those near the coal fields, to power stationary machinery and also to work ploughs in the fields. These heavy machines were never of great importance to the majority of working farmers, although in difficult conditions they were invaluable and made possible some of the more ambitious Victorian schemes, such as the breaking up of new ground on Exmoor (see pp. 151–4).

Although as we shall see artificial fertilisers, in the form of superphosphates were finding their way onto farms, manure was still seen as the basis of good husbandry. Its production and preservation became an essential consideration in farmstead design (Figure 56). As cattle prices rose in relation to cereals and railways opened up new markets, the fattening of cattle for sale increased in importance, and this again led to greater emphasis being placed on cattle housing. Buildings were still placed around yards, but increasingly these were covered to protect both manure and stock. Individual fattening of animals for

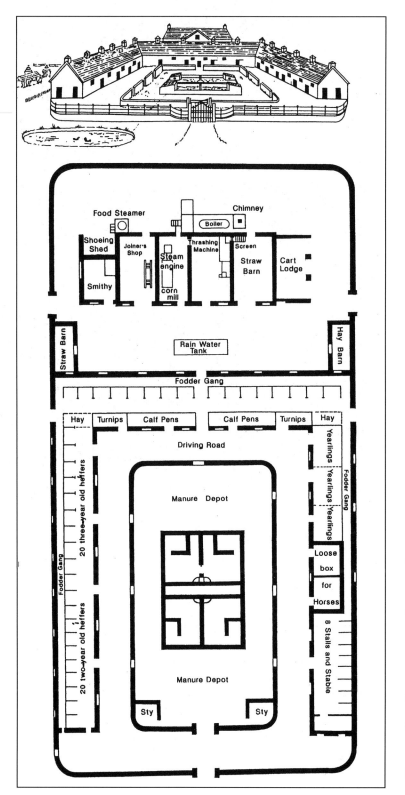

FIGURE 56.
This Lancashire dairy farmstead, illustrated in *The Agriculture of Lancashire* by J. Binns in 1851, demonstrates the importance attached by this time to collecting liquid manure from the cowhouses, the centre of the yard being entirely taken up by a 'manure depot' and tank. The steam-powered barn is in its own yard behind.

PLATE 1. The buildings at Betley (Staffordshire), built for and probably designed by George Tollet (1767–1855), comprise a fine example of a model farmstead from the early phase of the agricultural revolution, making good use of the fall of the land. Tollet was an agriculturalist, contributor to the *Annals of Agriculture*, breeder of Merino sheep, friend of Coke of Holkham and the Duke of Bedford and a regular visitor to their respective sheep shearings. The buildings of brick with tiled roofs, are on three levels down a slope with a yard, enclosed sheds entered through arched doorways, and shelter sheds supported on brick arcading at each level.

PLATE 2. The barn machinery, originally provided with a water wheel, is located in the central projecting wing.

PLATE 3. Interior of shelter sheds cut into the slope, with the brick vaulting supporting the granaries above.

PLATE 4. The barn and stables at Taynton, Gloucestershire. Three similarly proportioned late-seventeenth-century buildings, built of local brick with stone slate roofs, make up three sides of this fine gentry farmstead. The barn has two porches while the ox-house and stables have matching central doorways, the upper floors of which have been rebuilt.

PLATE 5. Arbour Hill Farm (North Yorkshire), showing the screen wall to the front of the house flanked by the stable/granary to the right and the barn to the left, hidden behind a later building.

PLATE 6. The barn, a conventional plan with two threshing floors, is located behind the castellated screen at Fort Putman (Cumbria).

PLATE 7. Trebartha Barton Farm (Cornwall) was built for the Rodd family as their home farm between 1820 and 1830. The bank barn with three threshing floors is entered at barn floor level from the north with south facing cattle accommodation below. Built of local stone and slate-hung, the buildings are arranged around a yard. The machinery was water-powered. The west range contained byres below and hayloft above, with pigeon holes below the eaves at the north end.

PLATE 8. A general view of Park Farm, Hulne Park, Denwick (Northumberland) designed by John Green for the Duke of Northumberland in 1827.

PLATE 9. The elaborate stable block at Croome House Farm, Sledmere (East Yorkshire), makes use of contrasting chalk and brick walling to good decorative effect.

PLATE 10.
The landscape around Belper
(Derbyshire).

PLATE 11.
The Great Barn at Holkham
(Norfolk).

PLATE 12. Chancellor's colourwash elevation of Stevens Farm, Chignall (Essex).

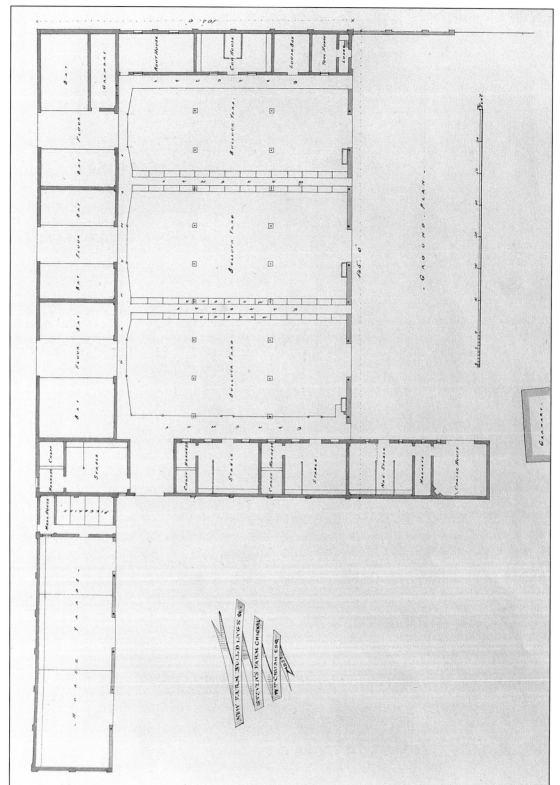

PLATE 13. Chancellor's colourwash plan of Stevens Farm, Chignall (Essex).

PLATE 14. The interior of the covered yards at Stevens Farm, Chignall (Essex).

PLATE 15. The remarkable covered yards at Home Farm, Apley Park (Shropshire).

PLATE 16.
General view of Olliver Farm, Aske (North Yorkshire), probably designed by the Duke of Zetland's agent W. J. Moscrop in the early 1870s.

PLATE 17.
The exterior of the covered yards at Kilworthy Farm, one of the Duke of Bedford's Devon farms.

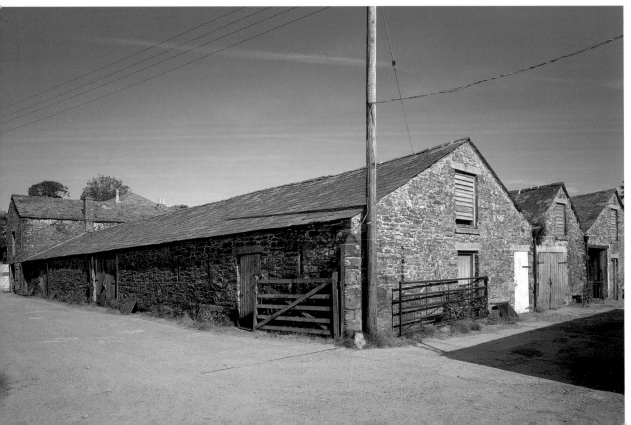

PLATE 18.
The huge chambers for manure collection are located below the covered yards at Kilworthy.

PLATE 19.
The bare hillside behind Warren Farm (Somerset) is a reminder of the elevated position of the Knight farms on Exmoor, sheltered by belts of beech trees, shown on the right of the picture. The house is on the left, with the cowhouse beside it and the barn to the right.

PLATE 20.
The dovecote on the roof
at Cheaveley Hall, on the
Duke of Westminster's
Cheshire estates.

PLATE 21.
The buildings dated 1883
at Aldford Hall, on the
Duke of Westminster's
Cheshire estates.

market might well be in loose boxes around this yard. Manure collecting systems such as the much advocated liquid manure tanks, and the manure houses and pits on the Duke of Bedford's Tavistock estates (see Figure 75 and Plate 18), show the importance still attached to organic fertilisers.

Architecturally, too, the change from the Georgian to the Victorian period was a marked one. This change in taste was reflected both in the more purely ornamental and eclectic designs of Victorian architects and in starkly functional examples such as Stevens Farm, Chignall (see Plates 12–14), designed by the prolific Essex architect, Frederick Chancellor, where the slim iron columns and low-pitched roofs feel surprisingly modern. Between these two extremes are a whole range of practical designs mostly produced in estate offices albeit sometimes on a very grand scale, as in the case of those for the Duke of Bedford at Woburn and Tavistock. The only well-known 'high farmer' to be placed as a winner in the farm building competition of 1851 was the Norfolk tenant, John Hudson, and his design was on a far simpler scale than those of the other competitors. However, he did agree that 'The supplying of extensive farm buildings by the landlord encourages high farming'.[2] His own Holkham estate farmstead was the only tenant farm there with a stationary steam engine, but it was not a single planned build and had nothing in the way of architectural pretensions.

From practical to professional farmer

The beginning of the Victorian age marked the start of a new scientific farming era. The depression of the post-Napoleonic War years finally came to an end with the stabilising of wheat prices after the mid-1830s at a level well below that of the 1790s, but one which provided a reasonable return for farmers. Meat prices, too, were beginning to rise to compensate for the level of grain and so agricultural development moved in new directions. Most of the land worth enclosing had been enclosed and improved, so new methods had to be sought to maximise profits by increasing productivity. The classic four-course rotation system, whereby the animals kept on the farm were fed off its produce and provided the main source of fertility through their manure, had also been fully exploited, and so again new directions needed to be explored if output was to be increased. Although cereal prices were improving, there was uncertainty about the future of the Corn Laws (finally repealed in 1846), and there was a realisation that prices would never again reach the inflated levels of the war years. In fact, grain prices held their own during the 1850s and 1860s, rising by between seven and ten per cent. This slow but steady growth rate encouraged farmers to make efforts to increase productivity, with the result that interest in improving both the quality and quantity of manure intensified. Meat prices rose faster, however, beef rising by an average of 31% and mutton by 27%.[3] It was this factor probably more than any other which encouraged greater emphasis on the quality of stock, inevitably involving the use of more imported feed. Although oil made from the residue from oil seeds such as rape and linseed, had been imported from the eighteenth century, its use as an animal feed did not become general until farming profits began to rise in the 1830s. By the 1850s some of the most intensive of the high farmers such as John Hudson of Castle Acre, Norfolk, was feeding his cattle between ten and twelve pounds a day.[4]

The new approaches associated with this phase of improvement came to be known as 'high farming', a phrase difficult to define and of obscure origin. It can be traced to the early-nineteenth century and implied a system of intensive farming based on high capital outlay by the farmer, in particular on fertilisers and feed. Ideally, this expenditure would, in turn, be balanced by landlord investment in land improvement and new buildings. Although many of the elements of 'high farming' have a long history, their active promotion can be seen as beginning with the founding of the Royal Agricultural Society (initially the English Agricultural Society) in 1838. Its aims, publicised through its *Journal,* were enshrined in the motto 'practice with science'. These included better land drainage, facilitated from the 1840s by new commercially produced pipe drains and, after 1846, encouraged by the grants available through land improvement loan companies. Another development was an increasingly significant relationship between the laboratory and agricultural improvement. There was nothing new about interest in experiment and scientific analysis, but those investigations reported regularly in the *Annals of Agriculture* through the 1790s were carried out by amateurs such as clergymen and gentlemen farmers. The contrast between the 'illiterate husbandmen' and the 'scientific farmer', who observed and recorded accurately, was then being made by Young, Kent, Marshall and other agricultural propagandists; but it took rather longer for the benefits of science to reach farmers at grass roots level. Sir Humphrey Davy's *Elements of Agricultural Chemistry,* published in 1813, demonstrated the value of the chemical analysis of soils and manures to cereal output; yet Francis Blaikie, the land agent at Holkham, remained sceptical of the academic approach. In his assessment of the estate's tenants in 1816 he frequently used as a compliment the phrase, 'a practical farmer – and no theorist'.[5] This attitude was slow to die, but by the 1840s, encouraged by the founding of the Cirencester Agricultural College in 1845 and the work on John Bennet Lawes' own home farm at Rothamstead, the value of science was becoming apparent. Lawes ran an experimental farm on scientific lines. He set up laboratories where his first success, by 1842, was to show the value of superphosphates as fertilisers and thus establish the importance of science to the practising farmer.[6] In 1858, the tenant farmer and agricultural commentator C. S. Read wrote that the days had passed when the greatest praise that could be given to a farmer was that he was a 'practical man'. Now it was scientific knowledge that was more important. Commenting on the merits of the many new fertilisers of variable quality that were flooding the market he wrote, 'Our practical ignorance cannot be bliss unless it is pleasant to buy things at double their value and lose crops into the bargain'.[7] Agricultural science was becoming a profession. To be innovative, farmers now had to keep abreast of the work carried out by chemists working in laboratories.

The increased use of imported and manufactured feeds and fertilisers, coupled with the purchase of the new mass-produced machinery that was gradually coming onto the market during the early years of Victoria's reign, meant that farmers needed more working capital than they had in the past. In years of agricultural instability it was difficult to find men willing to take the risks involved. Mr Wright, a Norwich land agent, claimed in 1833 that someone with £4–5,000 to invest would do better putting it in trade.[8] There was similar uncertainty in the 1840s when the future of the Corn Laws was in doubt and banks refused to lend to farmers. However, after an initial loss of confidence following their repeal in 1846, prices rose and with them an optimism which dominated British farming until the early 1870s. The basis of this prosperity had changed since the Napoleonic Wars. In the early phases of agricultural improvement, it had been the landlords' capital which had played an important part in providing the infrastructure for increasing yields. Now the pendulum was swinging towards the tenants' working capital. Not only did tenant farmers on the larger (ideally over 300 acres) and more commercial farms need more capital but also, as we have seen, a good scientific education. It was therefore well-educated, wealthy, or credit-worthy men whom the landlord sought. Tenants of this quality, realising that their bargaining position was strengthening, were able to demand the right to compensation for long-term benefits which they claimed artificial fertilisers gave to the soil.[9] Landlords, in their turn, realised that such men were worth encouraging, both through providing the fixed capital investment in the form of improved buildings needed for 'high farming' and through promoting the new methods. To do this they needed to build farms for their tenants suited to the mechanisation of crop processing for sale and animal feed, and with accommodation for additional livestock. The development of this type of building will be discussed in general, followed by examples of key estates and home farms.

The industrial farmstead

The 1830s had seen a lull in the building of planned and model farms, fewer than 20 being recorded for this decade. However, the next 40 years saw a massive increase in activity reaching a peak in the 1860s, with over 90 being identified (see Figure 3). With the gradual recovery in farming confidence at the beginning of the period, complaints about the general state of buildings were commonplace. In spite of the earlier wave of enthusiasm much remained to be done. John Grey, writing in 1843, was appalled at the 'ill-arranged and patchwork appearance of many farm buildings, which are often placed, in relation to their different parts, in utter defiance of the economy of labour in the case of cattle; and, what is still worse, with little regard to the production and preservation of manure'. With the increasing understanding of the importance of manure and the growing market for meat, it was the provision of good cattle accommodation that was to assume prime importance to the farmer. Grey was convinced that it was on the largest estates, with the wealthiest owners, that conditions were worst. 'In such cases the farmsteads near the residence, or near the roads approaching to it, may obtain some attention, but the remote ones are left to their fate.'[10] Grey's experience was mainly of Northumberland, but James Caird on his travels throughout England in 1851 described 'inconvenient and ill-arranged hovels' in many areas. 'With accommodation adapted to the requirements of the last century, the farmer is urged to meet the necessities of the present.' Comparisons with industrial buildings were unfavourable. 'The economies of arrangement and power which are absolutely necessary to ensure profit amid the active competition of manufacturers are totally lost sight of here. And even the waste of raw material, which would be ruinous in a cotton mill, is continued as a necessary evil, by the farmer.'[11] However, these generalisations hid great regional differences. Caird did find many landowners who were providing good buildings. The Duke of Wellington was busy on his Hampshire estates as was Mr Chaplin of Blankney in Lincolnshire, the Earl of Beverley in East Yorkshire and, as we shall see the Duke of Bedford.[12] In Leicestershire he found that the best landlords were 'capitalists from towns' who managed their estates with the same attention to detail that had made them successful businessmen. 'They drain the land thoroughly, remove useless timber and erect suitable farm buildings'.[13] The agricultural engineer, G. I. Andrews, pointed out that although examples of 'new simple and scientific steadings' were to be found in most counties, they were the exception rather than the rule. 'Indeed to deny the existence of such buildings in England would be doing a great injustice to those enlightened noblemen ... who have spent so much time and money in carrying out the most elaborate systems of farm steadings ... and at an outlay from which they can never expect such returns'.[14]

William Bearn, writing in the *Journal of the Royal Agricultural Society of England* in 1852, commented on the generally bad state of farm buildings in Northamptonshire. However, he noted a few exceptions, the most obvious of which were those of the Grafton estate in the parishes of Stoke Bruerne, Foscote, Abthorpe, Shutlanger, Blisworth, Greens Norton and Silverstone. Here, the Duke of Grafton had 'some years ago, remodelled some parts of his estate and erected a considerable quantity of new buildings'.[15] About £20,000 was spent on improvements between 1840 and 1848 under the directions of the agent, John Gardner, who designed the buildings himself. The planning and design of these farmsteads, dating from the very beginning of the Victorian era, hark back to the Georgian period. Here, as elsewhere, the traditional E and U-plan closely linked to substantial farmhouses on the fourth side of the yard continued to be the most usual farm layout (Figure 57). The original plans show shelter sheds arranged round large courts, designed to be divided into separate feeding yards.[16] Gardner made no provision for mechanised threshing, although one of the larger farmsteads included a barn at right-angles to the rear shelter sheds, extending into a stack yard allowing for a power source to be drawn alongside. In spite of these, and other well-publicised examples of improvement, much still remained to be done in

FIGURE 57. These designs for farmsteads were the work of John Gardner, the agent to the Duke of Grafton in Northamptonshire in the 1840s. About a dozen steadings in the Stoke Bruerne and Towcester area were rebuilt on similar layouts. No mechanisation is provided for the barns, and several of the yards were roofed over.

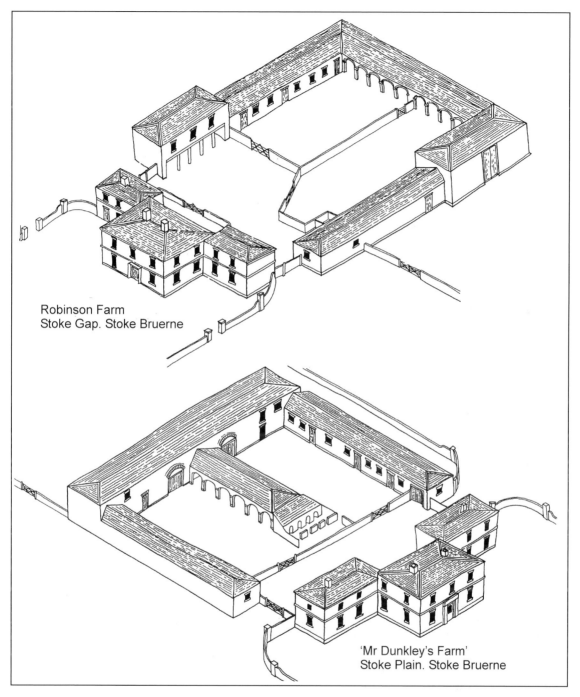

Robinson Farm
Stoke Gap. Stoke Bruerne

'Mr Dunkley's Farm'
Stoke Plain. Stoke Bruerne

the 1860s with writers such as Copland being outspoken in their criticism of
landlords who refused to provide the necessary capital investment.[17]

As we have seen, the distinctive feature of 'high farming', as contemporaries
called it, was the increased investment it demanded of both the tenant and
the landlord. If the farmer was investing heavily in raw materials he expected

a similar level of commitment from the landlord. Output was increased by the purchase of manufactured manures and feedstuffs. More animals could, therefore, be kept and more manure produced. The profits from animals increased as the railways extended into the agricultural regions, allowing for their swift transport to the London markets. The Norfolk 'high farmer', John Hudson, believed that sheep lost an average of seven pounds and bullocks 28 pounds of weight on the week-long walk from his farm to Smithfield. The arrival of the railways in the 1840s reduced the journey time to less than a day and meant there was no weight loss.[18] Urban populations were also increasing. Between 1820 and 1850 the population of South Lancashire doubled, three quarters of whom were not employed in agriculture, and Caird saw these urban consumers as a market waiting to be exploited.[19] To take full advantage of these new opportunities methods of livestock fattening became more intensive, and the increasing understanding of the valuable components of manure meant that the methods of its collection and storage would also influence farmstead design.

John Grey, writing as early as 1843, listed a few fundamental principles of design which he felt should be followed in farm building. The three points to be aimed at in construction were 'convenience, accommodation and economy'. By economy he meant not only keeping down the costs of construction and maintenance, but the saving of labour. He believed that the barn, straw house and turnip stores should be centrally situated with easy access to the cattle yards. In northern areas, on account of the prevalence of threshing machines by this date, farmsteads only needed one barn.[20]

The traditional barn therefore diminished in significance as, gradually, the threshing machine replaced hand-flailing. As the surplus of labourers declined mid-century in the south of the country, farmers here became increasingly interested in mechanisation and the efficient working of the farm.[21] Although the regional divide between the high wage counties of the north and the lower wages to the south remained, those in the south were beginning to rise in the 1840s. The average wage in southern counties for the period 1833–1845 was between seven shillings and ten pence and nine shillings and seven pence. By the period 1867–70, this had risen to eleven shillings and six pence to thirteen shillings and six pence.[22] This increased the incentive to mechanise, and so the flail and threshing floor became redundant. Where farms were not large enough to justify the installation of a stationary threshing machine, portable engines and machines, often owned by contractors who went from farm to farm, were beginning to appear.

George Dean, a member of a new profession describing themselves as 'agricultural engineers', emphasised the importance of labour efficiency. Writing in 1851, he stated, 'There ought not to be the smallest convenience on a farm, down to a pigsty, that is not so precisely in the right spot that to place it anywhere else would be a loss of labour and manure'.[23] Time management and process flow, as applied to the most advanced factory planning of the period, were thus applied to the farmstead. This theme was further explored by another agricultural engineer, John Bailey Denton, who wrote: 'To farm successfully with defective and ill-arranged buildings is no more practical than to manufacture profitably in scattered inconvenient work-shops in place of one harmoniously contrived, completely fitted mill'.[24] Andrews was keen to point out that this industrial analogy, although very neat, was not really accurate. On a farm most pieces of machinery were not used all the time, as in a factory, but only for a limited part of the year. Buildings therefore had to be more adaptable than those of a factory.[25] By 1878 the change was complete and Caird was able to write, 'our agriculture is no longer influenced by considerations of the means of finding employment for surplus labour, but is now developed on the principle of obtaining the largest produce at the least cost'.[26]

New designs

The late 1840s and early 1850s saw interest in farmstead design reach a new height with the publication of many practical plans in the farming journals and encyclopedias of the day (Figure 58). This culminated in the Royal Agricultural Society's farm prize competition, the results of which were publicised in its *Journal* for 1850. Six sets of plans were published as well as several essays, amounting in all to 130 pages. One of the competition's judges, H. S. Thompson, was of the opinion that more good entries had been sent in for this than for any of the other competitions run by the Society. A common thread running through all the essays was the fact that farm buildings were going through a period of change. As the *Journal*'s editor, Philip Pusey, put it: 'farm buildings, like certain countries, are really in a state of revol-ution'.[27] In his report on the competition in the *Journal* Thompson wrote, 'There are doubtless many who are not convinced of the advantage of thrashing by steam, box feeding, or other modern practices ... but there are probably very few who would be satisfied with any plan which was not capable of being adapted to such a system whenever it might be desirable to commence it'.[28] The chimneys for stationary steam engines were no doubt very impressive in the farming landscape, but could hardly be justified on any but the largest of farms where provision for smaller portable engines was perfectly adequate. These ideas can be seen in practice on the published plans. Buildings were still usually arranged around a yard, but this was often divided into several smaller yards surrounded by open sheds for the selective feeding of cattle. The house was placed at a greater distance from the group, emphasising the increasing social status and separation of the farmer from his work place, where he might by now be employing a foreman or bailiff to oversee the everyday business of the farmyard. Many designs included loose boxes for the individual fattening of cattle for sale. These could be placed around the yard, or in rows with a central feeding passage in a dividing wing between two yards. Occasionally the whole area within the yard would be filled with rows of boxes. A particularly early example survives at Enholmes Farm, Patrington,

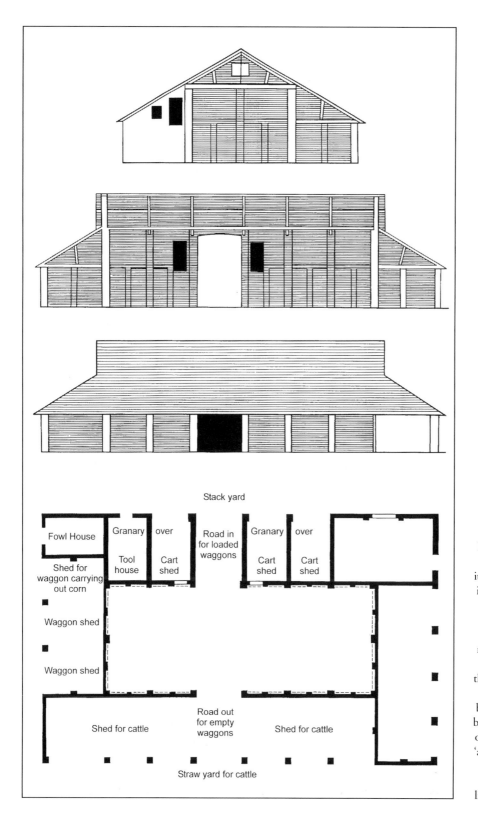

Stack yard

Fowl House | Granary | over | Road in for loaded waggons | Granary | over

Tool house | Cart shed | | Cart shed | Cart shed

Shed for waggon carrying out corn

Waggon shed

Waggon shed

Road out for empty waggons

Shed for cattle | Shed for cattle

Straw yard for cattle

FIGURE 58.
This rather strange looking 'nucleated farm' was erected at Langton near Spelby in Lincolnshire, and its plan was published in 1839. Like Wyatt's Great Barn at Holkham, it was designed to make maximum use of the barn walls by using them to form the side of more than one building. Strong iron bars were used instead of wooden king posts 'as giving more room' and 'presenting smaller obstacles to light and ventilation'.

(East Yorkshire) (Figure 59). The farmstead – centre of a farm that had grown to 1,000 acres by 1851 – was built in 1849 for William Marshall, a wealthy industrialist whose family had been responsible for the construction of fire-proof mills in Leeds since the early years of the century and whose residence, Enholmes Hall, stood half a mile to the west. Marshall was advised by a consulting engineer to the Royal Agricultural Society, the result being a steading that reflected the latest ideas on flow-line production. Five parallel ranges divided by passages filled the yard and were linked along the northern side by a feed preparation area. Another innovative feature was the manure shed with liquid manure tanks under it which took up the south-west side of the yard. Much thought was also given to the grouping of buildings for feed preparation to reduce the distances that bulky feeds were being moved, tramlines being included on which to move trucks of fodder. Tramlines ran from the stack yard into the barn so that corn could be taken directly to the threshing machine. In view of the fact that the work involved in taking down and moving a stack into a barn was a day's work for a team of men, this represented a considerable saving of labour, albeit at a considerable capital outlay.[29]

Steam and water power were frequently included in the prize designs, not only to work threshing machines but also for milling and feed-crushing mills and in workshops. John Elliott's plan for an unidentified farm of 300 acres was perhaps the most ambitious (Figure 60). Inside a conventional U-plan, with a steam-powered barn at one end and stables and livestock sheds down

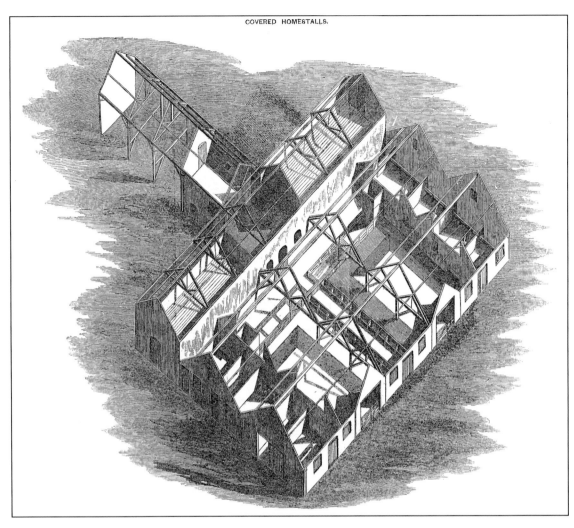

the two sides, was a central block containing four rows of eight loose boxes for cattle, served by two feeding passages. 'If it be a desirable practice that a number of animals should be allowed to range loose in a farm-yard, exposed, without any protection, to all the vicissitudes of the weather, and that the dung should be scattered about and drenched with rain throughout the winter, and loose its ammonia by evaporating during the summer, we are afraid our plans will not be approved'. Tramlines ran from the stack yard into the barn and on through the central block and out to a manure pit at the end of the yard. 'When the cattle are to be fed, the trucks take up their load of roots, cut or boiled in the root boiling and cutting store, or the chaff and linseed compound for another meal, obtained each from their respective store houses adjoining the rail, and proceed on their way through the cattle-boxes, giving out to each animal its accepted allowance. The trucks are again available for littering the animals, procuring the supply from the straw barn; and when the accumulation of the manure in the boxes has reached its limited height of

FIGURE 60.
The earliest published illustration of covered yards is that for Knapp Farm, owned by the Herefordshire land owner, Lord Somers, and published in the *Journal of the Royal Agricultural Society of England* in 1853. These buildings survive, almost unaltered, although an oast house has been inserted at one corner.

124

increase the trucks convey this mass of dung direct to the dungpit. One man could thus easily by means of the rail and truck, manage all these operations in a short time'.[30]

The covered yard was a further development in design which made its appearance in the early 1850s, although not in the farm prize competition. The importance of shelter, both to the efficient fattening of stock and the protection of manure, became appreciated as a result of the work of Lawes, at Rothamstead and his colleague Dr Augustus Voelcker, consultant chemist to the Royal Agricultural Society. Scientific analysis thus came to influence building design and the idea of covering the cattle yard, where animals could either be tied up or roam loose on an ever-deepening bed of straw was suggested. This new type of building was first described in 1853.[31] Built at Knapp Farm, near Ledbury on the Eastnor estate of Earl Somers, it was designed by a Worcester architect, James Day (Figure 61). Other examples are included in some of Frederick Chancellor's designs of the early 1850s. Providing enough ventilation to keep the animals healthy was a problem that was overcome in a variety of ways. One of the most elaborate was the provision of raised roof sections, with slatted ventilation panels between the sections, an idea clearly taken from industrial maltings and smitheries. At Park Farm, Bylaugh (Norfolk), two square covered yards opening southward across the

FIGURE 61.
John Elliott's entry for the Royal Agricultural Society's farm prize competition.

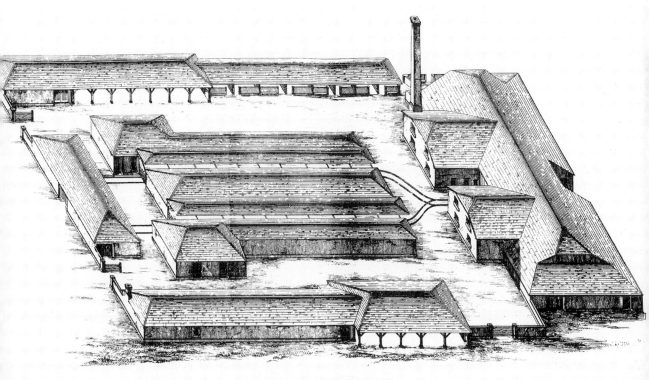

ISOMETRICAL ELEVATION.

valley provide a central area for loose stock, with boxes down two sides for final fattening. The central section of the roof is raised, with ventilation louvres between the two sections. There are also high-level louvres just below the roof line, the opening of which could be controlled from the ground by pulleys and levers (Figure 62). Similar systems can be seen at Northbrook Farm, Kirtlington (Oxfordshire) and Olliver Farm, Aske (Yorkshire). (See Figures 64 and 70.)

There was much scepticism amongst the farming community about the value of these planned farms. Farmers were critical of their expense, which

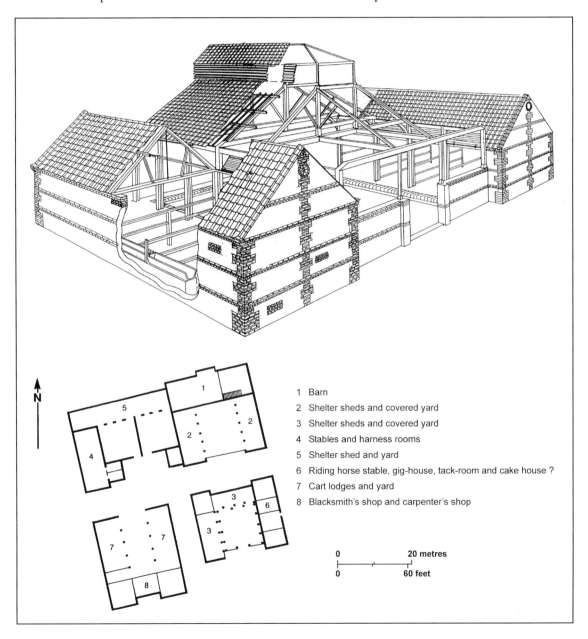

N

1 Barn
2 Shelter sheds and covered yard
3 Shelter sheds and covered yard
4 Stables and harness rooms
5 Shelter shed and yard
6 Riding horse stable, gig-house, tack-room and cake house ?
7 Cart lodges and yard
8 Blacksmith's shop and carpenter's shop

0   20 metres
0   60 feet

would then be passed on to the tenant as a rent charge. It had to be accepted that the capital investment needed for these new steadings, as in fact 'high farming' itself, could only be justified in economic terms on larger farms. Andrews thought that farms needed 400–500 acres of arable to make the buildings worthwhile. If the farm was large enough, the advantage of a good layout incorporating mechanisation resulted in 'extra-ordinary savings'.[32] Unlike many of the earlier plans, most of these were the work of engineers and land agents, with only a few architects being involved. As we have seen in the earlier period, agents were primarily concerned with economy and so where they were responsible, new buildings were usually of a simple and functional design. Unlike the earlier period, discussion was likely to be on the merits of covered manure pits or tramways rather than the niceties of different architectural styles. The new methods associated with high farming meant that well laid-out buildings with plenty of storage for feed and fertilisers as well as methods of conserving manure, good livestock accommodation and provision for mechanisation were necessary to attract innovative tenants.

Some plans were still the work of amateurs, with little immediate farming experience. Richard Barley was the actuary of the Savings Bank in Thirsk, but was responsible for the design of new buildings for George Crowe of Ornhams, near Boroughbridge, which he described in *The Farmer's Magazine* of 1851. In his introduction, he also emphasised the changes that were taking place in farm building design: 'It might be supposed that ere this, experience would have decided what particular form was best and most suitable for the disposition of farm buildings. But it is quite the contrary. We seem to be on the threshold of enquiry'. He also used the industrial analogy, considering the farmyard as the 'manufactory of the results of harvest into marketable ware'. The steam engine and barns were placed on one side of a square, with 'buildings calculated for converting the raw material of the stackyard into corn, meal, flour etc. to be distributed to the two remaining sides of the square as may be wanted for the horses and cattle respectively.' Many designers had therefore adopted the principal concepts of process flow taken from factory design and which, in contrast to the classical inspiration of a previous generation, looked forward to the next two decades and beyond.

The importance to architects of commissions for farm buildings was well-recognised by the profession by the middle of the century, and its journal *The Builder* published plans such as those for Coleshill (see Figure 104), the Home Farm at Blenheim and Wallscourt, Stoke Gifford (near Bristol).[33] It also produced a series of articles through 1860 entitled 'Maxims and Memoranda relating to the arrangement and construction of farm buildings' in which the position and site, arrangement of the farm, construction and fittings were all discussed. The more general magazines, with a readership stretching beyond farmers and gentry, also took an interest in farm building design. The degree of interest was such that the *London Illustrated News* featured the Earl of Macclesfield's new farm at Shirburn (Oxfordshire) in the winter of 1857; and in 1858, the Home Farm at Blenheim for the Duke of Marlborough, a model

FIGURE 62.
The date of the covered yards at Park Farm, Bylaugh, Norfolk, is not known, but they were built for the Evans Lombe estate, probably in the early 1850s when the family was building a new house and creating a park nearby. The block plan shows the barn to the north with a covered yard abutting to the south, and a further smaller freestanding yard to the south. Workshops and stables stand to the west. The covered yards represent a very sophisticated design, with elaborate louvre systems to control ventilation. Inside are rows of pens on a brick causeway with a central yard for loose cattle.

of which had been exhibited by the architect William Wilkinson, at the Baker Street Show. The paper reported that after its publication of the Shirburn farm, 'for some weeks … the buildings were visited daily by gentlemen from various parts of the kingdom, likewise by several distinguished foreigners'. This 'proves the considerable interest that is manifested in buildings of this class'.[34]

Country house architects received commissions for farm buildings from the more architecturally discerning members of the landed class, bringing to their designs their own individual interpretations of vernacular, Gothic and Tudor styles. Charles Devey worked for the Rothschilds around Waddesden as well as in Kent,[35] and S. S. Teulon was responsible for the design of new farmsteads on Sunk Island as well as farmhouses for the Duke of Bedford at Thorney. Some architects took a particular interest in this aspect of their practice. The prolific Chelmsford architect, Frederick Chancellor was one such man. His work included houses and public buildings as well as farmsteads. Over 750 of his plans survive in Essex Record Office, more than 50 of which are for farms. He did not claim to be an agricultural engineer, but as in all his work he was receptive to new ideas and worked closely with his clients.

Amongst the Chancellor plans in Essex Record Office are many loose drawings and a book of 23 designs, with watercolour perspective drawings, possibly put together as examples of his work to show prospective customers.[36] They cover farmsteads erected in Shropshire, Cambridgeshire, Huntingdonshire, Surrey and Kent, as well as Essex. Although the designs vary in scale and detail, they all have certain elements in common. Many have covered yards. The plan dated 1850 of Hormead Farm (Hertfordshire) is one of the earliest examples of a covered yard so far identified. This has not been located on the ground, but other examples include Stevens Farm at Chignall in Essex (1852) and Model Farm at Graffham in Cambridgeshire (1854), both of which are still standing. That at Chignall is particularly innovative and explicitly functional in its design (Plates 12–14). The high roof is supported on elegant,

FIGURE 63.
Chancellor's sketch for Model Farm, Graffham.

slim cast-iron columns and there are open hay and straw lofts above the stables and cattle stalls on either side, allowing for the feed and litter to be forked down into the yards and stalls. The ventilation is provided through sky-lights in the slate and boarded roof. Model Farm, Graffham, built for the Sparrow estate based at Gosfield (Essex), is of a more typical design, with the gables at right-angles to the barn at the rear. The two yards are divided by a feeding passage, set under a central gable. There are two gables over each yard and the valleys between are supported by wooden pillars with decorative supporting braces (Figure 63).

All the farmsteads are of a highly functional design (which does not preclude them also being elegant in their own right). A few have purely decorative features. Westwood Farm, Tunbridge, Haines Hill (Berkshire) and Rivenhall (Essex) have dovecotes, pigeon keeping on a large scale having become uneconomic as wheat prices had risen in the Napoleonic Wars.[37] Other farmsteads such as New Farm, Eye, (Cambridgeshire), have decorative façades of little practical use. Haines Hill and Sennowe Hill (Surrey), have timber-framed fronts, and there is the occasional Venetian, Gothic or classical window or arch. However, the overall impression is one of restraint with only the occasional touch of flamboyance. In spite of the interest in innovative cattle housing, as exemplified by the covered yard, there is little evidence for mechanisation on Chancellor's plans. Most of the barns have one or more threshing floors with no provision for a threshing machine or power source. New Farm, Elmington (Cambridgeshire) had a horse walk and at Little Bardwell there was a steam engine, but these are unusual. Here, in the rural south-east of the country, labour was still cheap and there was little incentive to replace manpower with machinery. Nevertheless, the arrangement of the buildings themselves is carefully thought-out for ease of movement of feed, litter, livestock and cereals.

By the 1850s, the engineering profession was added to those who were designing farm buildings on a professional basis. John Denton and George Dean were two men who would have described themselves as agricultural engineers. John Denton's background was that of a sanitary engineer, designing many of the urban sewage schemes that were being installed for urban corporations at this time. In 1863 he was appointed engineer to the General Land Drainage and Improvement Company and published a collection of plans of thirty newly-constructed farmsteads across England. Denton's extensive travels for the Company enabled him to select exemplar steadings which demonstrated the ideal for a variety of sizes of farm on a variety of soils. By this date, covered yards were an accepted aspect of good farmstead design and are included in six of his examples. Denton's main concern in the selection of his farms was to demonstrate what could be built at reasonable expense, and he suggested a sliding scale of outlay related to farm size. The smaller the farm, the greater the expenditure per acre was likely to be. Not more than £7 an acre should be spent on farms of 200 to 500 acres, whilst a farm of over 1,000 acres could be provided for at a cost of £4.10s. per acre. The designs he selected therefore tend to be good, functional layouts with little in the way of unnecessary elaboration.

Half of the farmsteads illustrated in Denton's book[38] were designed by men described as 'architects'. Some were the work of those with busy national practices such as the Oxford architect, William Wilkinson who was responsible for buildings at Longleat, Wiltshire (Figure 105) and Northbrook, Oxfordshire (Figure 64), and Frederick Chancellor's farmsteads at Haines Hill (Berkshire) and Nabbots Farm (Essex). Most of the architects, such as E. Browning of Stamford,[39] practised within their own localities and no further. Often the architect worked very closely with the agent, owner or occupier. At Downsplace Farm (Surrey), the farm was said to be 'designed by H. Peake, (architect) who embodied the suggestions of Mr Faviell', the owner[40] and at the Willows (Herefordshire) the 'farm designs were by Mr Thomas Fenn, the agent for the proprietor, Mr Charles Trubshaw of Stafford acting as architect.'[41] The work of Denton himself at Toothill (Hampshire) is the only example of the work of an agricultural engineer illustrated.[42]

Some agents continued their profession's tradition as farmstead designers, dispensing with the assistance of architects. Robert Mein, the Duke of Bedford's agent at Thorney, designed the new farmsteads there. Christopher Turnor's Lincolnshire agent, J. Young Mcvicar, designed the new farmsteads on the Stixwauld estate on an innovative and very workable plan (see p. 143), and the new buildings at Maisemore (Gloucestershire) were the work of Messrs Cluttons. Other farmsteads that found their way into Denton's book were the work of owners as at Sancton Hill (Yorkshire) or, as in the case of Brome Hall (Suffolk) 'erected by workmen on the estate under the supervision of [the otherwise unknown] Mr Goodrick'.[43]

George Dean was typical of the sort of person who was sought after to design farm buildings in the 1850s. He was not a trained architect, but a land agent. He wrote several books on agricultural matters, including, in 1851, *The Land Steward*, in which he bemoaned the lack of good farm buildings: 'A compact and well-arranged steading is of immense importance to the farmer; it is there his livestock are sheltered and fed a great portion of the year, it is there the produce of his farm is manufactured and consumed, and it is there he collects the means of enriching his lands and of increasing the quantity and improving the quality of his crops.' This meant animals should be well housed, implement sheds should be adequate as more wear and tear was caused through leaving tools outside than through actual work, and the buildings should be well-spaced so that there was plenty of room for extension.

Dean was employed at Holkham for the Earl of Leicester in the 1850s, and his work there demonstrates two elements of his designs. Firstly, at Egmere Farm he was responsible for the only complete re-build of a tenant farm on the estate during the 'high farming' period (Figure 65). It was built between 1850 and 1856, costing about £5,500, the most expensive building project on the estate. Here six cattle yards were created, with shelter sheds alongside them. Between the sheds were rows of sunken loose boxes with a central

FIGURE 64. Northbrook Farm, Kirtlington, Oxfordshire, was illustrated by Bailey Denton and built in 1858 by Sir Henry Dashwood. It is an example of the work of the Oxford architect William Wilkinson, who designed farm buildings in Oxfordshire and Wiltshire. The open and covered yards between them provided accommodation for 50 or 60 cattle and stalls allowed for the fattening of twelve beasts. There was stabling for fourteen horses and also fifteen pigsties. Small ground-level sliding hatches allowed for muck to be shovelled from the stables into the yard beyond.

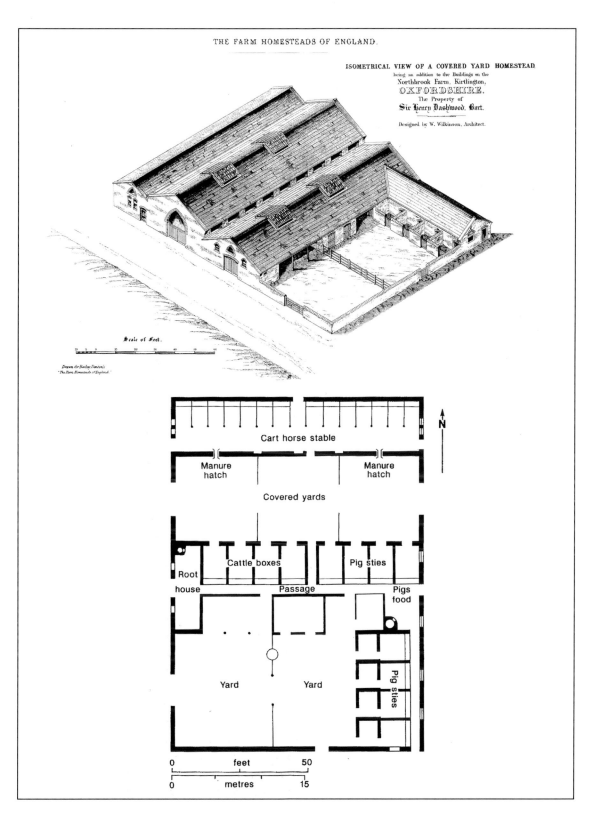

ISOMETRICAL VIEW OF A COVERED YARD HOMESTEAD,
being an addition to the Buildings on the
Northbrook Farm, Kirtlington,
OXFORDSHIRE.
The Property of
Sir Henry Dashwood, Bart.

Designed by W. Wilkinson, Architect.

Scale of Feet.

Drawn for Bailey Denton's
"The Farm Homesteads of England."

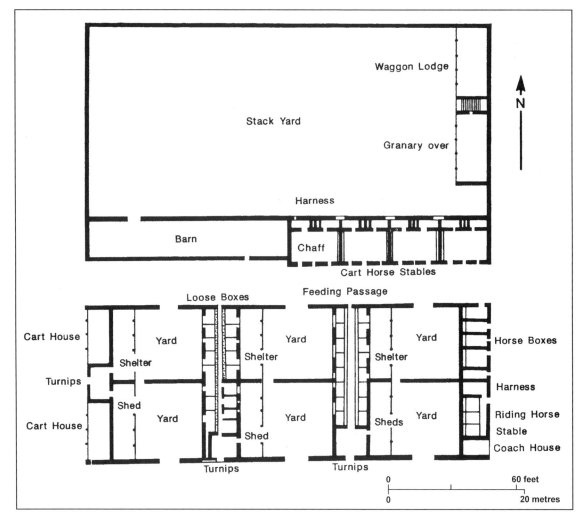

feeding passage for the individual fattening of cattle, indicating the increasing value being put on fattening stock and finishing it for transport, often via the railway station at Fakenham, to market. Behind these ranges and across a roadway, the old barn remains with the stables beside it and behind them a huge stack yard and new granary above cartsheds. The change in emphasis away from the barn as the dominant building, and towards cattle accommodation, is clearly demonstrated here.[44] The barn is, however, still in a central position between the cattle sheds, stables and granaries, emphasising the importance of the spent straw as bedding. Unlike the planned farmsteads of the Wyatt period at Holkham, these buildings had no architectural detailing. This is similar to other buildings by Dean, notably at Charlton in Dorset and on a larger scale at Lymm in Cheshire, a dairy farm where ninety fattening cattle and up to 200 pigs were to be housed.[45] However, another side to his work can be seen at Holkham, where he also designed the estate workshops at Longlands and a dairy steading (Model Farm, Holkham) to house the Earl's

FIGURE 65.
Plan of Egmere Farm on the Holkham estate (Norfolk), designed by the agricultural engineer G. A. Dean.

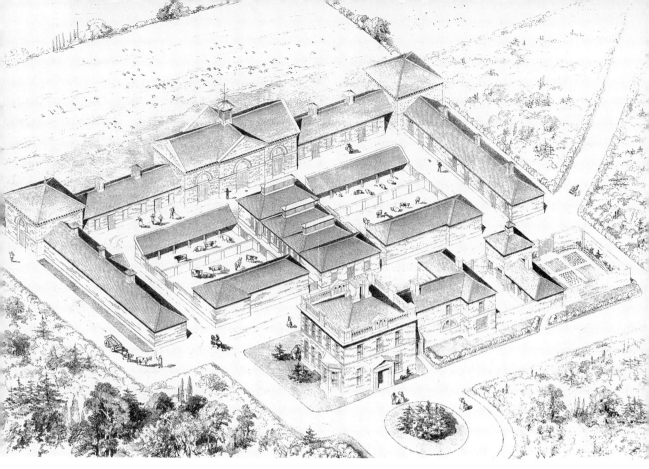

FIGURE 66.
Model Farm at
Holkham (Norfolk)
was designed about
the same time, again
by Dean, but its
parkland setting
demanded a more
architectural
treatment. It was
intended to house
dairy cows within the
park. The main
building is a large feed
store and mixing
house, while the
cowsheds and yards
fill the centre of the
complex. This
illustration is from
Dean's book, *Selected
Designs for Country
Residences, Entrance
Lodges, Farm Offices,
Cottages, etc.*,
published in 1867.

prize Red Poll cattle. These buildings are no less practical than Egmere in their layout, but include much more in the way of architectural, in this case Italianate, embellishment (Figure 66). This more ornate style can also be seen on the farmstead designed for Prince Albert in Windsor Great Park, to be discussed later.

Dean went on to publish a selection of his plans in 1867.[46] These range from the purely functional to Windsor Park and included steam engines, manure pits and tramlines. None included covered yards. The designs for Mr Brooke of Leamington comprised plain buildings which included a railway to bring stacks to the barn, where there was a threshing machine. The barn was connected to a central block of yards by a covered way. All Dean's published plans broke away from the conventional E or U-plan, the buildings being placed in a central block with barns and other ranges linked to them by a passageway or across a roadway, and sometimes wrapping round them.

New building materials; corrugated and cast iron, concrete and laminated timber

The creation of planned and model farmsteads reached a peak in the 1860s as farming confidence remained high. Building continued through the early 1870s, in spite of the fact that grain prices had already begun to fall. This fall served to increase emphasis on livestock accommodation, as well as on labour-saving devices which would help reduce the cost of labour. Interest in new building methods – usually imported from industry – also increased, especially if they could reduce building or maintenance costs, and these were most likely to be found on the home farm.

One of the most astounding home farm complexes is that designed by Frederick Knight's Exmoor agent, Robert Smith, for William Taylor's 900-acre farm at Eastwood Manor, East Harptree (Somerset) between 1858 and 1860 (Figure 67). It was automated from a huge 27-foot-diameter (9m) water wheel. Tramways brought the stacks to the threshing machine in the barn. Behind the fine limestone façade are two huge covered yards, with an underground manure pit The whole was roofed over with corrugated iron. The roof is supported by cast-iron pillars and trusses and the yards surrounded by first-floor storage areas. A fountain filling a water trough played in one of the yards and water was recycled through the hollow, cast-iron columns which fed the water troughs around the buildings.[47] Here we see the ultimate application of factory design to a farm, with nearly all the building materials coming from outside the locality. Iron fittings were foundry-made, either from the Bristol firm of Wrights, or Musgroves, with works in London and Belfast.

Another material being tried experimentally at the time was concrete. It was

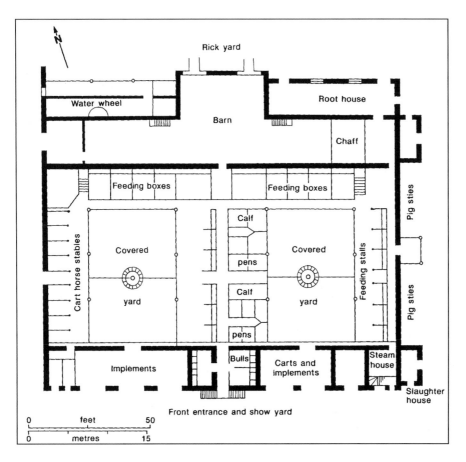

FIGURE 67
(*left and opposite*). The most remarkable farm complex of the 'high farming' era is Eastwood Manor Farm at East Harptree (Somerset). The plan shows buildings around two covered yards. It contains all the features associated with the best farmstead design for the next fifty years. Machinery was water-powered and iron trusses and the use of corrugated iron as a light roofing material allowed for wide roof trusses over two covered yards.

134

successfully used for docks in the 1860s and its merits discussed in an article in the *Journal of the Royal Agricultural Society of England* in 1874, in which it was pointed out that it was not always cheaper to use.[48] However, its main advantage was that labour costs in construction could be saved as unskilled workers could be used rather than stone masons of bricklayers. The first concrete buildings were erected at Buscot (Oxfordshire) where Robert Campbell, returning from Australia with a fortune, had bought the 3,500 acre estate and in 1870 erected a large barn.[49] However, several leading estates experimented with its use. In 1873, the Earl of Leicester bought Drakes Patent building apparatus to support the shuttering as the building went up and a few concrete buildings and cottages were built into the 1880s, but then the project was abandoned.[50] The harbour engineer, A. T. Peterson was responsible for building much of Southampton docks and was an enthusiastic user of concrete. In the 1880s he built himself a concrete mansion at Sway in the New Forest, and pigsties beside a concrete tower at Towers Farm.[51] Further examples are to be found on the Hanbury-Tracy Greynog estate in Wales,[52] the Poltolloch estates in Argyll,[53] and the Sutherland estates in northern Scotland,[54] but the experiments were mostly abandoned by 1890. The buildings were found to be damp and condensation was always a problem in cottages. The concrete often shrunk as it dried which meant window and door fittings were distorted. As a result, no more concrete buildings appear until the 1920s.

The Home Farm at Apley Park (Shropshire), dating from the final phase of building for 'high farming', provides another example of the very satisfactory unity of form and function. Owned by the Foster family of ironmasters, who did not rely on their estates for their income, it certainly demonstrated their wealth and their interest in progressive agriculture, but unfortunately no correspondence relating to its building survives. Dated 1875, it is built of red brick with decorative black brick detailing. It is on a traditional E-plan layout

FIGURE 68
Home Farm at Apley Park (Shropshire) is dated 1875. Its carefully designed exterior frames a highly practical arrangement, whereby the covered yards can be approached both at ground floor level and from a feeding gallery (Plate 15).

'*Practice with Science*', *1840–1875*

FIGURE 69
Louvres below roof
level provide
ventilation to the
covered yards at Apley
Park. A cast-iron
spiral staircase rises
from the mixing room
with its belt drive
from the steam engine
to the feed store above.

but with covered yards between the main wings and a barn with ornate
chimney for the steam-engine house that extends behind the long rear block:
a layout being advocated a quarter of a century before (see pp. 75–6). As at
East Harptree, it was the desire to cover a wide, open span which led to
exciting use of new materials, in this case in the form of laminated timber
for the huge curved arches over the covered yards (Figures 68 and 69, Plate
15). These are supported on cast-iron pillars and there are both ground-floor
and high-level walkways around the yards, the upper ones connecting with
the first-floor feed stores. Laminated timber was developed in the early-nineteenth century, firstly in bridge design in Germany and then for the wide
spans needed for indoor riding schools in France. In England they were
pioneered by the Newcastle architect Benjamin Green who used the technique
for railway bridges on the east coast line near Newcastle, and the new church
built at Cambo (Northumberland) in the 1840s. This did not, however, herald
a new era in timber engineering. It was overtaken by the development of cast
iron. The only other farm building known in which laminated timber was
used is the corn store at Poling, on the Duke of Norfolk's Arundel estate,
designed by the estate Clerk of the Works, George Hevingham in 1881.[55] The
end result at Apley is a distinguished example of industrial design and materials
being utilised in an agricultural context.

Similarly, there are no records of the building of Olliver Farm, near Aske
Hall, just north of Richmond, a home of the Duke of Zetland in North
Yorkshire. The estate was purchased from Lord Holderness by Sir Laurence
Dundas's family in 1762, a man whose considerable wealth had been largely
gained through the procurement of army contracts in the Seven Years War.
The estate, however, was in debt by the time his grandson Thomas inherited
in 1781, and a programme of improvements and building was put in hand to
maximise returns from the estate. A New Farm, where experiments in animal
and plant breeding could be carried out, was created in 1809. Richard Smithson
the agent, who took over in 1808, kept Sir Thomas informed of progress there.
The land was first drained and then limed and dressed with bone meal:
'many have criticised the large amount of lime put on, but they are now
silenced'.[56] In March the new buildings around a courtyard were laid out,
after some discussion as to whether the farmyard should face exactly south or
whether there would be a better aspect with a slightly different orienta-
tion.[57] A four horse-power water-powered threshing machine was later installed
after calculations had been made as to how much water would be needed to
operate it.[58] The family also owned land in Cleveland, between Redcar and
Marske, and in both areas fields were rearranged, drainage undertaken and
new farmsteads built. Indeed the coastland between Redcar and Marske
presented a typical 'improved' landscape, with straight roads, rectangular fields
and planned farmsteads on courtyard, U, E and octagonal plans by the 1840s.
New leases imposing rotations were agreed, but not until rent reductions were
negotiated for the first two years whilst the farming systems were changing.[59] Controls over farming were to be strict. When, for example, the tenants

gathered on rent day in 1813 they were told how much lime and manure they must put on the fallows, and were reminded that they could only claim back the cost of the lime if they could present receipts.[60] Rents rose, but how much this was the result of the improvements and how much simply the general rise in agricultural prices, is impossible to tell.

By 1816 there was an E-plan farmstead on the present site at Olliver Farm.[61] However, the existing steading had been rebuilt by the mid 1870s, when the Duke's agent W. J. Moscrop was experimenting with various methods of fattening cattle. Different groups were tied up in the stalls of a cowhouse, placed in loose boxes and put in open shelter sheds with yards. The temperature was carefully monitored and the rates of fattening noted. The result was to show that 'the greatest profit derived from a given consumption of food, is from cattle fed in boxes, while the least profitable mode of consumption is by cattle on open yards'.[62] These experiments were only confirming what Moscrop had already shown at Kirkleatham, where he had been responsible for building covered yards, and which he had written about with enthusiasm in the *Journal of the Royal Agricultural Society of England* for 1865.[63] On moving to the Aske estate, he may well have built those at Olliver Farm. Here an E-plan group of buildings is infilled by two covered yards on a smaller scale than those at Apley (Figure 70, Plate 16). A separate building housed a steam engine for powering farm machinery. A tramway runs through one covered yard to the barn and feed preparation room behind. The stall divisions and feeding troughs are all cast-iron as are the troughs and rails separating the covered yard from the passageway around it. Here the yard roofs are held up by cast-iron columns and wrought-iron trusses, with a cobweb of supporting tension rods. The roofs of the yard have central raised sections, with ventilator panels controlled by pulleys. Again this is a technically advanced group making full use of wrought and cast-iron, both for stall fittings and tramways, and also in the roof structure.

Tenanted farms

In spite of the criticisms levelled by Caird and others at the landowners, it is clear that many persisted in their expensive enthusiasm for improvement and rebuilding. Nowhere was this more true than in Northumberland, where many landowners continued to generate wealth from outside agriculture which they could then invest in their farms. The existence of good building stone meant that solid buildings were erected and, as we have seen, a shortage of cheap labour meant that horse, wind and steam power were likely to be adopted at an early date. On visiting and commenting upon developments in Northumberland in 1841, John Grey described the 'comfortable and substantial farm houses' which had been built, and 'the commodious sets of farm offices, laid out on compact plans ... in central situations with roads diverging from them.'[64] As we have seen, new building had been going on steadily from the 1760s, but it was not until 1836 that Matthew White, fourth Baron Ridley,

inherited the 10,000 acre Blagdon estate just north of Newcastle, and, severing the family connection with collieries and banking, concentrated on improving the agriculture on his estates. He maintained this interest until his death in 1877. An estate survey of 1836, and field book with plans dating from 1889, shows how much progress was made in this period. In 1835, most of this heavy-land estate had only recently been enclosed, and was still used for pasture. Few turnips were grown and a great variety of rotations used in the arable, mostly including a fallow year and several years of grass, emphasising the importance of cattle on the farms.[65] By 1889 nearly all the farmsteads illustrated had either a U or E-plan and several had round houses for horse engines or stationary steam engines with chimneys. Although these impressive estate buildings demonstrate planning on a grand scale, there are no indications of covered yards, suggesting that the tried and tested techniques of farmstead planning were considered to be more appropriate than innovative ideas.[66] No architect is mentioned in the estate records and, like so many other buildings, they were probably the work of the agent with advice from both the farmer and local builder. New Horton Grange, with datestones of 1856 and 1863, was described in *Kelly's Directory* of 1858 as 'the most complete and extensive model farm in Northumberland' (Figure 71). It was one of the largest farms on the estate, amounting to 776 acres. In plan, it is similar to a farmstead built at

FIGURE 71.
The 'poultiggery' at New Horton Grange on the Ridleys' Northumberland estate. The poultry helped keep the pigs warm, while the pigs deterred foxes.

Outchester for the Greenwich Hospital estate and illustrated by Grey.[67] Two two-storey wings, comprising open shelter sheds below extensive granaries extend either side of the barn forming the back of a range of yards, separated internally by either walls or turnip troughs and with byres or stables in the end wings. Along the front of the yards is a wall with freestanding pavilion-type turnip houses on the end of the yard walls entered by double cart doors to

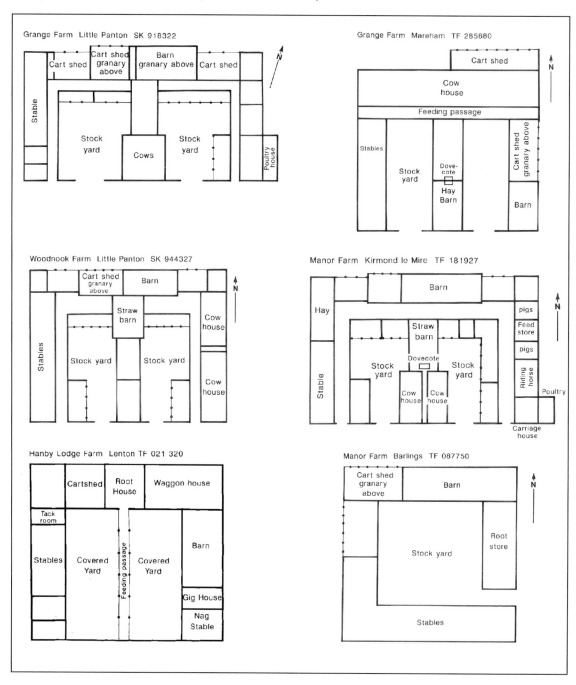

the roadway and single-width doors into the yards. Further cattle yards, and a poultry house with pigsties below, complete the buildings on this site.

More innovative in plan form were the farmsteads built for Christopher Turnor of Stoke Rochford Hall, who inherited about 20,000 acres in Lincolnshire in 1829 and controlled the estate until his death in 1886. Although he was the third largest landowner in the county, and an extremely wealthy man, little is known of his life and no estate documents survive. However, it is clear from the number of farmsteads and cottages that still stand that he was an active improver and 'probably responsible for erecting more buildings in Lincolnshire than any other single person'.[68] His estates were widely dispersed, ranging from the mixed soils to the east of Lincoln into the Wolds near Louth. About twenty farmsteads were rebuilt either in whole or in part between 1847 and 1870 on recently enclosed land, with the finest examples dating from the 1860s. As was so often the case they were not designed by an architect but by Turnor's agent, Mr J. Young Macvicar, and they impressed John Bailey Denton to such an extent that he chose to illustrate the one at Wispington in his book. Built in 1855, it was described by Denton as 'one of several … all of which are either enlargements or modifications of the same design'.[69] Their unusual layout, which is typical of the estate, consists of an external U, with an internal E, linked to the outer range through a central straw barn (Figure 72). The threshing barn is in a conventional position along the back of the U. Here the grain was separated from the straw by hand flailing, there being no sign of a mechanical power source or stand for a threshing machine. The grain was then stored in an adjacent granary, which could be reached via a staircase from the barn. There was also access to the straw barn where the threshed-out straw would be stored after threshing. Doors from the straw barn and the passageway between the E and U ranges enabled the straw to be taken to the stables and cowhouses in the outer range, whilst doors at the other end of the straw barn allowed access to the yards of the inner range. Although there was no mechanical power source or covered yard this was an extremely efficient layout, enabling the flow of feed, litter, animals and manure. Nevertheless, it does not seem to have been copied on other estates. Whilst Wispington Farm was just over 300 acres the more ornate examples served farms of between 500 and 560 acres, all replacing village farmsteads and located in the centre of the fields that they served.[70] Dovecotes rise from the central blocks at Newstead Farm, Stixwauld, Grange Farm, Little Ponton, Manor Farm, Kirmond-Le-Mire and Grange Farm, Marham-on-the-Hill (Figure 73).

Also mainly in the east of the country were the extensive estates of the Duke of Bedford. Following the death of the fifth Duke in 1805 and the short-lived enthusiasm for agriculture of the sixth Duke, there was a period of stagnation before the seventh Duke inherited in 1839. An estate report of 1835 emphasised the dilapidation of the estate buildings on 37 farmsteads, stating that: 'The outgoings for repairs of buildings will for a number of years be considerable owing to the great majority of buildings being wood and thatched'.[71] It is clear that there had been a change in building policy between

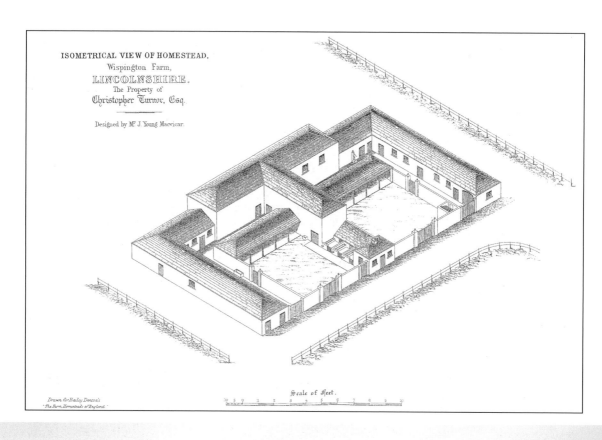

FIGURE 73.
(*opposite and right*)
The Turnor
farmsteads. The layout
illustrated by Bailey
Denton at
Whispington (1), now
demolished, was of a
plain, small-scale
example.

At Manor Farm,
Kirmond-le-Mire (2)
the buildings were
more elaborate with a
central dovecote
forming a decorative
feature. Tripartite
windows were a
feature of several
estate farmsteads.
Innovatory features
included the sliding
panels, as at Grange
Farm (3), which
facilitated feeding
directly from the
passage into the stalls,
and water troughs for
the stables which
could be filled from
the walkway between
the inner and outer
buildings. There were
no stationary
steam-engine houses
on any of the
farmsteads, but at
Grange Farm a wheel
took belting from the
portable engine placed
outside the barn (4).

145

the days of the fifth and seventh Duke. The fifth Duke's efforts were concentrated on the Home Farm, where his sheep shearings took place. Whilst some of the outlying farmsteads had been rebuilt, they were of *pisé*, wood and thatch, and therefore impermanent. With the accession of the seventh Duke, a period of high investment and estate improvements began, with wood and thatch being replaced by brick and slate or tiled buildings. An annual average of over £10,000 was spent on the Bedfordshire estates of the Duke, covering just over 30,000 acres, and producing a rent averaging £43,600 between 1858 and 1875.[72] The estate's *Annual Reports*, which began in 1844, listed the amount spent on various improvements. From these it is clear that the late 1840s and the 1850s were years of great building activity, not only in the arable east but also on the Duke's Devon estates. In this way, the ideas of the 'high farmers' of the cereal counties were introduced to the pastoral west. On all three estates expenditure was needed, in Bedfordshire because of 'a total neglect'. In Thorney (in the Cambridgeshire fens) the new drainage meant that there were new farms to be created and equipped, and in Devon new farms were being laid out as the life leases of small farmers expired and their lands amalgamated.[73] The reason for such high expenditure compared with neighbouring estates was given in a report of 1853 as the need to 'satisfy the requirements and take advantage of the recent improvements in agriculture and to enable tenants to meet the competition to which free trade in corn and other agricultural produce has given rise, and through building in brick to protect against incendiarism and to ensure the durability of the buildings'.[74] This reference to arson is an isolated one, but may well have influenced the decisions of other landowners in the years following the Swing riots of the early 1830s. Much of the anger of the rioters was directed against threshing machines, which were taking away winter work, and certainly delayed the uptake of machinery in regions such as East Anglia where underemployment remained a problem into the 1850s. The inscription on a brick horse-engine house at Hengrave in Suffolk reads, 'Burnt 1849, Sir T. R. Gage rebuilt 1849' and reminds us that arson remained a problem well after the main period of unrest in the 1830s.

The Duke of Bedford's expenditure reached a peak in the 1850s, with outgoings of over £17,000 in several years. It is clear that this investment never produced the hoped-for returns,[75] but it did result in some of the most expensive and extensive buildings for 'high farming' erected in England. Most estate offices imprinted their own hallmark on the buildings of their farms and the Bedford farms in Bedfordshire had certain typical elements in common. The estate dominated farm building in the Bedfordshire parishes of Thurleigh, Stevington, Steppingley, Eversholt, Milton Bryan, Houghton Conquest, Ridgmont as well as Woburn and further afield at Cople. Many included a wide and well-ventilated stockhouse, with a higher central section, used for fattening cattle and pigs. As well as these, there were also often long, narrow dormer-style roof ventilators along other stock buildings. Perhaps surprisingly for such a progressive and highly capitalised estate, covered yards were not part of the original design of any of the Duke's Bedfordshire or Cambridgeshire farmsteads although they were built in Devon, possibly reflecting the wetter climate and greater emphasis on livestock in the west. The buildings were instead arranged in a traditional south-facing E-plan layout, often with more than two yards. Several farmsteads included steam-engine houses with tall impressive chimneys, or the unusual arrangement of standings for portable engines in open porches (Figure 74). Details of the buildings erected are sometimes given in the *Annual Reports*. New buildings at Brogborough Farm are described in 1853 as 'cart hovel, with granary and chaff loft, barn, engine house, cow house, two open hovels, nag and carthorse stables, poultry, implement and gig house, double feeding house with boiling house'.[76] Over 40 farmsteads were remodelled on improved lines. However, the exceptionally high costs involved and the lack of return in terms of increased rent, makes it clear that it was only the wealthiest of estates that could afford to build on this scale. When Caird visited in 1851 he commented on the amount of building activity around Woburn, but wrote that the new farm buildings were 'not designed with that regard for economy and arrangement which would render them models for other estates'.[77]

It was not only in the Woburn area that this level of expense was being lavished. A further area of the Bedford estate where improvements were carried out mid-century was in Devon, where the Duke's copper mine – the largest in the world – dominated the economy and financed the building of workers' housing and schools as well as large-scale development of municipal buildings in Tavistock and its surrounding villages.[78] In the early-nineteenth century this area of west Devon consisted of small, mainly pastoral farms with anciently-enclosed fields, but from the 1840s the Bedford estate had a policy of farm amalgamation and rationalisation, creating at least six new farms. These new farms were intended to be more commercial enterprises than the small dairy farms they replaced. In order to educate the tenants in a more entreprenurial style of farming, the agent Mr Benson suggested in 1847 taking a farm in hand so that 'the double purpose of bringing it into good condition, which it stands much in need of, and making it serve as an example farm, might be answered and therefore farming there has been commenced'.[79] This farm has not so far been located, but it is clear from the *Annual Reports* that the estate surveyor, Mr Jones, was sent to look at best practice in the neighbourhood, one notable example being at Prince Hall on Dartmoor, designed by the well-known promoter of improved agriculture, J. C. Morton, where rows of cattle boxes backed onto a manure house.[80] As a consequence, local conditions strongly influenced the design of these farmsteads. Indeed, all the Bedford farmsteads in west Devon placed great emphasis on manure protection in the form of manure houses, and employed established regional features such as bank barns and the use of water and horse power for farm machinery (Figure 75).

The most monumental surviving example is that at Kilworthy, just outside Tavistock (Figure 76, Plates 17 and 18). This was built in 1851 'upon a new plan, which, if it should be found to answer, may become a model for the other farm buildings … the main feature … being a great compactness, having the farm buildings nearly all under one roof, keeping the manure under cover free from the influence of the rain, wind and sun, economising labour by means of tramways and providing extensive housing for cattle'. The plan exhibits much thought and apparently a judicious adoption of the improvements which Mr Jones had inspected.[81] Not only was all the feed processing and threshing entirely mechanised but under the cattle houses is a large manure pit. Gaps between the granite slabs which made up the cattle shed floors allowed the liquid to drain into it and chutes along the side walls of the shed meant that the manure could be shovelled down. The sheds were supported over the pits by six rows of five massive granite pillars and could be approached by manure carts down the slope along a roadway. Threshing and feed preparation machinery was powered by a huge iron water wheel over 30 feet (10m) in diameter, fed from a stone-lined circular reservoir at the top of the hill. Similar buildings were built on several farms, including nearby Week

The English Model Farm

FIGURE 74
(*left and opposite*).
Lower Farm at Millbrook (Bedfordshire) stands within the planned landscape created by the Bedford estate (1). It is a compact set of red brick buildings dominated by the tall chimney of its steam-engine house (2). Dividing the yard is a wide stock house typical of the estateAt Park Farm, Steppingley, (3) is another feature found on several farmsteads: a covered standing with a chimney for a portable steam engine.

148

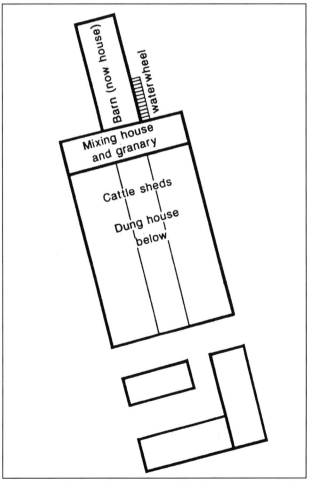

FIGURE 75.
Week and Beara
Farms, Milton Abbot
(Devon) were both
built around a
courtyard with central
manure houses. The
view into the yard at
Beara shows the
manure house to the
left with to the rear
an open-fronted
shelter shed with
upper granary and a
bank barn with
ground-floor cattle
housing. The barn
machinery was
powered by a horse
engine, located in an
engine house to the
rear of the barn.

Barn (now house)

waterwheel

Mixing house
and granary

Cattle sheds

Dung house
below

some ten years later, where a water wheel powered machinery in the three-storey barn and a manure house was centrally placed in the yard.

In contrast to the ancient landscape of west Devon, the Bedford estates in the parish of Thorney (Cambridgeshire) were one of the few areas of England still largely unreclaimed in the late-eighteenth century. There had been attempts to drain the Fens from the seventeenth century, but all had failed because of the problems of keeping the mouth of the Nene beyond Wisbech clear, so that the drains could empty. A new outfall was built following parliamentary acts in 1826 and 1827, a new drain for the North Level (of which Thorney was a part) was built between 1831 and 1834, and steam engines installed to replace the windmills which had only been capable of lifting the water up to four feet. The agent to the Duke of Bedford at Thorney, Tycho Wing, was confident enough in the new system to write to the Duke in 1834: 'I am preparing to take down and sell as fast as I can dispose of them, the windmills formerly used for drainage on this estate ... it is impossible that they can ever be required again for purposes of drainage'.[82] As a result of Wing and those like him, no windpumps survive in the Fens. Once drainage was under control, the work of building farmsteads began. Previous steadings had been concentrated on the 'high ground' immediately around the village, but now new farms were created out in the fen. Expenditure rose through the 1840s and 1850s, reaching a peak in 1861, when £19,326 was spent.[83] By 1880, there were eighty farms of varying size within the parish, many on new sites. John Bailey Denton illustrated two types of building designed by the agent, Robert Mein, and very similar to those erected near Woburn.[84] The larger set of buildings was to serve a farm of 500 acres and included a steam engine to work a threshing machine and other barn machinery, and four yards to house 76 cattle, as well as seven loose boxes (Figure 77). Many farmsteads have disappeared over the years because of the problems of building sound foundations in the Fens. By the 1890s, they were being replaced by timber buildings needing less substantial footings.

Another unreclaimed area still waiting to be developed for intensive agriculture in the 1820s was the 20,000 acres of Exmoor Forest, which was bought from the Crown by John Knight in 1820. He was a Worcestershire landowner whose family had made their money in the iron industry, but members of whom had been prominent agriculturalists.[85] Unlike the Fens, however, Exmoor was unsuited to cereal growing. Although the entire area was over 240 metres (800 feet) above sea level, Knight unwisely planned to break up much of it for arable and graze lowland sheep on the rest, farming it as a single farm. John Knight had hoped to inherit a considerable fortune from another branch of the family who owned the Downton estate in Shropshire, but in 1840 the courts decided against this claim and this limited what could be done on Exmoor. In 1841, he handed over control to his son, Frederick, who decided to lay out tenant farms and place more emphasis on livestock. Between 1844 and 1852 eleven farms were created and buildings put up. As on so many other estates, the farmsteads were designed partly by the landowner and partly by

151

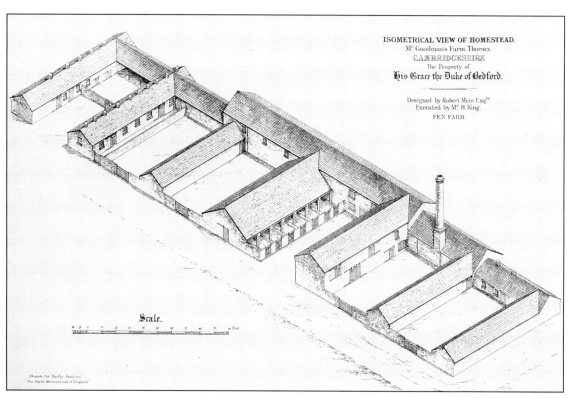

ISOMETRICAL VIEW OF HOMESTEAD.
Mr Goodman's Farm, Thorney.
CAMBRIDGESHIRE
The Property of
His Grace the Duke of Bedford.

Designed by Robert Mein Esqr
Executed by Mr H. King.
FEN FARM.

Scale.

'Drawn for Bayley Denton'
'The Farm Homesteads of England'

152

his agent, in this case Robert Smith. One was illustrated in the *Journal of the Royal Agricultural Society of England* as an example of a steading suited for a 300 acre farm in hill country (Figure 78).[86] They are amongst the simplest of planned farmsteads. Sheltered by belts of beech trees, the two-storey, white-washed double fronted, hipped roofed houses are flanked by grey stone buildings, enclosing a yard (Plate 19). In some cases the house is central whilst in others, such as the plan published by Smith, the house is in one corner.[87] Buildings included a barn, stables, cartsheds, calf and cow houses and pigsties, with a paved roadway leading into the yard and entrances to the four separate divisions. Built of local materials, the buildings are entirely functional and there is little in the way of architectural embellishment. Unlike the other estates so far discussed, the Knights were always short of money. New buildings were often not complete when the first occupants came to take up their tenancies. As we have seen, water power was introduced to many west-country farms in the mid-nineteenth century, and in the example illustrated by Smith a water wheel provided power to the barn. Certainly there was always a shortage of labour on the moor, which was virtually unpopulated when the Knights bought it. The parish of Exmoor, with its church at Simonsbath, was created in 1856. Despite deep ploughing and liming it proved impossible to grow wheat and barley across much of the newly reclaimed land, and tenants were

FIGURE 77.
(*opposite and right*)
The Thorney farmsteads in the Cambridgeshire Fens have more in common with the Bedfordshire examples than the Devon steadings. Some of the larger ones, such as that illustrated by Bailey Denton (1) had steam engines, but no chimneys have survived. Typical detailing at St Vincent's Cross (2) includes the sliding doors (3).

153

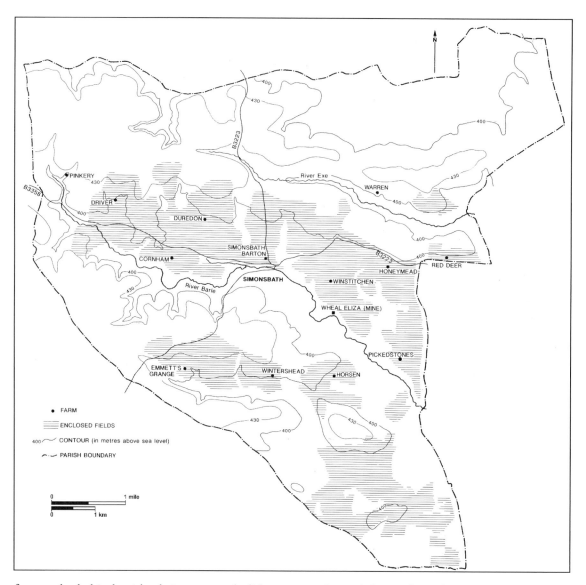

frequently behind with their rent and did not stay long. These planned farmsteads are examples of buildings designed primarily for livestock farms at a time when cereals were still regarded as the backbone of profitable farming. The barns are small and would rarely have housed a crop for sale. By the 1860s very few cereals were grown and a cattle and sheep rearing system based on pasture had been established. After these difficult beginnings, these livestock farms weathered the depression of the 1880s better than many lowland arable ones.[88]

Away from the great farms of the north-east, there was one other part of England where over 20% of farms were over 300 acres in 1851: this was the chalk lands of the south in the counties of Hampshire, Berkshire, Wiltshire and Dorset. The region's proximity to London and the ports of Bristol and

FIGURE 78.
The map shows the
boundaries of the new
parish of Exmoor
(Somerset), created
when the Royal Forest
was sold, and the sites
of the farmsteads built
by John Knight
within their newly
enclosed fields. The
Exmoor farmsteads
were all built on the
same simple courtyard
layout, and the
detailed plan of one
was published in the
*Journal of the Royal
Agricultural Society of
England* in 1856, a
redrawing of which is
reproduced here.

Southampton also made it a popular area for the *nouveaux riches* and during the mid-century prosperous farming years, men with wealth made in industry were still investing in land. Unlike John and Frederick Knight, William Nicholson of the Nicholson Gin Company was never short of money to invest in the Basing Park estate which he purchased in 1863. Again, unlike Exmoor, the area had long been productive farming land but like most of Hampshire the buildings were said to be 'very inadequate in extent, and entirely without plan or convenience'. In neglecting to provide suitable buildings, the landlords had 'failed to perform the most important part of their duties'.[89] By 1909 the estate had grown to cover over 8,000 acres and 38 farms, several of which had been rebuilt in the 1860s in a distinctive estate style. They were designed as simple, functional buildings, using the local flint and brick and based on a conventional E-plan, originally with open yards. Typical of an area renowned for its huge barns, those on Nicholson's farms were not designed for mechanisation, although at the more elaborate home farm there was an engine house as well as an ornate octagonal dairy. The buildings are modest and would have served the farms adequately, as well as acting as examples of practical architecture for a neighbourhood where impermanent timber and thatch were still the main building materials.[90]

The downlands of southern England supported some of the largest farms, often covering over 500 acres, and the wealthiest farmers in England in the mid-nineteenth century. The new farms, laid out in huge rectangular fields as the chalks were enclosed in the early-nineteenth century, were ideally suited to large-scale sheep and corn husbandry with cattle kept on the lush pastures of the valley floors. The farmsteads built for the twelfth Earl of Pembroke and his widowed step-mother, Catherine Woronzow, who were embarking on a grand building programme on their 30,000 acre estate around Wilton in south Wiltshire, unashamedly embraced industrial farming techniques. Many of the farms were rebuilt in the 1850s in a variety of styles, the most remarkable being the Italianate dairy farm at Bremerton with its strange crazy-paving façade. The farms were large enough to justify the most lavish provision of covered yards and ample cattle accommodation. In this area, far from any industrial centres, labour was in abundant supply and steam engines were all later additions. Estate features include Romanesque window detailing and cast-iron Gothic or Romanesque sliding windows.

By contrast, some landowners continued to place a great emphasis on the picturesque with little interest in the model plans published in the literature of the time. The buildings of Joseph Neeld of Grittleton, a parish set in the wood pasture landscape of north Wiltshire, are of an entirely different type to those at Basing. Instead of rejecting the local building styles, the work of Neeld provides an early example of the Vernacular Revival. A merchant from Bath, who had inherited a fortune from his uncle, Neeld bought the Grittleton estate near Chippenham in 1828 and during the following 28 years continued to accumulate surrounding land. By his death in 1856 he owned nearly 16,000 acres, mainly in the four neighbouring parishes. He rebuilt Grittleton Hall and the village of Grittleton, as well as seven large farmhouses and their buildings. The farms were all mixed holdings of between 150 and 200 acres on light soils, the farming landscape requiring little modification to serve this size and type of holding. The farmhouses were large, and sometimes contained elements of earlier buildings. The existence of two-storey cheese rooms behind two of them emphasises the importance of dairy cattle within the economy, although flocks of sheep were also kept. The farm buildings erected are similar on all the farms and date from around 1850. They are traditional in style, of Cotswold stone with stone slate roofs (Figure 79). A stock yard is enclosed on one side by the house with barn, stables, cow byres and shelter sheds around. In some cases these are continuous ranges, but elsewhere they are freestanding structures originally linked by walls. On the larger farms, there is a stack yard with implement sheds, carthouses and granaries on the far side of the barn. The barns mostly have half-hipped roofs, a central porch and lean-to loose boxes either side under a continuous roof pitch. The buildings are well-built and sound, but by 1850 they would have been regarded as old-fashioned. There is no mechanisation, although at a later date horse walks and portable engines were incorporated. The cattle were kept in shelter sheds

FIGURE 79.
The farmstead at West Sevington (Wiltshire), one of those erected by Joseph Neeld on his Grittleton estates, was typically dominated by its barn.

156

around open yards with no provision for the yard divisions and loose boxes required for intensive fattening or manure preservation. They would have been adequate for the system of farming usually associated with the early phases of the agricultural revolution, rather than the intensive systems of high farming. There is no indication that an architect was employed. Their traditional design and materials suggests that they were seen as promoting the image of a timeless, prosperous rural idyll so obvious in the estate village with its church, cottages and school, rather than as the necessary infrastructure for innovative commercial agriculture.

Constraints on new building

The importance of these buildings to improved farming, and indeed the value of splitting responsibility for fixed and working capital which the landlord–tenant system entailed, will be considered in the final chapter of this book. However, it is important, as part of this debate, that the wide distribution of planned farmsteads (mainly, but not only, across the arable areas of England) and the variety of types of buildings which the landlords were providing is appreciated. Whether they ever paid for themselves in increased rents has been frequently questioned.[91]

We have already seen that although this was a period of increased capital investment in agricultural improvement, there were still much to criticise in the 1860s, and one of the reasons put forward for this was the problem of settled estates. Under this arrangement, designed by owners to keep their estates intact down the generations, the owner was legally no more than a tenant for life and so only had control of the estate income and not the capital. This prevented the sale of the settled lands and the use of it as security against loans, which made it difficult for the owner to raise money for improvements. To appease the landed interest, which had opposed the repeal of the Corn Laws in 1846, companies empowered to lend money for agricultural improvement, particularly drainage, were set up by parliamentary act. Attempts were made to overcome the perceived problem of settled estates by allowing landowners to borrow for agricultural improvement on the security of their estates. From 1846, both government and private sources were available and this money was used for drainage, farm buildings and cottages. Information on the exact use of loan money is limited, but figures available for Staffordshire indicate that little of this money found its way into major rebuilding schemes. Instead it was used for modifications or extensions to existing plans.[92]

The large sums needed to build complete farmsteads limited their distribution to the wealthy estates of committed landowners. These sets of buildings, erected typically between 1850 and 1870, reveal the extent to which landlords were prepared to fulfill their side of the farming bargain and invest in the infrastructure of their tenants' farms. They also demonstrate significant changes in farming practice and the degree to which changes advocated in the text books were actually being taken up on the ground. Finally, they reflect the optimism and prosperity of an age which believed that farming progress would last so long as the standards of living of an increasingly urban and growing population continued to rise, and that science was the key to ever-increasing yields.

It follows that the estates most likely to embark on expensive building schemes were those great reserves of landed wealth, such as the Turnors, Bedfords, Leicesters of Holkham, Earls of Pembroke at Wilton, Greenwich Hospital and the Ridleys of Blagdon, or ones with money from elsewhere such as the Neelds and Nicholsons. Those without this strong financial backing, such as the Knights on Exmoor, found it much more difficult to invest heavily with only a very distant prospect of financial returns. It is significant that the smaller estates, which were more likely to be applying for loans from the improvement companies, very rarely submitted schemes for completely new planned farmsteads; rather they were adding to and altering already existing ones.[93]

Home farms

The main reason given for rebuilding tenant farmsteads was to attract the much sought-after men of intelligence and capital who would improve the farms, thus increasing their long-term value. Most home farms continued to be regarded as the suppliers of fresh produce to the house. Their ornate dairies are an indication both of the importance of their role in supplying milk and cream, and the fact that the lady of the house often took an interest, if only a very superficial one, in its activities. A visit to friends and neighbours, however, could well include a tour of the home farm, and certainly it was here that the more enthusiastic owners could demonstrate improved techniques. The need for new buildings on the Home Farm at Windsor in 1852 was supported by the argument that 'Situated as they are in the very centre of the Queen's private walks, they are naturally an object of much interest and ought to be such as her Majesty could herself visit with comfort and might have some satisfaction in showing to her royal and other visitors. They ought besides to be of the most approved construction and should combine all the most useful modern equipment – in short, while executed with a due attention to economy, they should be model buildings for the purpose for which they are required'.[94]

One of the earliest of the home farms to be associated with the new ideas of high farming was that for Henry Howard at Greystoke (Cumbria) (Figure 80). Built between 1833 and 1837 to the designs of John Barker, an otherwise unknown architect, the restrained classical front block has a central pedimented portico and matching smaller pedimented entrances at each end. It is of a conventional layout around a yard. Because it is built into a slope there is a two-storey bank barn along one side and other split-level buildings. In one corner of the yard, beside the barn, is a chute leading down into a vaulted root store which would have been unloaded into the yard below. Hatches for

FIGURE 80.
The Home Farm at Greystoke (Cumbria) was built by Henry Howard between 1833 and 1837. A bank barn along one side (1) opens onto a roadway at first floor level (2).

158

emptying the sawdust from the estate saw mill on one side also open into the yard, originally providing bedding for the livestock sheds. A two-storey building in the corner of the yard was later (probably in the 1880s) opened up so that it could be used as a silo. The grass was loaded in through the outer upper doors, trodden down by horses until it was fully compressed, and then cut out as it was needed through a low-level door opening into the yard. Although the technique of silage making was known on the continent earlier, the first references in Britain are from 1839 and 1843.[95] It did not gain popularity until the disastrous hay harvests of the 1880s, and then enthusiasm was only short-lived. Perhaps it is not surprising that this rare example should be on a home farm, in one of the wettest parts of England and ideally suited to silage making.

In the early years of the Royal Agricultural Society there was much interest in the idea of 'example farms'. Building on the idea first put into practice by Neil Malcolm of Poltolloch, Argyll, who built his Experiment Farm in 1798, these were to be placed in the various agricultural regions of the country and be used both for experimentation and to demonstrate best practice. This idea was taken up by the farmer and author, John Morton, who recognised that many landlords aspired to this role on their home farms, but that on the whole they were more concerned with the improvement of livestock than arable farming. The fact that home farms were 'a losing concern for the proprietor affords the strongest argument to the farmer against the adoption of any of the proposed plans and strengthens his prejudice in favour of his old habits'.[96] The Duke of Bedford was unusual in hoping to make a profit at Woburn's Park Farm, considering that it would set a bad example if he was seen to lose at farming.[97] As agent for Lord Ducie of Tortworth, Gloucestershire, Morton persuaded his employer to allow him to establish an example farm on his estate at Whitfield, near Bristol. The work of improvement began in 1838 and involved drainage and road making. The farm covered 250 acres and the buildings were intended to house nine horses, ten milking cows and 40 young stock, as well as a barn and its machinery. One of the aims was to demonstrate, in addition to the benefits to farmers, the certainty of a return to the landlord from permanent improvements. However, the costs were all much higher than estimated. Although the buildings are by no means ostentatious, the original estimate of £860 rose to a final figure of £2,978. Over 2,000 people, mostly from the locality, visited the farm over its first four years to view demonstrations of improved farming techniques. The possibility of increasing yields was proven, but the cost of permanent improvements could not be expected to produce a return in the short-term, and the figures published by Morton in 1842 were not encouraging.[98] The buildings themselves are of interest because they demonstrate the work of a practical farmer rather than an architect, representing an early example of a steam-powered barn with extensive mixing rooms for animal feed orientated towards feed preparation as advocated by the high farmers (Figure 81).

Because of its nature as a showpiece, outside professional help was far more

likely to be employed to design the home than the tenant farms. For example, as we have seen, the agricultural engineer, George Dean, not only worked in Windsor Great Park, but also on the Home Farm at Holkham, and the Oxford architect William Wilkinson worked at Longleat (see Figure 105). There is also plenty of evidence, as with other examples of Victorian industrial architecture, for collaboration between agents and architects. The Earl of Radnor's home farm at Coleshill, Oxfordshire, was designed by the agent, Edward Wells Moore, in 1852. Moore, an active member of the Royal Agricultural Society and acquainted with some of the most pioneering agriculturalists of the day such as Philip Pusey and Sir John Conroy, had been appointed in 1840 on the recommendation of Earl Spencer. These buildings were very much state of the art, designed to facilitate the flow of raw materials through the buildings from the stack yards to the feeding boxes, with a covered storage pit for manure in the central core (see Figure 104).[99]

Prince Albert was an earnest and enthusiastic supporter of all branches of scientific improvement. His interest in agriculture is reflected in his involvement in building projects within Windsor Great Park and on the Osborne estates on the Isle of Wight. He was the president elect of the Royal Agricultural Society at the time of his death in 1861. The buildings at Windsor were designed by the resident architect, J. R. Turnbull, and the agricultural engineer, George Dean, and were extensively publicised at the time of their constructuion by John Morton, John Bailey Denton and J. B. Spearing.[100] New farmsteads were built at Shaw Farm and at the Dairy Farm at Frogmore, where the existing buildings were described as 'ruinous, unsightly and inconvenient, not only ill-adapted for their purposes, but a positive disgrace to a royal park'.[101] The buildings for which George III had been responsible at Flemish Farm were also replaced.

The new dairy farmstead was completed by 1855. It was illustrated in Morton's book[102] and survives, externally, very much as shown (Figure 82). It was built to house a dairy herd and is of a conventional E-plan design with a wide central block, containing the cow stalls for 60 cows either side of a central gangway with a central raised ventilator along the roof. On either side are the sheds and yards for young stock, with pigsties and loose boxes in the outer ranges. The hay barn and more yards make up the connecting range. The buildings are ornate but practical, with a clock tower in front of the hay house. An innovative feature is the manure house, for both solid and liquid manure, which stands to one side of the buildings and is fed by drains from the yards and stable.

Both Norfolk Farm and Flemish Farm had been taken in hand in 1841, and in 1858 Prince Albert agreed to pay for the rebuilding of Flemish Farm to

FIGURE 82.
The ornate appearance of the Dairy Farm hides a practical dairy farmstead in which cows were stalled down two sides of a wide central building with a central feeding passage and mucking-out passages behind.

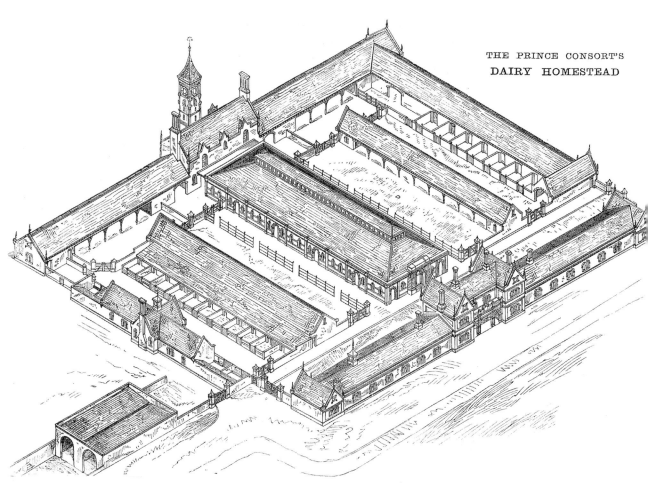

THE PRINCE CONSORT'S
DAIRY HOMESTEAD

ISOMETRICAL PERSPECTIVE OF THE PRINCE CONSORT'S DAIRY HOMESTEAD

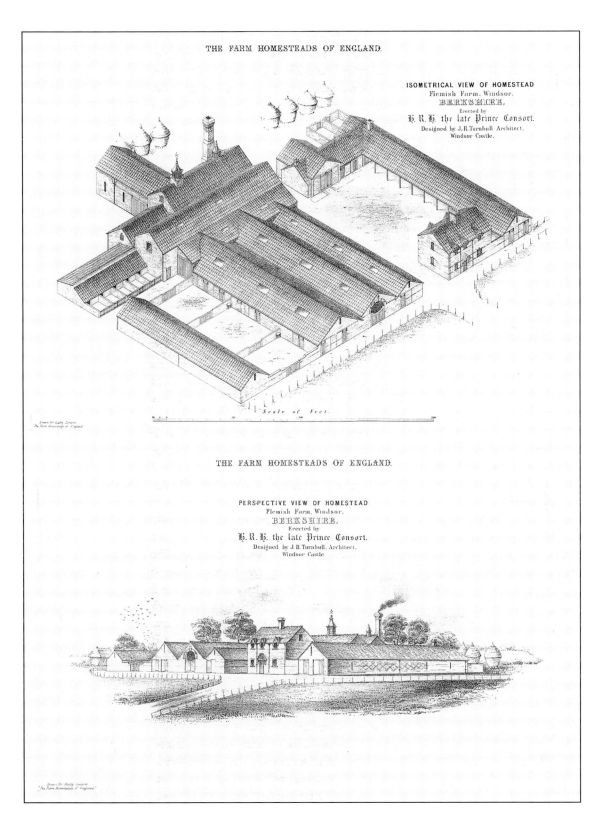

ISOMETRICAL VIEW OF HOMESTEAD
Flemish Farm, Windsor,
BERKSHIRE,
Erected by
H. R. H. the late Prince Consort.
Designed by J. R. Turnbull Architect,
Windsor Castle.

Scale of Feet.

THE FARM HOMESTEADS OF ENGLAND.

PERSPECTIVE VIEW OF HOMESTEAD
Flemish Farm, Windsor,
BERKSHIRE,
Erected by
H. R. H. the late Prince Consort.
Designed by J. R. Turnbull, Architect,
Windsor Castle.

163

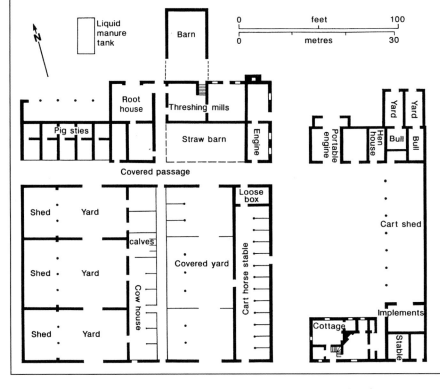

Liquid
manure
tank

Barn

0   feet   100

0   metres   30

Root
house

Threshing mills

Yard

Yard

Pig sties

Straw barn

Engine

Portable engine

Hen house

Bull

Bull

Covered passage

Loose
box

Shed   Yard

Cart shed

calves

Shed   Yard

Covered yard

Cow house

Cart horse stable

Shed   Yard

Implements

Cottage

Stable

FIGURE 83 (*previous
page and left*).
Flemish Farm at
Windsor represents a
conventional mid-
century plan. The
chaff and litter cutters
were placed over the
chaff room and straw
barn so that the cut
materials fell through
ready for use in the
covered yards and
stables. This drawing
appeared in
J. B. Denton's book of
1863.

designs submitted by Turnbull and widely published in the farming press
thereafter. It served a farm of 390 acres, providing stabling for 12 horses and
housing for 40 fatting and 60 store beasts. They represent a typical set of
mid-century buildings, with covered yards separated by a covered passage from
the straw barn, a steam-powered threshing barn and feed preparation room
(Figure 83). The Prince Consort was said to have 'highly approved of this
homestead and recommended the plan to his friends abroad'. Whether any
similar farmsteads were built on the continent is not clear, but the Reverend
Canon Jefferson is said to have followed the design at Thicket Priory (Yorkshire).[103]

By far the most extensive and ornate farmstead at Windsor was that designed
by George Dean at Shaw Farm (Figure 84).[104] Prince Albert took on the
tenancy of Shaw Farm in 1851 and agreed to pay half the cost of the new
buildings as the existing ones were 'by no means adapted for a model farm
in the immediate vicinity of Windsor Castle and which is to be cultivated on
the most improved system of modern husbandry.'[105] Its increased cost, the
result of additions to the original plans, became the subject of much disagree-
ment between the Prince Consort and the Commissioners for the Crown
Estate. As a result of the Prince's intervention, a stationary steam engine
replaced the portable one and an extra floor for additional machinery was
inserted in the barn. A clock tower and bell were added, as well as an extra
implement shed and one more shed in each cattle yard. Dean justified these

FIGURE 84.
The most elaborate
and extensive of the
Prince Consort's
farmsteads at Windsor
was Shaw Farm,
which typically for
Dean contained no
covered yards. This
illustration appeared
in Dean's book of
1867.

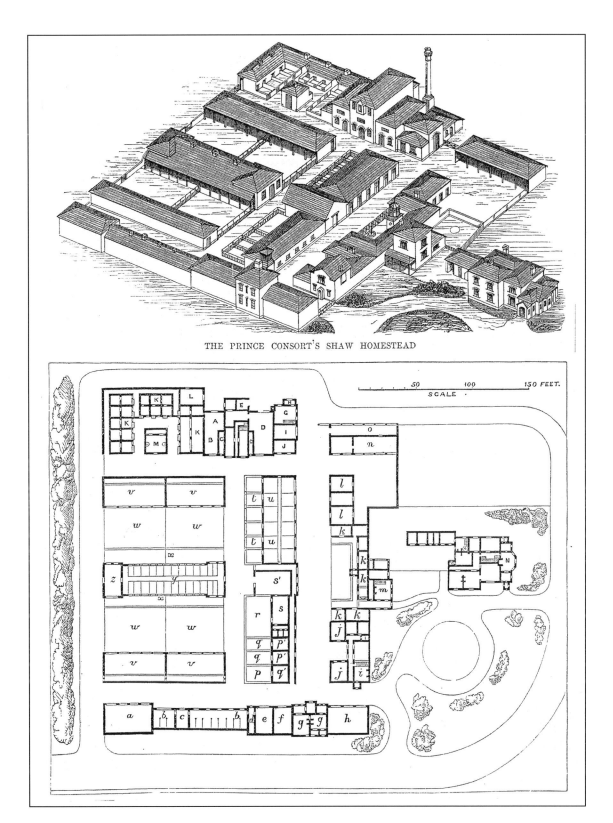

THE PRINCE CONSORT'S SHAW HOMESTEAD

changes, which cost over £3,000, by writing 'I have always viewed these works in the light of a national undertaking. No greater benefit in my opinion could be conferred upon agriculturalists or the agricultural labourer than the erection of such buildings as many Noblemen and landed proprietors of this and other countries will doubtless inspect them when built and go and do likewise.'[106] The result was a huge complex of extensive ranges around four open yards, with two rows of loose boxes opening off a central passage down the centre. Across a roadway was the barn, with steam engine and feed preparation rooms. The plan that appears in Morton's book is less ornate than the final version in Dean's. The Italianate clock towers and façades were no doubt thought necessary for a building so near Windsor Castle. As a model, it was really far too extensive for all but the most ambitious to follow, but it certainly identified Prince Albert with the agricultural cause. He was made a president of the Royal Agricultural Society in the last year of his life and no doubt, if he had lived, he would have been an active one.

A very different model for consideration on a national scale was Mechi Farm, Blennerhassett (Cumbria), built by William Lawson between 1863 and 1865 as a co-operative (Figure 85). The co-operative philosophy has its origins with Robert Owen and his publication in 1814 of *A New View of Society*. He envisaged the creation of communities who would live together and work on the land and his ideas were taken up by others who saw them as the answer to the social ills of an industrialising Scotland. However, the Orbiston community, set up with great publicity in 1824, was a failure and his ideas were only briefly revived by the Chartists in the late 1840s. A new type of co-operation received a further airing in the *Journal of the Royal Agricultural Society of England* in 1863 where Mr Gurdon, owner of estates in Assington (Suffolk), described the running of two co-operative farms, the first one created in 1830 and the second in 1852.[107] His aim had been to improve the lot of the farm labourer (and so reduce rural crime such as poaching), by letting a 100-acre farm to a group of 20 labourers. A second farm of 150 acres was let to 30 more labourers twelve years later. The farms were managed by all the tenants, some of whom worked on the farm, while the rest continued to work on other farms in the neighbourhood. The profits were shared amongst all the tenants and the benefits – besides a general reduction in marauding and poaching – were said to be great. 'Fifty families were not only taken off the rates, but interested in keeping them low as being themselves rate payers'. However, there is no evidence that any new buildings were constructed, and those remaining are very typical of a south Suffolk farm.

It cannot be a coincidence that this article appeared just at the time that William Lawson was setting up his farm. Lawson, a small Cumbrian land-owner, inherited the farm in 1862 with the idea of improving and running it partly on an experimental basis. He began by steam ploughing and draining and then putting in new fences and roads. Mechi Farm differed from the Assington experiment in that Lawson was very much in control. The profits were to be divided between the 'public good' fund and a tenth between the

FIGURE 85.
Blennerhassett. There are two groups of buildings at Mechi Farm (Cumbria) as well as the house with its laboratory wing behind. The sheep house (1), with pens opening onto a yard, contained a slaughter house at one end and an office/store at the other.

The huge double hay barn (2) stands close to the covered yards, which were built between the engine house on the far side and stables on the near side.

167

workers. Farm decisions were to be made by all, in a 'parliament', firstly held for half an hour every day after lunch, and later from three until six on Saturday afternoons. He was much influenced by John Mechi and named his farm after him. Mechi, the son of an Italian immigrant, was an example of a businessman who had made a fortune which he used to indulge his enthusiasm for improved agriculture. He bought 130 acres of poor land at Tiptree in Essex which he intended to make productive. No expense was spared, as his critics were quick to point out. He piped liquid manure to all parts of the farm with the aid of a steam pump. It required three men to operate, but allowed a hundred tons of manure per acre to be spread annually.[108] A similar scheme was installed at Blennerhasset with three-quarters of a mile of irrigation pipe, and pumps allowing the liquid manure to 'rain down fertility'. As well as farming, Lawson employed a chemist to make fertilisers and analyse them. In later years he ran a market garden, manure works, flax and starch mill, all close to the farmstead. All this is described in detail in his book, published in 1874.[109]

The farmhouse was the first building to be erected, with its back wing containing a laboratory upstairs, followed by the U-plan barn and byres enclosing covered yards. Alongside the barn was a pulping room for preparing animal feed. The grooves for tramlines can still be seen in the floor of the barn, showing where feed trucks from the pulping room turned into the covered yards in which the animals were tied in two rows. The floors were to be slatted, in order 'to facilitate the washing of their droppings into a channel under the boards ... and pipe, draining all into the liquid manure tank'. This was an innovation that had already been developed in the early 1850s at Earl Radnor's farmstead at Coleshill (Oxfordshire) (see Figure 104) and the Duke of Bedford's Kilworthy Farm (Plate 18). Above the threshing machine was the water tower and beside it the pump house for pumping up the manure from the underground manure tanks, a technique we have seen was introduced on the Strutt farms in Derbyshire in the 1840s. One side of the U-shape contained an engine house and cart lodges with a granary above, and the other cattle stalls and stables. 'For safety and dignity' the whole range was lit by gas.[110] Behind were two enormous, open-sided hay barns.

The second building to be erected was a sheep and implement shed. Fronting onto the yard was a row of five arched openings with implement sheds, coach house, butchery and granary above. Behind was the sheep shed, entered through ten small doors. An impressive clock tower rose above this range to dominate the neighbouring fields. The whole is solidly built of local pink sandstone (Figure 85). The steading was typical of the more extravagant buildings of the high farming era but is extremely unusual in Cumbria, a region of small, owner-occupied farms. The farm was not a financial success, partly because of the enormous outlay involved and partly because of the temperament of Lawson, who frequently changed his mind and left projects unfinished.

New farming techniques were thus reflected in farm buildings more than at any previous time, as new farming technology came to be represented in the application of factory planning to farmstead design. They mark the high point of confidence in British agriculture before the onset of farming depression from the late 1870s.

CHAPTER SIX

Retrenchment,
1875–1939

The final years of model farmstead design, *c.* 1870–1900

The end of agricultural prosperity, signalled by the collapse of rents in arable areas, heralded the decline of interest in model farmsteads on all but the most affluent estates. A few new farmsteads which incorporated the most developed of the high farming ideas were built during the 1880s, as on the Dysart estates in Lincolnshire, but it was mainly in the dairying districts that profits were maintained. Innovation was likely to be concentrated in a search for cheap building materials, such as concrete and corrugated iron. An increased emphasis on stock promoted the construction of many more covered yards, and feed preparation and loose boxes were increasingly important. As agricultural labour became more expensive nationwide, interest in labour-saving devices such as tramlines to move feed around became more common. Only on the estates of the most wealthy, such as the Duke of Westminster, were architects employed and extravagant, highly decorative styles adopted. Elsewhere it was clear that the days when the landed estate dominated the countryside were nearly over, and with it the landlord-built planned and model farmsteads.

As imports of American grain began to flood the British market from the early 1870s, confidence in cereal farming collapsed and the optimism of the high farming philosophy was undermined. The almost unending rain and cold of the summer of 1879 brought the worst harvest of the nineteenth century. In the past a poor harvest would have meant higher grain prices, but in 1879 and 1880 both wheat and barley values were substantially lower than in the preceding two years. The belief that an ever-increasing urban population was a captive market for British goods was shown to be flawed. The opening up of the virgin soils of the Canadian and American prairies, by the westward advance of the railways across the continent, allowed a flow of cheap foreign grain to enter Britain. As a result, the price of wheat dropped by 50% between 1871 and 1875 and continued to fall until the end of the century, being two-thirds lower by 1900. It was not only cereals that suffered. The invention of refrigeration and iron steam ships allowed beef and mutton to be imported, principally from Argentina, New Zealand and Australia.

Very few commentators had foreseen the disaster. The Duke of Bedford wrote in 1880: 'Agriculturalists and the nation at large were alike insensible to the real character of the depression ... it is easy to be wise after the event, but it is strange that a catastrophe which was no longer merely impending but had actually taken place should have been regarded by those best able to judge as a passing cloud'.[1] Clare Sewell Read, an agricultural writer, tenant farmer and Norfolk MP from 1865, had always pointed out that 'high farming' could only be profitable so long as prices were also high. He visited America in 1879, as part of a parliamentary enquiry team, and realised that the British farmer would not be able to compete as this vast land was further opened up and its produce exported by rail and ship to Europe.[2] The costly, high-input systems operated by the 'high farmers' would be obsolete and diversification was required. As the search for alternatives grew much advice was available, mostly based on the theme: 'It no longer pays to plough, it pays to graze'.[3] The number of articles in the *Journal of the Royal Agricultural Society of England* on laying down arable to pasture increased in the 1880s. Between 1875 and 1900 the acreage of permanent grass went up 25%. The shift to grass was greatest in traditional pastoral areas, especially where improvements in transport meant that feed grain could be brought in and livestock products, particularly dairy, could be taken out. In Northumberland, for example, the area of arable cropping dropped by 40% between 1870 and 1890 with most of the Wallington estate being put down to grass. Permanent pasture's share of the total acreage in Essex rose by 67% between 1875 and 1900 as the county became the major milk producer for the London market.[4]

One of the few estates to appreciate what was happening was the Leveson Gower estates in Staffordshire and Shropshire. The agent wrote to his employer in 1879 that the lack of profit in growing grain on heavy land 'has long been recognised here and a great deal has been done in the direction of this change'.[5] The chief enterprise had long been cattle fattening, which stood up well to the depression. In order to make farms more efficient, tenants were offered open-sided corrugated ('Dutch') barns, covered yards and the installation of a small railway along which small fodder crops could be pushed.[6]

Rents followed the collapse of prices, often by as much as a third to a half in arable areas, with the consequence that there was limited money available for investment. The implementation of the improvements necessary for high farming had involved landowners in unprecedented expenditure. Costs of land drainage and building were estimated at £5 per acre in the 1850s, as distinct from £1–£2 an acre in the age of parliamentary enclosure. While some great magnates could finance this type of expenditure from their own resources, others had taken out loans and the Land Drainage Companies had encouraged borrowing on an unprecedented scale. As a result, landowners as a class were heavily in debt and with a decline in rents this debt was difficult to service.[7] The owning of a country estate could no longer provide an adequate income for its owner, but instead was an expensive luxury, still valued for the social prestige which it brought but not as a viable investment. The old landed families with little income from outside agriculture could not afford elaborate building programmes. Here work was limited to essential repairs and additions to tenant farms, such as livestock accommodation and implement sheds, in a desperate effort to keep farms tenanted.[8]

However, it is easy to exaggerate the level of decline, and the number of recorded new planned and model farmsteads only dropped substantially after 1900 (see Figure 3). An analysis of the figures provided to the Royal Commission on Agriculture between 1894 and 1897 shows that landlords in livestock areas were generally more willing to spend money on their estates than those in arable regions, the result being that rents retained their value there.[9] Many of the largest landowners obtained their income from a variety of sources,

such as London property and mineral wealth. Others had diversified during the good years and bought into the stock market. The landowning class had always been remarkably fluid, with new entrants from other walks of life and this continued to be the case after 1875 as sales to industrialists, who were quickly assimilated into the aristocracy, continued. For example, Lord Armstrong, the engineer and munitions manufacturer from Newcastle, bought Cragside (Northumberland), and the Cunliffe-Listers, mill-owners from Bradford and later Earls of Swinton, bought the Swinton Castle estates (Yorkshire). The Luton Hoo estate (Bedfordshire) was purchased by Sir Julius Wernher whose fortune had been made in South African diamonds. All these landowners ran their new acquisitions on traditional lines, carrying out improvements in 'the time honoured manner',[10] valuing the prestige that interest in country and farming matters could bring. They spent on farm buildings, often extravagantly.

Inevitably, new economic circumstances found their expression in new building types (Figure 86). While farm incomes were declining, those of the urban workforce continued to rise and with them the demand for meat and dairy produce. The main growth area was therefore in dairying, particularly the production of liquid milk, and this as we shall see was reflected in the buildings. The number of dairy cows steadily increased throughout the last quarter of the nineteenth century and by 1930 the British farmer gained more of his income from milk than all his arable crops put together.[11] Store cattle also increased, with numbers up by 15% in the last thirty years of the century. These were sold during their second year, younger than previously, thus allowing for a quicker financial return. They, too, would need winter housing to increase the speed of fattening.[12] All over the country arable land was either being put back into permanent grass or sown grass left for an extra year. The rich dairy farms of Cheshire suffered less during the depression than those elsewhere, with rents on average within the county dropping only by 10–12%.[13] On the Earl of Derby's Lancashire estates they actually rose by 18% between 1870 and 1896.[14] Marketing relied on fast railway links to the towns and cities, especially London, and some dairy farms were benefiting directly from the new industries. In 1882, for example, the main source of income for Mr Ratcliff of The Priory, Beech Hill, near Reading, was his milk sales directly to Huntley and Palmer's biscuit factory in Reading. The cows were kept in 'an admirably arranged, well ventilated and roomy house, having a central pathway from which the animals are fed.'[15] Industrialisation was also coming to the dairy itself, with cheese factories being set up in Somerset and on the Cheshire estates of the Duke of Westminster.

The advice of the experts

Declining agricultural fortunes could mean that tenants were difficult to find, even at reduced rents. A major incentive in keeping farms occupied was the provision of labour-saving buildings suited to the types of farming remaining

173

profitable, such as dairying. In 1879, for the second time in its history, the
Royal Agricultural Society ran a farm building competition and the results
were published in its *Journal.* The comments of the judges and the emphasis
of the designs were very different from those thirty years previously. Cost had
become the paramount factor. Indeed the design that the judges 'considered
exhibited the greatest merit in arrangement and detail' was not eligible for
the prize because it was too expensive. At £6,146 (not including the dwelling
house or roadways) it amounted to £18 per acre or an increase in rent of 24s
1d per acre to repay the debt at an interest of 4.5% in 25 years. This was not
considered to be economic at a time of falling rents, and so the design was
only commended. One of the reasons for the exceptionally high cost was that
most of these steadings provided for the covering of both stock and manure
– 'a principle that has gained ground considerably since the Society offered
prizes for plans of farm buildings thirty years ago.' Other than this it was the
saving of labour in the mixing and preparation of food, the conveying of it
to stock and the removal of manure, that were judged to be most important.[16]
Most of the plans included covered yards, but where they did not provision
was made for the covering of them at a later date. The barn had become little
more than a feed store and mixing room, still powered by steam engines.
Several of the plans included tramways for carrying feed, manure and stacks.
However, even though they were built on several farms, the judges were not
sure that this was an extra expense that could be justified.

'Experimentia' was a design submitted by Mr J. E. Watson of Newcastle
and consisted of an entirely roofed complex: 'consequently the servants
attending the stock at night and in stormy weather can do so with every
comfort; the dung is also protected from the weather' (Figure 87). The cost
was estimated at just over £3,000.[17] Although few examples of this type of
building survive, one in the parish of Kilham in Northumberland, built for
the Earl of Tankerville of Chillingham Castle, is very similar to the Watson
design. Here the barn along the north side of the complex is powered by a
water wheel, while in 'Experimentia' it was a steam engine. The Kilham
buildings were built to serve a holding of over 800 acres, nearly 200 of which
were pasture. Good corn crops were grown and excellent sheep produced, but
the extensive covered yards show that cattle too were important. This model
design replaced an extensive, but unplanned group some time between 1860
and 1898. The rent in 1910 was high at £750, but how much this was influenced
by the quality of the buildings is impossible to say.[18]

Farm text books continued to contain information on farm buildings.
Perhaps the most informative is Professor John Scott's *Text Book of Farm
Engineering*, published in 1885, the fourth part of which covered farm buildings.
Like the judges of the farm prize competition, he felt that the time had come
to re-write John Morton's classic *Cyclopaedia of Agriculture* (1855) because of
the changes of the previous thirty years. Again, echoing the judges, he stressed
the need to economise 'in the present conditions of British agriculture'. There
was, therefore, a need for a better arrangement of buildings rather than more

of them, and for cheaper materials such as corrugated iron. On the Leveson Gower estates in Shropshire tenants were provided with Dutch barns with iron frames and corrugated iron roofs, which considerably reduced the annual expense of thatching stacks – an important saving in terms of labour costs.[19] Roofing felt, rubber roofing and 'Willesden roofing paper' were also recommended.[20] Scott describes a corrugated iron and concrete dairy homestead for 48 cows and another built entirely of iron by Mr Humphries of Albert Gate Works (Figure 88). It was for a farm of 400 acres and could accommodate

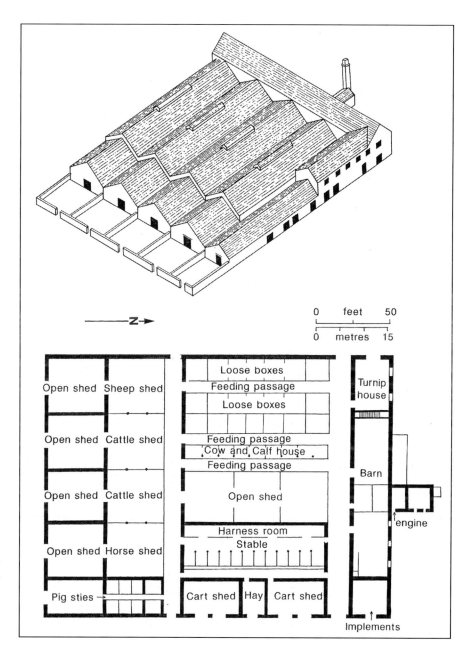

FIGURE 87.
'Experimentia' illustrates the ultimate in covered yard design with all the functions of the farmstead combined under one roof.

175

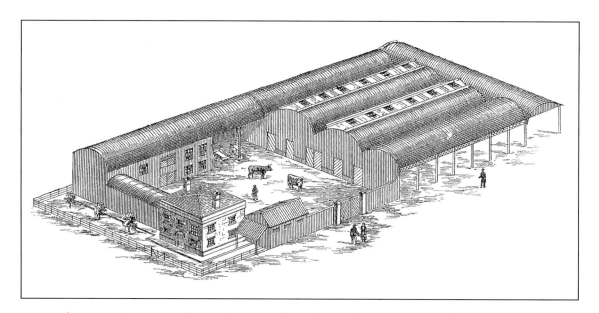

100 cattle, some in open and some in covered yards, 12 calves, 30 pigs and nine working horses. 'The various classes of animals are brought as near as possible to their food, and the arrangements for their health and profitable progress will be found all that can be desired'.[21] As with so many of the new designs, the needs of a dairy herd were paramount. They were to be housed in the lower portion of the building, nearest the calves. Access to the cattle stalls did not involve disturbing cattle in the yards and the straw, roots and hay were all placed close to the mixing floor and the motive power for chaffing, pulping and grinding. The stable had direct communication to the straw and chaff house, with the cart and implement sheds nearby. All these points were well-established principles by the 1850s, but new requirements resulted from improved farm machinery, more sophisticated preparation of feed for stock and more stock. The gradual move towards covered yards was accompanied by increased demand for fodder storage which included buildings for hay and grain and silos for the green crop.

Enthusiasm for silage was short-lived. It was known as a technique by 1840 (see p. 160), but the real period of interest began with the wet years of the early 1880s when hay crops could not be harvested. As emphasis on dairy farming increased, a new winter feed which did not rely on good weather at haymaking time seemed attractive. In 1884, the Royal Agricultural Society published the findings of its investigation into silage.[22] It found that a few English farmers had been making silage for several years. Lord Cathcart had had a silo on his farm near Thirsk since 1875. However, it was the publication of a book on the subject by the French agriculturalist Auguste Goffart, in 1877, which really brought the technique to the attention of British farmers. In order to conduct its investigation, the Royal Agricultural Society sent out questionnaires. Replies were received from about forty British farmers who were already caught up with the enthusiasm for the new practice and were

FIGURE 88.
In 1885 Professor John Scott published designs for a complete corrugated iron farmstead, made by the Albert Gate Works.

176

prepared to give descriptions of their silos and the methods they used. Some were placed partly below ground or built into slopes, others were constructed within redundant barns which were partitioned off into cement-lined sections. Generally the grass was tipped in, trodden down by horses and then topped by a layer of weighted boards. Some of the silos were on small 'hobby' farms or the home farms of great landowners, such as the Duke of Hamilton at Easton Park (Suffolk), Lord Walsingham at Merton (Norfolk), Lord Egerton at Tatton Park (Cheshire), Earl Fortesque at South Molton (Devon) and Lord Londsborough, at Market Weighton (East Yorkshire). Many of these constructions were relatively inexpensive, but a tower built by Mr Johnston near Darlington to house eighty tons of silage cost £150.[23] An example built of concrete, in 1882, still stands at the home farm of the Ashburton estate near Arlesford (Hampshire). It is built into the slope, with access at a higher level for loading, and unloading doors on the lower side.[24] The pastoral areas such as Herefordshire[25] also saw some silos being built in the 1880s, but problems in keeping silos air-tight meant that most were abandoned and little progress was made until after the First World War.

A final type of building, illustrated by Sheldon in 1879 and again by Scott in 1885, was the 'American Barn' where the barns, feed stores and buildings for stock are all under one roof, but on different floors.[26] The example illustrated by Sheldon was octagonal, several surviving ones in New England being round 'to enclose a maximum area with minimum walling' (Figure 89). The hay loft and grain bins are at the top and the hay is fed down to the cattle and horses below. Underneath, again, is the manure store and the root cellar where the roots are chopped by machine and lifted up to the animals above. In some designs there were pigsties at this level as well and a silo up

FIGURE 89.
Scott also illustrated a three-storied 'American Barn' where the emphasis was on the vertical movement of feed from the hay loft above and root bins below to the animals in the middle.

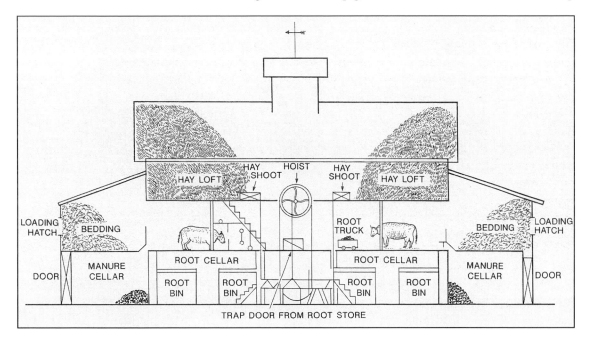

through the middle of the building. Scott thought the design had much to recommend it. It provided the ultimate combination of covered yard and mixing house, with vernacular predecessors in the bank barns of north and central Europe. One cowhouse similar to Scott's design was built at Cae'r lan, Abercraf, Breconshire, but it does not survive.[27] The idea does not seem to have been taken up in England.

The farmsteads on the ground

The last quarter of the nineteenth century also witnessed an increased number of many new families, often with wealth derived from commerce and industry, joining the landowning class. It was the smaller landowners (those with under 5,000 acres) who suffered most, as they were the people least likely to have incomes from outside agriculture.[28] The large estates of long-established landowning families often had non-agricultural interests which allowed them to continue investing in improvements, not only on home farmsteads but also on tenanted holdings in an effort to keep them tenanted. In many cases money was no object and the textbook advice on the need for economy went unheeded.

Cheshire is the county for which the most model farmsteads have been recorded. References to 45 sites have been found, and the sites of 33 located. There are several reasons for this large number. First, the county contained good agricultural land and a mild, wet climate particularly suited to rich pastures where rents were amongst the highest in England. Another factor was the county's proximity and good rail links to large urban centres such as Manchester and Liverpool. Moreover, the wealth of many of the county's major landowners was gained from outside agriculture, from commercial and industrial interests in Manchester and Liverpool or, as was the case with the Duke of Westminster, property in London. Over half the county was in estates of over 3,000 acres in 1873 and there had been an active land market during the early-nineteenth century, allowing new wealth into the area.[29] Cheshire had long been known as a dairying county with specialisation on the Cheshire Plain dating back at least to the years immediately after the Black Death. By the late-sixteenth century factors provided the London market with cheese[30] and its proximity to urban markets meant that, as transport improved, the region was able to take full advantage of the growing liquid milk market. The region did not suffer from the post-1870 depression, but instead prosperity increased. Typical of the county, therefore, are late-nineteenth-century L and U-plan cow houses, sometimes with open-sided hay and manure houses nearby. Unlike planned and model farmsteads elsewhere, they frequently do not include a barn for the processing and storage of corn (Figure 90).

Because of the increased wealth of the area in the later nineteenth century, farm buildings dating from before 1850 are rare, but a survey of the Tollemache estates in Bunbury made in 1795 shows what the estate buildings were like before improvement.[31] The Tollemache estate was greatly expanded between

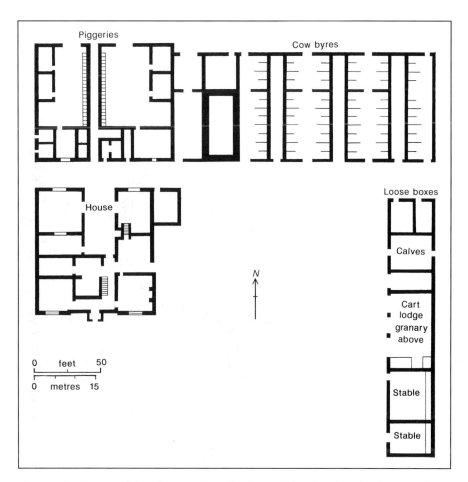

FIGURE 90.
By the end of the
century there had
been much rebuilding
on the Tollemache
estate, with L-plan
buildings such as
those illustrated in
Sheldon's book on
British dairying
published in 1908
becoming the norm.
Six rows of cows of
twelve cows each face
three feeding passages,
and there are milking
and mucking out
passages behind.

1820 and 1840 resulting in a rationalisation of the farming landscape: about
fifty new holdings were created in the Peckforton area alone, mostly requiring
new buildings.[32] An illustration in Sheldon's book shows one of these new
farmsteads,[33] and there are many similar examples in the region today. The
older buildings were timber-framed and thatched, whilst the newer ones were
brick and slated. The older buildings were mostly multi-purpose, again a
design which continued into the later buildings. The description of the farm
buildings at Singleton's 76-acre farm at Tiverton is typical: 'a thrashing floor
and two corn bays of timber boarding covered with thatch, a drifthouse
(covered way) joins the roof of this to two cowhouses for twelve cows, a
fodder bing, a stable for four horses of bricks covered with thatch, to which
is added a shed or tying for six cows, a cart house with a granary or cheese
room over, of brick, thatched'. The tradition of substantial two or three-store-
yed combination barns goes back to the eighteenth century in north-west
England.[34] In many ways, therefore, the buildings of the late-nineteenth century
were simply following established precedents (Figure 91).

The dairy farms of Cheshire were featured in an article in the *Journal of
the Royal Society of England* in 1893.[35] The plans show the cows housed down

West view of the Buildings on Ferny Ley Tenem.[t]

the length of the building in two rows of up to ten stalls each, back-to-back, with feeding passages in front and a mucking out passage behind. Above was a substantial hay house. It was this arrangement, on different scales, that was to be found across all the dairy lands of Cheshire. Cows in the north-west of the country were kept indoors for at least half the year, and this in turn involved the provision of enough hay to keep them fed for that length of time.[36] Unusually, none of the cowhouses featured contain provision for any form of motive power to work machinery. The only differences between individual farmsteads were in the degree of decoration and architectural detail. Indeed, there is hardly a Cheshire dairy farm that is not planned, and many were rebuilt as single units in the late-nineteenth century. Extensive cowhouses with large open-sided hay barns, such as the fine one illustrated by John Bailey Denton at Tattenhall,[37] were typical of the region.

From this general picture, those designed by John Douglas for the Duke of Westminster stand out for their particularly high architectural standard. The block plans of some of his farmsteads, built in Cheshire for the Duke of Westminster in the last thirty years of the nineteenth century, show a great variety of layout, mostly based, however loosely, upon the established U or L-plan (Figure 92). Even though rents were declining on the Duke of Westminster's farms in the 1880s his income from mines and London property allowed him to rebuild Eaton Hall with its stables, stud farm, gas works and private railway. Over the thirty-year period from 1869 the first Duke also rebuilt four churches, eight parsonages, 15 schools and 300 cottages, as well

FIGURE 91.
These farm buildings at Ferny Lea, Tiverton (Cheshire), were drawn for a Tollemache estate survey of 1790. It can be seen that the general principle of building haylofts over cow byres did not change over the next hundred years.

FIGURE 92.
Block plans of some of the farmsteads built by John Douglas for the Duke of Westminster's Cheshire estates. Douglas's designs were mostly based on an L-plan but show a refreshing variety, breaking away from the classical symmetry of his predecessors.

180

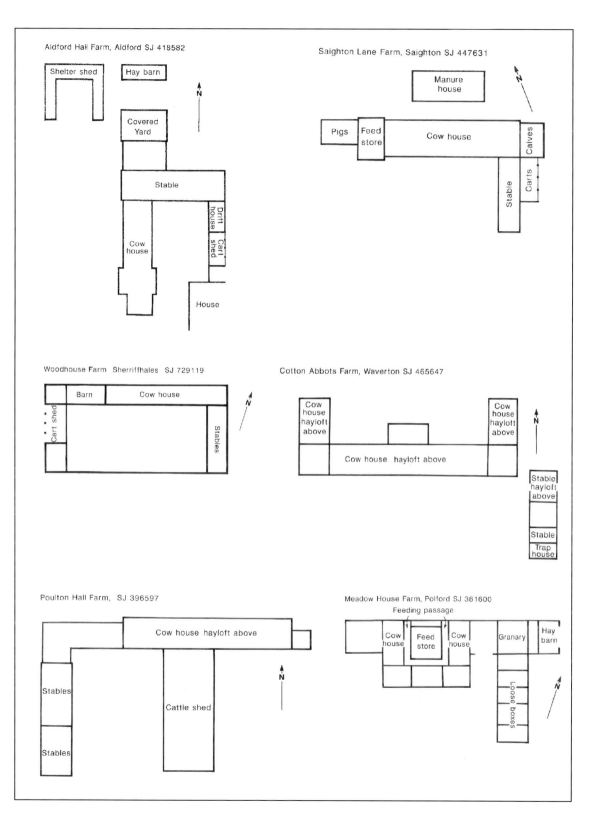

Aldford Hall Farm, Aldford SJ 418582

Shelter shed

Hay barn

N

Covered Yard

Stable

Drift house

Cart shed

Cow house

House

Saighton Lane Farm, Saighton SJ 447631

N

Manure house

Pigs

Feed store

Cow house

Calves

Stable

Carts

Woodhouse Farm Sherriffhales SJ 729119

N

Cart shed

Barn

Cow house

Stables

Cotton Abbots Farm, Waverton SJ 465647

N

Cow house hayloft above

Cow house hayloft above

Cow house hayloft above

Stable hayloft above

Stable

Trap house

Poulton Hall Farm, SJ 396597

N

Cow house hayloft above

Stables

Stables

Cattle shed

Meadow House Farm, Polford SJ 361600

Feeding passage

N

Cow house

Feed store

Cow house

Granary

Hay barn

Loose boxes

as about 50 farmsteads.[38] The designs varied greatly, but they were very much part of the domestic revival in architectural style. They exhibited a great decorative use of half-timbering, conveying a sense of confidence and continuity when in fact the fortunes of farming indicated no such thing.[39] The majority of the floor space was devoted to cowhouses, with stables in a separate wing or building. Hay was mostly housed at first floor level, sometimes with a freestanding hay or manure house nearby. Within the strictly functional limits imposed by their use as farm buildings, Douglas was able to create a refreshingly varied range of elevations and styles, providing an architectural foil to his equally impressive farmhouses. The drift-house, or covered entrance way, was characteristic of these farms and particularly suited to decorative treatment.

One of Douglas's earliest farms was Cheaveley Hall, built between 1875 and 1878. Its prominent position, on the edge of Eaton Park, ensured that proper consideration was taken of its architectural detail. It is a carefully massed composition with a variety of roof levels, surmounted by a low tower with pigeon holes, under a steep conical roof (Plate 20). The many gables are either half-timbered or contain ornamental brickwork, and the drifthouse too is

FIGURE 93.
Plan of Cheaveley Hall, Huntingdon (1), where forty cows were stalled around three sides of the turnip house (2). Cheaveley Hall (Plate 20 also) was visible from the Duke of Westminster's house at Eaton Park.

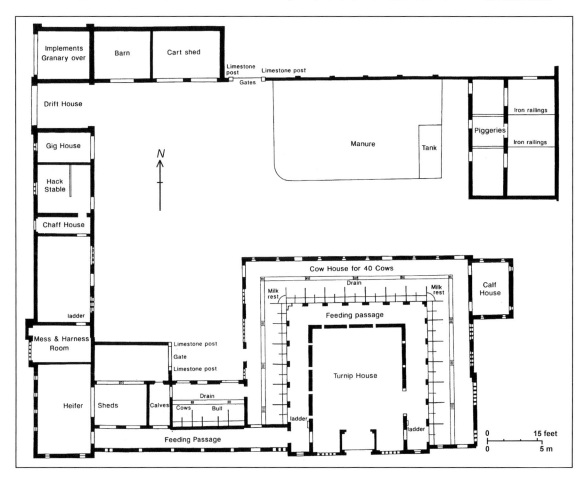

treated decoratively. However, under all these embellishments is a well-planned farmstead with some innovative details (Figure 93). Instead of being housed in parallel rows down the length of a rectangular cowhouse, with feeding passages and feed stores between the rows, the cattle were housed around three sides of an enclosed square. In the centre was a turnip house entered through a double door in the fourth side. A feeding passage runs round the outside of the central turnip house and a double door from the store opens into the passage. The stalls were divided from the feeding passage by a Gothic arcade through which the mangers could be filled. A drain ran around behind the cows and doors opened into this outer passage for mucking out and milking. In the angles of the U were small shelves for resting milking buckets. Across the yard was a walled manure store with an underground tank for liquid manure which could be pumped out to the fields. This highly practical arrangement, which provided stalls for forty cows, was only adopted elsewhere on the estate at Meadow House Farm in Pulford. More typical of the well-built, impressive yet practical buildings of the Westminster estate are those at Saighton Lane, built in 1888 (Figure 94). Here sixty cows were housed in a long building in six rows of ten, divided by three feeding and three milking and mucking out passages. Many other farmsteads demonstrate the variety and quality of Douglas's work (Figures 95 and Plate 21).

Although the buildings of the Duke of Westminster are the most extravagant, he was not the only landowner to continue building in Cheshire throughout the depression. Bowen Jones illustrated farmsteads built by Lord Crewe, the Marquis of Cholmondeley, and Lord Tollemache as well as the Duke of Westminster. He noted that agriculture had not suffered here as much as in many other counties, and explained this in part by the efforts of landlords to provide 'superior buildings ... so as to economise the cost of production'. However, he also acknowledged that a key factor was the county's reliance 'as of old' on dairying and the feeding and breeding of pigs where there 'has been a smaller decline in prices'.[40] These buildings provide testament to the fact that Cheshire remained relatively prosperous throughout the depression years.

The existence of wealthy landlords also played its role. The Dysart estate, held by a branch of the wealthy Tollemache family, with major estates in Cheshire and Suffolk, was one of the largest in Lincolnshire. It covered about 18,000 acres centred on Buckminster Park, just outside Grantham. A period of farm building took place in the 1880s, with several farmsteads of exactly the same design being built. No documentation survives to help explain this rare example of large-scale investment and the architect for the schemes is not known. In 1878, the ninth Earl inherited from his grandfather at the age of only 19. Until 1892, it seems that the late Earl's brothers had an interest in the running of the estate, but it is possible that the coming of age of the ninth Earl, in 1880, may have stimulated a period of building activity.[41] At least five farmsteads, all dated 1883, were built. That at Hanby was built on an old site, replacing earlier buildings, while The Pines on Little Ponton Heath

Manure

Cobbled paving

N

Pig yards

Ducks

Root house

Calves

20 cows

20 cows

20 cows

Tank

Young stock

Pigs

Pigs

Pigs

Boiling house

Chop house

Calves

Pigs

Pigs

Pigs

Gangway

Roadway

Loose box

Privy

Coals

4 Stall or stable

Cart shed

Grass

Stall or box

Milk house

Press room

Scullery

Pantry

0   feet   30

Kitchen

Living room

Entrance

0   metres   10

Gig house

FIGURE 94.
The plan of Saighton
Lane Farm (Cheshire)
shows the L-plan
buildings with stables
and gig house in one
wing and six rows of
twenty cows each in
the main, wider wing
with a feed store at
the end. The piggery,
located behind the
house, was an
important element of
all dairy farmsteads.
The covered manure
house is a feature
found on many of the
Duke of
Westminster's
farmsteads by 1900.
As with so many dairy
steadings the original
windows have had to
be replaced to
conform with modern
regulations. The
photographs show the
unity of house and
farm buildings typical
of Douglas's work (1),
the two-storey
cowhouse with its
hayloft (2) and a
detail of the stabling
(3).

185

FIGURE 95.
Many of the
farmsteads on the
Duke of
Westminster's
Cheshire estates
demonstrate the
variety of John
Douglas's work and
the quality of detail
employed, such as the
loading doors above
the cowhouse (1) and
ventilators in the roof
(2) at Aldford Hall.

186

FIGURE 96.
The Pines, Little
Ponton (Lincolnshire)
is centred on two
covered yards entered
through wide double
doors divided by a
narrow feeding
passage. Detailing
includes cast-iron
hit-and-miss windows
for ventilation.

187

was a new creation (Figure 96). All are built of brick except for Grange Farm, North Witham, which is of stone. They were all planned on a U-plan layout with two covered yards divided by a raised feeding passage within the U. The feeding passage, which is wide enough to take a hand cart, is open down to trough height on either side between the pillars that support the roof. The roof of the feeding passage is higher than those of the yards either side, allowing for ventilation into them through a row of adjustable shutters under the eaves. The barn on one side consists merely of the lower floor of a two-storey building with granary above. There is access from the barn into the nearest yard so that straw could be taken directly to it. There is no sign of a power source on any of the farms, the barn machinery being worked by portable machines. These compact farmsteads, which served mixed arable farms of between 250 and 300 acres, provided well-ventilated, easily-serviced cattle accommodation and represented an important and almost final stage in the sophistication of farm building design at a practical, tenant farm level.

The improvement of dairy breeds had long been very much a gentlemanly pursuit which had increased in importance in this period. The Earl of Leicester at Holkham, for example, kept a prize herd at the Model Farm there. On the small Buckhold estate, near Pangbourne (Berkshire) Dr Herbert Watney kept prize Jersey cattle. In the late 1880s he built an octagonal cowhouse 'with a double circle of standings within its lofty interior. Between them ran a tramway for horse-drawn trucks'.[42] Lord Cadogan was another Jersey cow enthusiast, and when he bought the Culford Hall estate (Suffolk) in 1889 he immediately began improvements at the Home Farm to house his cows. The buildings, originally erected by the Reverend Benyon in the 1830s, were remodelled to include two covered yards. The eighteenth-century barn behind became a feed preparation room with machinery powered by the already existing water wheel which also lifted all the water needed for the cow stalls and yards. Tramlines took feed to the feeding passages and troughs. Turntables were provided to allow the carts to be turned though ninety degrees at the corners of the yard (Figure 97). A new cowhouse for 48 beasts was also built. The walls were tiled and patent cast-iron stalls and sliding doors installed. Drains led to an underground liquid manure tank and a pump lifted the liquid for spreading on the fields. The Cadogan coat of arms and the date 1890 are emblazoned on one gable.

In the great majority of cases, investment in new buildings on this scale was only made possible by income from outside agriculture. The Gibbs family, who built up their estate at Tyntesfield near Bristol between 1843 and 1861 with money from banking and trade, turned attention to the home farm in 1881 after completing their house (Figure 98). This was built on sloping ground so that the long rear building was approached at an upper level from an estate yard. At the lower level it contained feed stores opening into the covered yards where a prize herd of Alderney cows was stalled. A portable steam engine stood at the end of the long rear building and powered feed preparation machinery throughout the upper part of the building. Chutes in the floor

FIGURE 97.
An interior view of
Home Farm, Culford
(Suffolk), showing the
tramway and cast-iron
troughs and stalls.

allowed the milled and crushed feed to be moved into the storage space below. The covered area contained iron cow stalls, a midden, pigsties and calf pens. Drains fed into an underground manure tank, which could be pumped out through a trap door near the midden. The whole complex was carefully planned for efficiency and well-built, with fine architectural detailing.

The main area of farm building development, therefore, was in the form of the provision of good buildings for cattle housing and dairying, and here a new spirit of enterprise developed. The earliest developments in commercial cowhouse design came from Scotland, where in 1810 William Harley had developed systems of roof ventilators which allowed the cows plenty of fresh air without creating draughts. He built a ventilated cow house for 24 cows on a site near Glasgow which he soon expanded, so that by 1814 he was keeping 300 cows on a much-visited model farm providing milk for the Glasgow market.[43] London dairy farms were slow to follow suit. The London market had long been provided with milk by town cows, but it was not until the 1860s that they were kept in well-designed dairies. The systems adopted in both urban and suburban dairies were described in 1868 in an article by

189

James Morton. Having touched upon the problems resulting from the adulteration of town milk through watering it down, he then describes the keeping of cows in towns. Whilst green feed might be difficult to come by there was plenty of brewers' grain which formed the major part of their diet. The cowhouses themselves varied greatly from 'rickety old stabling' to the establishment of Mr Dannock of Chelsea which was entered through a passage roofed with glass and covered with vines. Inside was a yard with a clean and comfortable cowhouse on one side and stabling, hay house and feed store on the other. The largest of the London dairies milked 200 cows and the one that most impressed Morton was at Barking, where London sewage was used for irrigation and produced rich crops of grass. Here there were several cowhouses accommodating 60 cows each, scattered around 50 acres of land. Each shed, where the cows stood in rows back-to-back, contained feed stores and a sleeping room for the farm workers. The sheds were said to be clean and airy. 'The whole thing is compendious, not very expensive (costing about £4 per cow) and economical of the labour performed in it; and this is a very important consideration'.[44]

Morton admitted there could often be problems with the cleanliness of town milk and that the standards between dairies could vary greatly. To help improve the image of milk drinking, and ensure their share of the market,

FIGURE 98.
(*below and opposite*)
The buildings at Tyntesfield (Somerset) were designed in 1881 and built shortly afterwards (1). The stalling in the stables (2) and the covered yard (3) was provided by Musgrove, iron founders of London and Belfast with a national distribution network. The covered yard incorporated a midden, shown to the left.

some of the more enterprising dairymen built model dairy farms to act as an advertisement for their clean and pure product. Holland Park Dairy was widely publicised and described in Sheldon's book on dairy farming in 1879. Based on seventy acres of pasture in Kensington, a new farm was built on the High Street with a shop for selling milk in the front. The shop featured decorative tiles, marble-topped tables and a fountain, and a glazed observation area from which customers could see into the cowsheds.[45] Similar was George Barham's Express Dairy Company (so-called because it relied for much of its supply on milk deliveries by express trains from London's hinterland) at College Farm, Finchley (Figure 99). Designed by Frederick Chancellor in 1883 it provided, behind a timber-framed gabled façade, a tiled shop with a viewing area into the cattle sheds. 'Up the centre of this main building is laid a tasteful but inexpensive aisle of Minton's tiles, which look clean and pleasant. On either side of this roomy aisle is a long row of intelligent faces of the cows that give the milk ... The stalls and mangers are all of pleasing design. The stalls are all littered with small chips or shavings of wood obtained from some workshop in town, and while answering the purpose very well, they look clean, crisp and pleasing.'[46] Brick silos were built alongside for preserving grass although, by 1891, Mr Barham had ceased using them. Across the road was a tiled dairy, of the type normally found on estate farms with a thatched roof and overhanging eaves. By 1891 it was disused, and Sheldon points out that many

FIGURE 99. College Farm, Finchley, built in 1883 for the Express Dairy Company, is one of the finest of the farmsteads designed by Frederick Chancellor as a show-piece dairy and advertisement for drinking fresh milk.

such buildings, with their shallow cream settling dishes, were by then redundant as cream separators and refrigeration had taken over.[47] Here we see the farming industry confronting the very modern problem of improving its image with the consumer: something which would have seemed unimaginable in the prosperous days of high farming when the British farmer had the monopoly of the British market.

Conclusion

As farming moved into the twentieth century conditions did not improve and landed estates continued to be sold. The loss of sons of the landed families

FIGURE 100.
(*right and overleaf*)
The buildings at
Aston Wold
(Northamptonshire)
are a charming
reminder that even
through the
depression the rural
idyll remained a
powerful image and
the *ferme ornée* still
held the appeal that it
had had for Marie
Antoinette.

in the First World War, coupled with Lloyd George's tax reforms and their affects on the gentry, accelerated this trend. The temporary improvement in agricultural prices brought about by wartime demands encouraged further sales and the *Estates Gazette* estimated that a quarter of the land of England changed hands between 1917 and 1921. Not only was this exchange of land on a far larger scale than at any time since the Dissolution of the Monasteries, it was of a different type. Farms were often bought on an individual basis to their sitting tenants, who did not have the money to build extravagantly. The era of the model farm was over. Occasionally there was a wealthy owner, such as Lord Rothschild at Aston Wold (Northamptonshire), who could afford to build a *ferme ornée* for his own amusement, but these are rare (Figure 100). Such places have great architectural charm, but are looking back to a rural idyll rather than initiating new farming techniques. As such they have little relevance to the farming story and show a final break with the link between beauty and utility which was at the heart of the Enlightenment and the philosophy of the early 'improvers'.

The Royal Agricultural Society held a building competition in 1908 and published the plans of the four winning entries in its *Journal* for that year.

The main points in design that were taken into account by the judges were economy in planning, cost of construction and maintenance, convenience of arrangement for working, and accommodation for animals, especially lighting, ventilation, and drainage of sheds, particularly of those for dairy cattle.[48] Significantly, as we have seen, it was the needs of dairy cattle, the one remaining profitable part of the farming industry, which was of most interest to farm building designers. The resulting plans are plain and utilitarian; a far cry from the elegant Georgian and often flamboyant mid-Victorian creations of a powerful and confident landed class (Figure 101).

FIGURE 101.
Drawings submitted to the *Journal of the Royal Agricultural Society of England* competition of 1908 show almost completely enclosed farmsteads with straw barns and feed mills along the back. Hay is stored in stacks or Dutch barns and power is provided by portable engines rather than by stationary engines needing tall chimneys.

The spirit of improvement which had resided with the landed gentry was reduced to a shadow of its former self. As landed power declined, municipal, institutional and commercial power increased. New building was more likely to be undertaken in the form of the many farmsteads built as part of asylums or the sewage farms built by public health authorities, or by industry. Express Dairy's Finchley Farm provides an early example of the power and wealth of the new food manufacturers. This was followed in the 1930s by the Ovaltine farms at Kings Langley near Welwyn Garden City (Figure 102). Along with malt extract, thousands of gallons of milk and large numbers of eggs were required each day in the manufacturing process. In 1929, 450 acres was bought so that the raw materials could be produced on site and modern methods of production under scientific conditions could be investigated. The Ovaltine

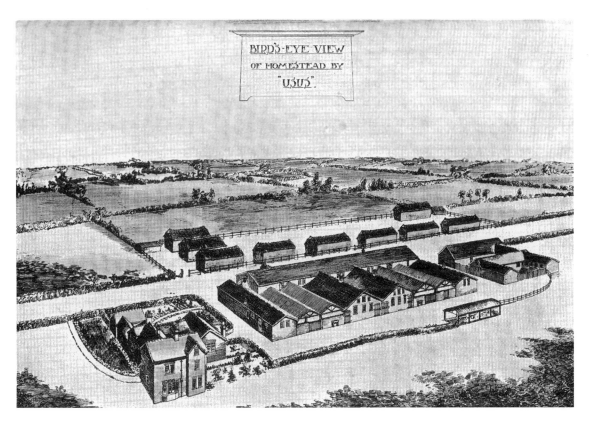

BIRD'S-EYE VIEW
OF HOMESTEAD BY
"USUS".

Egg Farm was built in 1929, and the Dairy Farm three years later. The managing director worked with the company architect, J. A. Bowden, to combine in the farm an outer shell of charm and tradition with an interior that was devoted to the best modern methods of dairy practice. 'The Ovaltine drinkers of suburbia would thus be satisfied on all counts: the product was of impeccable quality while the rustic illusion remained reassuringly intact'.[49] The farmstead was therefore a central plank of the company's marketing policy, backed by the resources of a limited company. By contrast, as the fortunes of the landed aristocracy and particularly the gentry declined so did the era of the planned and model farmstead come to an end, having influenced farm building design for hardly more than 150 years.

FIGURE 102.
The Dairy Farm
(Berkshire) built in
1931 to the designs of
Bowden, Son and
Partners.

CHAPTER SEVEN

Epilogue

The history of the rise and fall of the planned and model farmstead mirrors that of the landed estate and its importance within the context of fashion and society, as well as agriculture. The planned and model farmstead was an entirely new and uniquely British building type of the Georgian and Victorian period, initially owing more to Palladio's villa-farms than vernacular traditions. It was able to gain importance as landowners, through enclosure and reclamation, created new farmsteads and tightened their grip on an ever diminishing independent peasant class in a way that happened nowhere else in Europe. Those farmsteads built as home farms, as eye-catchers or sited within newly-enclosed farmland can be seen as visible evidence, alongside the great house and park, of that increasing influence over the countryside. They also indicated to his peers and neighbours that the landlord was performing his patriotic duties and taking his new-found power seriously. Some patrons regarded farm buildings as little more than symbolic elements within a parkland landscape, whilst for many others an interest in practical farming was paramount as they aimed to meet the national need for increased food production. Home farms were both an example for the tenants and a place for individual experiment and observation, which would provide a topic for discussion between neighbours. New buildings for tenant farms, especially improved housing, would encourage a more intelligent class of tenantry who would be prepared to share the owner's enthusiasm for improvement. Finally, all owners appreciated the increased rent roll that the encouragement of more intensive agriculture might bring. The tripartite aims of beauty, utility and profit were inextricably linked and interdependent in the philosophy of the improving landlord.

It follows that for landowners these buildings had far more than agricultural significance. As in the design of parks and gardens, the preference for certain architectural styles conveyed specific messages, demonstrating man's dominance over nature, as well as the dominance of the status-conscious landlord over the land. These styles displayed a diverse approach to the issues of functionalism and ornamentation, a balance that was not always struck. Sometimes, as in the case of the castellated parkland follies at Greystoke, Cumbria, functionalism – albeit in an 'improved' landscape – lost out. The Palladian designs of Samuel Wyatt, on the other hand, could serve both architectural and agricultural aspirations well. Whilst the Palladian farmsteads of the eighteenth century reflected the country gentleman's admiration for order and all things classical, the designs of many mid-nineteenth-century farmsteads demonstrated to a wide audience the application of new materials and factory planning to farmstead architecture. Indeed, as agricultural writers such as Copland began to break away from the patronage of the landowners and were prepared to be more critical of them, the need for landlords to justify their position grew. Articles in the *Journal of the Royal Agricultural Society of England* in the 1840s began to support tenants' demands for compensation for improvements made during a tenancy, and so the need for the landlord to be seen as an improver to justify his ownership of land increased. Pusey's remarks, made in the context of water meadows and upland improvement, are equally relevant to farm building: 'If the plain means of improvement and employment are still neglected, it will be impossible not to tax the owners of these needless deserts with supineness, and difficult to deny that they hold in their hands more of the country's surface than they are able to manage for their own good or for the good of the community'.[1]

Some owners had always preferred more functional styles, which became more prevalent in the difficult years at the end of the nineteenth century. Tenant farms were also typically of a simpler build than the home farms. Where buildings were designed by estate managers or farmers they were likely to be much simpler (as in the case of John Hudson's prize plan of 1850, or John Morton's Example Farm of 1839) than those designed by architects or landowners. Although the origins of model farmstead design are to be found in polite rather than vernacular architecture, regional traditions also find expression in the plan and form of these buildings. Bank barns were included in the farmsteads of Cumbria and the western fringes, while linhays are also to be found in the pastoral west. The courtyard layout gave way to an L-plan arrangement, often with a free standing stable, in the dairying areas of Cheshire.

The influence of model farmsteads on agricultural improvement has often been dismissed by agricultural historians, particularly those eager to promote the formerly little appreciated role of the tenant farmer. Macdonald, for example, dismissed model farmsteads as irrelevant because 'they displayed the latest agricultural techniques, not necessarily because they were profitable, but because they were remarkable'.[2] There undoubtedly were well-publicised examples, such as that of William Lawson at Blennerhassett whose expensive farmstead and his idealistic schemes for a co-operative ended in failure. As we have seen, however, Lawson's ideas received a great deal of publicity just at the time when the co-operative wholesale movement started by the Rochdale Society of Equitable Pioneers was expanding fast. The lack of official backing for such schemes as Morton's network of example farms meant that, as so often is the case in the history of British technological advance, the initiative was left to private individuals.[3]

Planned and model farmsteads never made up anything like the majority of farmsteads, even those holdings of over 300 acres which were considered as the smallest on which 'high farming' could be practised.[4] Nevertheless, they were widely distributed and publicised, providing an example and a standard to which others could aspire. Perhaps what this research has contributed most to the debate on the importance of planned and model farmsteads to improvement is in the number of such farmsteads which have been located. Only a handful attracted enough publicity to reach the pages of the agricultural journals and textbooks of the time, but the 800 or so which have been found through documentary research and fieldwork show how widespread they in fact were. The survival of such a large sample suggests that they were certainly not ephemeral. Scattered about the country and in the hands of the owners of more than 3,000 acres who made up the landed gentry, their influence on farming practice and design must have been considerable. Of course the majority of farmsteads were not completely rebuilt in the eighteenth and nineteenth centuries, but have evolved with new buildings added as they were needed. However, even here, the principles of the planned farm design were applied to the positioning of new buildings within old farmyards.

Model farmsteads satisfied the need for the owner to be seen at the cutting edge of agriculture improvement, and many were visited by both farmers and fellow landowners. There was widespread interest, for example, in the pure-bred stock that was kept by Lord Leicester at Holkham, the Duke of Bedford at Woburn and Lord Cadogan at Culford, and a curiosity in the innovations tried there. As we have seen, descriptions of some of these farmsteads found their way into the pages of the *Journal of the Royal Agricultural Society of England* and other journals. It is, indeed, as examples and foci for publicity that model farms must be seen in the context of agricultural progress. One promoter of plain neat buildings, Mr Browick of Stoneleigh, recognised in 1862 that while some model farms were a 'bye-word of how things should not be done, others set a good example'.[5] As experimental farms – 'shop windows of innovation'[6] – they demonstrated the possibilities of increased yields and the value of manure. In the case of some of the more elaborate model farmsteads, they also demonstrated the value of mechanisation and good layout to efficient farming, the reduction of labour costs and the quality of livestock produced. Many included innovative and practical design elements on the cutting edge of the available technology. Whilst they may well have been part of a fashion, that fashion could well have beneficial results. Developments such as the storage of silage, slatted floors in livestock sheds and liquid manure tanks, tramways and mechanised feed preparation were pioneered from 1850, but were not generally taken up until farming circumstances allowed, one hundred years later.

A comparison of the layouts of model farmsteads over the 150 years after 1750 shows that they were very much in the forefront of farmstead design. Layouts changed to suit new conditions, and new building materials such as laminated wooden beams, corrugated iron, cast iron and concrete were introduced. The variety of buildings for housing implements and farm produce as well animals, and for food preparation, proliferated, and covered yards were to be found on many of the new farmsteads built after 1850.[7] Mechanisation too was often a feature of model farmsteads, with elaborate systems of gearing from a power source allowing a bewildering variety of barn and feed crushing machinery to be turned. However, even in the context of home farms, mechanisation made slow progress outside its main areas of acceptance in the north-east and the south-west. Innovation slowed down after the 1870s. The timing of these innovations and the speed with which they were transferred from theory to practice can be seen in planned and model farmsteads. Whilst some farmsteads such as those on the Strutt estates may seem to be extremely innovative for the early-nineteenth century, many of their features, such as feeding tubes, and the mixing of feed on upper floors before moving down to livestock below, had been suggested by Young in 1770. Conventional layouts, such as those on the Grittleton estates, continued to be built as part of estate building projects through much of the nineteenth century, reflecting the mixture of continuity and innovation which is so typical of the farming community.

While agricultural prices were buoyant and tenants could afford high rents, both landlord and farmers were prepared to try new methods. As cereal prices declined after 1870, and rents followed prices down, this spirit of experiment departed. C. S. Read, never a supporter of the intensive high-cost methods of 'high farming', wrote as early as 1854: 'The only true and systematic incentive to improvement is the certainty of profit in the expenditure of capital'.[8] The truth of this comment was only now beginning to be appreciated. While exact figures are impossible to find or interpret, there is no doubt that there was little 'certainty of profit' on the investment involved in the building of tenant farmsteads. However, their value cannot simply be judged on these terms. The rents of well-equipped tenant farms no doubt withstood recession for longer than those which found it more difficult to adapt to increased livestock or dairy production. Added to this, well-built steadings did not need the regular maintenance required on less stalwart premises and, to this extent, capital invested in planned farm buildings for tenants could be said to have been 'worthwhile'. The situation as far as model home farmsteads is concerned is more complicated. They probably were never economically viable and many were built by long-established landowners such as the Dukes of Westminster, Bedford, and Northumberland who had made money outside agriculture. Others were the work of the *nouveaux riches* such as the Ridleys at Blagdon and Curwens of Workington who had benefited from the shipping of coal from Newcastle and Workington, and the Daintry family in Cheshire who had been textile manufacturers and bankers in Macclesfield.

As landowning ceased to be the major wealth-producer in the country with the rise of commerce and industry, so the landowner's economic superiority was undermined. Gradually, too, his political and social influence declined. The various reform acts beginning in 1832 and most significantly, the secret ballot of 1870, reduced his control over voting for national government. Poor Law Unions, and after 1888 County Councils, took over many of the roles of magistrates. The Agricultural Holdings Act of 1885 established tenants' rights on a legal basis. In contrast to earlier periods, the owner now appeared as an 'acceptor rather than as an originator of change' and leadership was transferred from landowners to farmers in a variety of rural spheres.[9] With some notable exceptions, this was also true of farm buildings. Owners were more likely to respond to requests for individual additions, such as increased livestock accommodation, than initiate a complete rebuild.[10] As the influence of the landlord declined socially, politically and economically, so did his domination of the agricultural scene. By the end of the nineteenth century, the ownership of land became an expensive luxury which many of the old families could barely afford. Rents fell, land was laid down to pasture and an increasing number of landlords relied on their investments outside agriculture for their income. Interest in agricultural improvement seemed futile and the model farmstead became an anachronism. Its importance declined with that of its builders.

Conclusion

The significance of the model farmstead as one of the strands that make up the 'Agricultural Revolution' has long been underestimated, and has continued to lose ground as the importance of farmer – as distinct from landlord-led – innovation has come to be appreciated by agricultural historians. However, the landlord was the provider of the infrastructure within which improved farming practice in key areas could flourish. This infrastructure included, along with drainage, reclamation and enclosure, the buildings to serve the farming system. On the home farm, the owner could demonstrate and experiment and follow up in practice some of the theories of the day. It was on model farms that the ideas of scientific planning began.[11] An annual visit to the home farm was part of the social calendar for the tenants of many an estate. The practical experience gained here allowed the owner or his agent to take an informed interest in the progress of his tenants, and his pure-bred livestock might well provide the sires to improve the quality of the tenants' flocks and herds. The buildings and their management could also provide an example of best practice. Model farms are as much part of the evidence for the country estate, the philosophies which had helped shape it, and the social order which it controlled, as its great house and park. Beauty was to be found in a tamed, productive, useful and profitable landscape rather than a wild and barren one. The buildings demonstrate, in a physical way, the importance of both the landlords' attitudes and their capital to agricultural improvement during the formative years of the eighteenth and nineteenth centuries. They inform our understanding of social and agricultural history, as well as delight us as architectural achievements and features in the rural landscape.

County Synopses

English Heritage commissioned a survey of planned and model farmsteads in order to determine how many examples were built, how many survive and where they are located. Initially it was necessary to identify as many examples as possible, through documentary sources and records of surviving examples, from those recorded prior to demolition or conversion to those that have been listed as buildings of special architectural or historic interest. Building on this preliminary work sample areas across the country were chosen for detailed study of different periods and types of building. As far as possible, the study areas were chosen to represent different agricultural regions of England as well as the different periods of building. Estates where the documentary sources were good were also favoured. The first phase of model farmstead building up to about 1820 was represented by estates in Nottinghamshire (Parkyns of Bunny), East Yorkshire (Sykes of Sledmere), Derbyshire (Strutt of Belper), Cumbria (Howards of Greystoke and Lord Lonsdale of Lowther), Northumberland (Blacketts at Wallington), Bedfordshire (The Dukes of Bedford at Woburn), North Yorkshire (Earl of Holderness at Hornby) the royal estates at Windsor and the Shropshire and Staffordshire of the Marquis of Stafford. The buildings of high farming are discussed in the context of Prince Albert's work at Windsor, estates in Devon and Bedfordshire (Duke of Bedford), Northamptonshire (Duke of Grafton), Lincolnshire (Christopher Turnor), Northumberland (the Greenwich Hospital estates, the Ridley estates at Blagdon and the Duke of Northumberland estates at Alnwick) and the work of the Essex architect, Frederick Chancellor. For the period after 1870 the Cheshire estates of the Duke of Westminster and the Lincolnshire estates of the Dysart family have been chosen.

Sites have been identified in a variety of ways and only a limited number of those included have been visited. Contemporary printed sources include the Board of Agriculture's *General Views* produced for most counties between 1797 and 1815, encyclopedias, such as that by Loudon, which went through various editions from 1827, journals such as *The Annals of Agriculture, The Farmers' Magazine, The Builder,* and *The Journal of the Royal Agricultural Society of England* (published from 1839). There were also several farming text books and books of plans published by land agents and engineers such as G. A. Dean and J. B. Denton. Contemporary manuscript sources, such as the plans of Frederick Chancellor which survive in Essex Record Office and the collection of drawings, principally by Soane and Adam in Sir John Soane's Museum, were also consulted. Modern printed sources included the *Buildings of England* series, books by Robinson, Brigden, Lake, Peters and Harvey (see bibliography), articles in *Country Life,* and the RCHME inventory volumes. Surveys of individual farmsteads, in the form of drawings, photographs and written reports, are available for inspection at the National Monuments Record at Swindon. The Council for British Archaeology, local history and vernacular architecture groups, conservation officers and county sites and monuments records were also contacted. Without their help the full gazetteer would have been far less complete.

The list below provides a summary of some of the best examples of planned and model farms in each county as well as a short analysis of the county's relationship to the history of these buildings. Necessarily, these vignettes rely heavily on secondary sources such as *The General Views,* the County Reports presented as Prize Essays to the *Journal of the Royal Agricultural Society of England* from the 1840s and commentators such as James Caird. Caird started his agricultural career in 1841 as a tenant farmer at Baldoon, near Wigtown in Scotland, having spent several years in Northumberland as a farm student. He was unusual amongst the farming community in that he supported free trade and came to the notice of the Prime Minister, Sir Robert Peel, after writing *High Farming as the best substitute for Protection* in 1849. In 1851, encouraged by Peel, he toured the country for *The Times,* writing reports in which he set out to show that farming could be profitable if farmers were only prepared to adapt to changed circumstances and intensify their methods. His pieces, therefore, presented a more optimistic picture than was painted by the complaints of landowners and farmers about the distressed state of agriculture as a result of the repeal of the Corn Laws. He would certainly have written with enthusiasm about any new farms designed for high farming that he came across. His articles were then published as a book *English Farming in 1850–51.*

Reference has also been made to the census of landownership in Britain and Ireland which was taken in 1871 and produced by J. Bateman as *The Great Landowners of Great Britain and Ireland,* the final edition of which was published in 1883. The number of large-scale landowners will obviously be of significance when considering the importance of planned and model farmsteads in each county.

Present use

Model farmsteads' solidity, quality and capacity to absorb change have also ensured that many have survived to the present day. In contrast to more traditional farm buildings of the eighteenth and nineteenth centuries – a sizeable proportion (over 300 out of 800 documented examples) have been listed as buildings of special architectural or historic interest, a means of protection that aims to ensure that their special character is conserved for the enjoyment of future generations. This number is a direct reflection of the high architectural and technological interest of these buildings. The great majority of listed model farm buildings have been listed at grade II, a grade that affects 92 per cent of all listed buildings. Eastwood Manor Farm in Somerset, the ultimate example of an industrial farmstead of the 'high farming' period, is one of only two (the other being Norris Castle Farm on the Isle of Wight) that have been listed at grade I, this grade comprising the top two per cent of all listed buildings. Some twenty others – such as Home Farm at Coleshill in Oxfordshire and Dalley and Moscow Farms in Belper – have been listed at grade II*. These fine farmsteads all enjoy a variety of uses, from continuing agricultural use (Eastwood Manor Farm, Dalley Farm) to offices (Coleshill) and even housing (Moscow Farm).

Buildings will only survive so long as they have a use, and this is as true of planned and model farmsteads as of any other building type. Historic farm buildings in general provide a challenge for the working farmer, but in many cases the problems of continuing agricultural use for planned and model farmsteads are less than those for some more traditional building types. Model farmsteads tend to be larger and thus more able to accommodate tractors or modern machinery. By definition they were carefully laid out and in some examples, particularly the later ones, the cattle accommodation is well suited to modern use. It is always a pleasure to visit sites such as Park Farm, Apley (Shropshire), where grain dust still fills the air and machinery is humming at harvest time, and where cattle are comfortably housed during the winter. Some have remained in agricultural use, but of a more specialised nature. Livery stables and riding schools for instance, as at Woodhouse Farm, Sherrifhales (Shropshire), provide a solution requiring only the minimum of alterations. The buildings at Easton (Suffolk), Sandwell (West Midlands), and Wimpole (Cambridgeshire) provide attractive settings for farm parks, while Chancellor's buildings at Purleigh (Essex), are the home of a thriving vineyard business.

Many successful conversions of model farmsteads to a variety of non-agricultural uses have been encountered during this research. Long low ranges of well-lit stables may lend themselves to office conversion while cattle sheds may require more windows if they are to be suitable. Lofty barns and covered yards may be suitable for larger workshops and cart sheds provide storage areas. Such conversions for industrial and commercial use as Fornham St Genevieve (Suffolk), with easy access to Bury St Edmunds, can help bring much needed economic activity to the countryside and provide pleasant working environment. A fine industrial farmstead, originally on the Duke of Bedford's estates, at Water End Farm, Eversholt (Bedfordshire), has been successfully converted to six office suites in an attractive rural setting but with easy access to the M1 (Figure 103). This group, with its engine house and tall chimney, was built in 1857 and would have employed at least thirty farm workers in its heyday. It is satisfying that this is the number of people who are now working there in the offices. The impressive buildings designed by John Douglas for the Duke of Westminster have similarly lent themselves to

FIGURE 103.
Water End Farm,
Eversholt,
Bedfordshire.

re-use as offices and workshops with very little external modification. The large complex at Wrexham Road Farm, Ecclestone (Cheshire), has been converted to highly individual office accommodation while smaller shippons in Aldford are now used for craft workshops for businesses such as cabinet makers. Their proximity to Chester has made them desirable to tenants. The re-use of the buildings in this way not only provides them with a sustainable future, but helps in much needed rural regeneration. The Country Landowners' Association, The Royal Institution of Chartered Surveyors and local amenity societies support these types of re-use by award schemes, and publicity given to award-winners provides encouragement for others.

In only a limited number of cases can these steadings be opened for the public. There are several successful farm parks, sometimes, as at both Wimpole and Shugborough Halls, providing added interest to an already popular visitor attraction and enabling the education of the public on farming matters. The advantage here is that in spite of the necessarily sanitised and artificial atmosphere, the animals are still in the buildings and fields and the hay and corn in the barns. Other groups provide the home for interpretation centres, field study centres, restaurants, gift shops, or even health clubs and shopping malls. Again there is always the danger that the original purpose of the buildings is lost on visitors, especially where the commercial element overshadows everything else. An indication of which farmsteads were known to be open to the public at the time of going to press is given in the county synopses.

Sadly, continued agricultural use or conversion to a new purpose are not options open to a sizeable minority of the buildings recorded in this research. Many are derelict or crumbling because their remoteness means that their useful life is over. Nearly a century of agricultural depression, from the 1870s into the 1950s, took its toll and many are structurally unsound. Wall's Court Farm, in South Gloucestershire on the outskirts of Bristol, was designed by the architect and editor of *The Builder,* George Godwin for the successful Bristol businessmen and founder of a fertiliser company, Alderman Proctor in 1855. A huge E-plan range contained not only the usual agricultural buildings, but also a school for local children. They were built of local stone with decorative Gothic detailing and the central wing was surmounted by a dovecote (now gone). By the 1980s, when the site was taken over by the computer company, Hewlett Packard, it was derelict. However, parts of the buildings have been restored and are used for storage and form attractive features beside the cafeteria. Some features uncovered during restoration, such as tramways and turntables for the tramline system, have been kept and displayed. A second Proctor farm nearby is now part of the Ministry of Defence complex and has also been restored as a landscape feature, but with little functional use. There will be occasions when no possible economic use can be found and the funds to stabilise the fabric as an historic shell are not available. Even if the farmstead is lost to the landscape it is essential that the historic information that it can provide is not. To ensure this a proper record should be made before it disappears. If this book strengthens appreciation of the significance of planned and model farmsteads to our understanding of the period in which they were built, then an important aim will have been achieved.

Guide to the list below

The numbers of documented and recorded examples are included in brackets after each county heading. This number should not be taken to include all examples in any given county. In some areas more information was available than elsewhere, but it is the result of exhaustive efforts to tap as many sources as possible and does provide a springboard for future research. It also needs to be noted that that there is no automatic link between landlord involvement in planned landscapes and buildings for social improvement such as cottages and schools, and areas where planned and model farmsteads are found. The full gazetteer, which is available for inspection at the National Monuments Record in Swindon, provides statutory listing, mapping and bibliographical references.

Bedfordshire (83)

The Duke of Bedford was by far the largest landowner in the county with 35,589 acres in 1871. With the help of the architect Henry Holland and his agent, Robert Salmon, the fifth Duke began improvements on the estate shortly after he inherited in 1787, but most of his building work was superseded by that of his successor, the seventh Duke. He was responsible for a programme of rebuilding on most of his farms in the 1840s and 1850s, each set of steadings costing as much as five years' rent.[1] No architect is recorded for any of this phase of building. The result is a planned landscape of distinctive new farms in the parishes surrounding Woburn in mid Bedfordshire.

The second largest estate in the county was that of the Whitbreads, based at Southill. Here the Home Farm was said to have been designed by Henry Holland in about 1800, but limited interest was taken in estate building generally.[2] Away from these two centres Caird found little to admire in the farm steadings, describing them as being of wood and thatch, although he did comment on the Home Farm at Putteridge being built for Colonel Sowerby, writing that when it was finished 'it will be one of the best'.[3] Unfortunately this farmstead was not located during the survey.

The main period of building in the county was after 1850 with work, not only on at least 35 of the Duke of Bedford farms, but also on the Lucas West estate in the area of Silsoe and Gravenhurst. An impressive farmstead, whose future is still uncertain is the Home Farm at Luton Hoo, built in about 1860 and for which plans survive in Bedfordshire Record Office.[4]

Figures 49, 50, 51, 74, 103.

Berkshire (13)

This county's soils vary from light chalk to heavy clays. Only 22 landowners of more than 3,000 acres were recorded in 1871, but in 1860 Spearing believed that Berkshire was 'favoured with as wealthy and influential a body of landed proprietors as most counties, who are ever foremost in giving a stimulus to agricultural improvements'. Several home farms were cultivated 'on the most improved systems'.[5] However these 'improved systems' did not often include planned farmsteads. One described by Spearing was Chalk Pit Farm, built by the Reverend Benyon at Englefield: 'Not perhaps so compact and uniform as some others, but in their selection, much practical judgement has been displayed.'[6] It contained cattle yards, open sheds and loose boxes as well as a steam engine house to power barn machinery.

The Essex architect, Frederick Chancellor designed two farmsteads for the Garth family. One, at Haines Hill, was illustrated by Denton, but has since been demolished.[7]

The Berkshire farmsteads that always excited most interest were those of George III and later, Prince Albert at Windsor. There were four farms within the Great Park. Shaw Farm was rebuilt to a plan of G. A Dean whilst the Home Farm (primarily a dairy farm) and Flemish Farm were the work of the estate architect, George Turnbull. Norfolk Farm was originally built as part of George III's improvement and not replaced by Prince Albert. Very little survives of the original Norfolk Farm, but Prince Albert's Home Farm, Shaw Farm and Flemish Farm are relatively intact.

Figures 31, 32, 82, 83, 84.

Buckinghamshire (16)

Buckinghamshire was a county of few landed estates with only 22 over 3,000 acres being recorded in 1871. Caird was critical of the landowners in the county who took little interest in their tenants. Farm buildings were inadequate, of wood and thatch, 'grown up by successive additions, as the necessities of the occupier dictated'.[8] The Duke of Wellington's estate, based at Stowe, was at the head of county society, but few new farms were built. The Home Farm, built around a courtyard now houses the National Trust offices. However, there were exceptions to this general pattern. Chalfont Lodge, now demolished, was illustrated by Loudon in 1833[9] and was said to have been built in 1796. The buildings consisted of a square of cow stalls and pig sties with a strange central building with granaries above cart lodges surrounded by a covered area to house and protect dung, the whole surmounted by a pigeon loft. A second early group at West Wycombe Park consisted of sheds and barns around a rectangular yard. It was built when the park was extended in the 1770s.[10] The second half of the nineteenth century saw more model farm building, especially on the Rothschild estate around Waddesden, where Charles Devey was extensively employed, mostly to design farm houses. The set of buildings at Fawley Court was described in 1855 as having been erected by the 'wealthy and enterprising tenant' rather than the landlord – an unusual situation, but perhaps typical of Buckinghamshire where, according to Caird, tenants were even expected to pay for pipe draining.[11] The buildings at Staceyhill near Wolverton, Milton Keynes, now house the Stacey Bushes Museum.

Cambridgeshire (21)

Cambridgeshire was a county of few landed estates, the Duke of Bedford's fenland possessions being one of the most significant. Apart from Wimpole Hall, all documented farmsteads date from the middle years of the nineteenth century. Those built by the Duke of Bedford on the Thorney level result from the improvement of drainage by the 1840s. They include such innovations as steam engines, sliding doors and hit-and-miss ventilator windows.[12] Similar buildings are illustrated by Denton at Woodhouse and Rectory Farm, Ely, built for the Ecclesiastical Commissioners and at Buckden built for Colonel Lynton by Peter Purves.[13] Chancellor also worked in the county and a fine set of his buildings survives unaltered in Graffham.[14] An unusually late example is the farm designed in 1937 for H. D. Watson by R. T Perry and partners. It is of wooden construction, built around a courtyard to house a dairy herd and breeding mares for Suffolk Punch horses. It now houses the offices of Thriplow Farms, Ltd.[15] The National Trust's rare breeds farm at Wimpole Hall is centred around the farmstead built in the 1790s to the designs of Sir John Soane.
Figures 63, 77.

Cheshire (58)

Cheshire was a county with a large number of landowners of over 3,000 acres (32) and over a third of its area in estates of over 10,000 acres in 1871. There were several wealthy estates in the county, including those of Lord Tollemache, the Warburton family, Lord Crewe, and the Duke of Westminster, as well as many smaller estates bought by the *nouveaux riches* with wealth made in commerce or industry. The increase in the importance of dairying during the nineteenth century, particularly of liquid milk after 1870, also contributed to the above-average density of model farmsteads.

The finest Georgian farmstead in the county is that at Doddington, designed by Samuel Wyatt for the Broughton estate. With a central barn and radiating livestock sheds, it is of an innovatory layout pioneered by Wyatt.[16] In the early years of the nineteenth century the Daintry family rebuilt five farmsteads in the parish of North Rode, where they were accumulating estates. They are all of a similar U or L-plan with porched barns.[17] An early documented dairying farmstead, at Liscard, was recorded in the *Farmers' Magazine* for 1848. A barn equipped with steam power working a ten horse-power engine worked threshing, winnowing and dressing machines as well as cake crushers, hay steamers and corn drying. It stood behind a yard divided by four ranges of single-depth cow sheds to house eighty cows. In all the buildings covered four acres and were a credit to their architect, Mr Torr of Lincolnshire and an example for others to follow.[18] The plan of a huge complex at Crouchley Hall, Lymm, was published by George Dean in 1850: much of it survives. The barn machinery was steam driven and there were tramways for moving feed to sheep, pigs and cows.[19] Hall Farm, Tattenhall, is one of two Cheshire farmsteads illustrated by Denton. It housed eighty cows in a long building with central feeding passage between a double row of stalls. Connected to the cow house by a root store was an open-sided hay barn (although Denton described it as for corn).[20] Broxton Farm is also illustrated by Denton. It is on a smaller scale and served a 75-acre holding. A long rear building contained a barn and stable with a central cow house at right angles for twenty cows.[21] A distinctive group of small dairy farmsteads are those built for the Tollemache estate, mainly in Peckforton, Baddiley and Spurstow. Typically they conform to L-plan with one side housing cows with hay store above and the other, a small barn, stable and cart sheds.[22] John Douglas was employed by the Westminster estate where he completely redesigned at least eight farmsteads. Wrexham Road Farm, Ecclestone and Cheaveley Hall, Huntington, are the finest examples of his work.

Two farmsteads, both managed by the National Trust, are open to the public: Home Farm, at Tatton Park, a late-eighteenth-century farmstead built for Lord Egerton, and Home Farm, Dunham Massey, a courtyard farm of 1822 with a central dovecote.
Figures 91, 92, 93, 94, 95; Plates 20, 21.

Cornwall (22)

Although there were 35 estates of over 3,000 acres in Cornwall in 1871, only a minority are known to have undertaken extensive improvements to the buildings of their farmsteads. Contemporaries agreed that the major period of agricultural development in the county did not begin until after the Napoleonic Wars,[23] and the building evidence would support this. The finest example is the showpiece of Trebartha Barton, built by the Rodd family who owned most of the parish of North Hill. Cornish courtyard farms were often on a small scale, (one plan published by Worgan in his *General View* of 1811 was for a farm of only 45 acres) [24] indicating the low acreages and pastoral nature of the farms. Many were powered by water, emphasising both the shortage of labour in a county where tin extraction was so important, and also the technical skills which had been developed for powering pumps in the mines. Ford Farm, St Cleer, illustrated by Denton,[25] was built to serve a farm of 188 acres which, typically for the area, was created by the amalgamation of small holdings. The buildings consisted of cattle sheds placed around a yard with sheds for storing feed. The barn, with water-powered machinery, was at first-floor level above cattle sheds. Because there was a shortage of straw, the cattle were all fed under cover with the dung being stored in a walled area in the middle of the yard.

The Mucklow family undertook ambitious improvements in the parish of Pound-stock and Whitstone in the 1880s. Penfold Farm, Poundstock, has impressive buildings around a yard, including a covered dung store, whilst The Barton, Whitstone is a simpler courtyard design. The Duchy of Cornwall rebuilt farmsteads in North Hill in the late-nineteenth century, mostly U-plan groups for livestock. The Rogers family built courtyard farmsteads in the Helston area, of which Methleigh Farm, just to the west of Porthleven and sited in a regular grid of fields contrasting with irregular and anciently-enclosed field boundaries around it, is the finest example.
Plate 7.

Cumbria (22)

The old counties of Cumberland and Westmorland were never areas of great estates, being generally dominated by independent yeoman or 'statesmen' farmers. One of the largest landowners in Cumberland was Sir James Graham with 30,000 acres centred on Netherby, near the Scottish border. Over the years 1820 to 1850, farms were consolidated to holdings of between 300 and 400 acres and new stone and slate farmsteads built.[26] The most publicised farmstead (much of which survives) was the Home Farm at Schoose, built by J. C. Curwen of Workington. Curwen achieved publicity through his writings, particularly on the feeding of cattle, and his farm was seen as an experimental one as well as the home for the Workington agricultural shows. The eccentric 11th Duke of Norfolk, with his architect, Francis Hiorne of Warwick, was responsible for several castellated farmsteads near his park at Greystoke and a fine planned farmstead was built near the castle in 1836. The buildings of Lord Frederick Cavendish, erected in about 1800 at Flookborough as part of his scheme to reclaim the moss in the edge of Moorcombe Bay have now been converted to residential use.[27] The Lowther estate produced elaborate plans for farmsteads between 1797 and 1815, but only a few – mostly still in farming use – were executed.[28] Much of William Lawson's farmstead at Blennerhassett survives intact and is the visual evidence for his mid-century agricultural and social experiments.

Figures 13, 30, 48, 80, 85; Plate 6.

Derbyshire (11)

Although there were 27 owners of more than 3,000 acres in 1871, this is not a county with many model farmsteads. One of the earliest is that by Robert Adam for Lord Scarsdale at Ireton, Kedleston, Weston Underwood and built between 1815 and 1817.[29] It is now owned by the National Trust. The most interesting group are those built by the Strutt family around Belper in the early-mid nineteenth century. Later examples include the Duke of Devonshire's Home Farm at Chatsworth which was built in 1840 to designs of Decimus Burton[30] and is open to the public. The Home Farm at Shipley, was designed by W. E. Nesfield in 1861 and is now converted to housing.[31]

Figures 22, 23, 26, 46, 47; Plate 10.

Devon (43)

Devon was a county with one of the highest number of landowners over 3,000 acres listed in 1871 (59). A farmstead at Tor Royal was built as part of plans to reclaim Dartmoor by the Duchy of Cornwall in the 1790s 'as an example for others to follow'[32] and in 1796 Lord Heathfield employed William Marshall to design a farmstead for him at Buckland of which only one building remains.[33] A further eighteenth-century example, built for the Killerton estate, survives on the National Trust property at Broadclyst. Sir Lawrence Palk's plan and elevations for his Home Farm at Haldon, appear in Vancouver's report on the county of 1808[34] but this interest seems to have been a rarity at the time. 'A good homestead is rarely to be met with', wrote Henry Tanner in his report on Devonshire in the *Journal of the Royal Society of England* in 1848. Three years later, Caird also reported that there were many landlords who left the upkeep of rickety old buildings entirely to their tenants.[35] The main reason for this lack of interest was probably the small size of many of the farms, the great majority being below 200 acres. Most model farmsteads are mid-nineteenth century in date, those erected by the Duke of Bedford on his Tavistock and Milton Abbot estate being the most impressive. Not only did they include covered yards and dung pits, but water or horse-powered barn machinery. The finest example is that at Kilworthy, near Tavistock with a huge water wheel reminiscent of those found working pumping machinery in the near-by mines. Both the Clinton-Devon estate, extending to 14,000 acres, and the huge Rolle estate, covering 47,000, were owned by the Rolle family. Many of their farmsteads around East Budleigh and

Otterton were rebuilt from the 1860s, plans of these courtyard steadings surviving in the estate office.
Figures 75, 76; Plates 17, 18.

Dorset (4)

The variety of soils in Dorset has resulted in several different farming regions. These range from light chalk soils, much of it downland which was not cultivated until the mid-nineteenth century and most suited to a sheep-corn system, to heavier clays where dairying was more important, as well as some areas of heath of little agricultural use. Enclosure of the chalk areas was accompanied by the building of new farmsteads, particularly on the estates of Lords Rivers, Portman and Westminster, as well as those of Mr Sturt and the Duke of Bedford.[36] Steam power was often included in these new designs. However, while these estates have left their mark on the Dorset landscape with distinctive architecture, the building of new planned or model farmsteads appears to have been very uncommon.

Durham (9)

Only 17 owners of more than 3,000 acres were recorded in 1871, which confirms the view of Thomas Bell who wrote in 1856 that the prevalence of small properties which were frequently changing hands was one of the reasons for the lack of progress in the county.[37] Caird supported Bell's view of the backwardness of agriculture in the county.[38] Farm buildings were said in general to be below the standard of those elsewhere. There were obvious exceptions; indeed, Garrett's book of farm plans was aimed at the county of Durham as well as Northumberland. At Raby are two early examples of planned farmsteads, both built about 1755 for the Earl of Darlington who was probably actively involved in their designs, although Garrett also influenced the design of Hill Farm which was built around a courtyard behind the house. One wing has been demolished. The Home Farm is hidden behind a spectacular Gothic screen and consists of a U-plan range of buildings. At Rokeby is another eighteenth-century planned farmstead, and a cow house designed by Sir John Soane in 1783–4 stands at Burn Hall, near Durham. It has recently been restored. The only example of a mid-nineteenth-century farmstead so far recorded in the county was designed for Mr Laycock at Tanfield by John Ewart, who submitted his plans to the *Journal of the Royal Society of England* competition of 1850.[39] However, this has not been located.

The Home Farm at Beamish, which has changed little in layout since the 1790s, is now part of the Open Air Museum.
Figure 21.

Essex (37)

It was not until the development of dairy farming providing liquid milk for the London market, that full advantage of the county's proximity to the metropolis was taken. There are fine examples of early-medieval timber-framed farm buildings in this county and the lack of building stone meant that timber remained the main material used. Frequently it was provided by the landlord, it being left to the tenant to erect his own buildings. Indeed landlords in general were described as being short of money and taking little interest in their tenants.[40] Lord Petre was an exception to this rule, and his buildings at Thorndon Hall are an early example of Samuel Wyatt's work, being designed in 1777. The large number of model farmsteads recorded in the county is explained in part by the plans of the mid-to-late-nineteenth-century architect, Frederick Chancellor, which survive in Essex Record Office: 27 of these were for Essex farms. Several of these are still standing although some have been converted to other uses: one at Rivenhall, built in 1856,[41] is now a leisure centre. Ongar Park Farm, Stanford Rivers, a Chancellor Farm of 1854 built for the Capel Cure estate, was remodelled as a dairy farm in 1884 by Primrose McConnell.[42] McConnell was typical of many west-country Scots who moved to Essex as dairy farmers in the 1880s. High rents and a shortage of farms had driven them south to form what was known as the 'Scotch Colony' around Ongar, Brentwood and Chelmsford. He became a vocal advocate of improved dairying methods and the eastern region reporter for the Royal Commission on Agricultural Depression of 1894–96.

Figures 28, 63, 99; Plates 12, 13, 14.

Gloucestershire (29)

Gloucestershire's contrasting landscapes include the light soils of the Cotswolds, not enclosed until the nineteenth century, and the heavier soils of the Vale of Evesham and the Severn Valley, more suited to dairy farming. One of the earliest courtyard groups located in this study is at Taynton House Farm where three late-seventeenth-century blocks – stable, barn and cowhouse – are on three sides of a yard behind the house. Generally it was not until the early-nineteenth century that landlords took much interest in improving buildings. One of the most dramatic examples was Home Farm at Sezincote, built in 1800–1805 to the designs of Samuel Cockerill for his brother, Sir Charles Cockerill, as part of his Indian-style extravaganza.[43] The house and gardens are open at certain times during the summer, but the farm is not.

In 1839 Lord Ducie's agent, John Morton set up Whitfield Example Farm at Cromhall. Within its rectangular fields, the farm buildings included a steam engine and barns with cattle yards behind.[44] As late as 1850 – when Lewis Vulliamy was at work on Home Farm at Westonbirt,[45] now successfully converted into housing – much remained to be done in the county. There was a lack of cattle accommodation meaning that cattle were still wintered in the fields in some areas.[46] College Farm, just to the west of Cirencester, was built in about 1845 for the new agricultural college as a model farmstead. It was provided with covered yards with slatted floors for sheep, boxes and stalls for cattle, tramways and a steam engine for thrashing. It has been converted into offices.[47] Maisemore Farm is an E-plan group, built in 1860 for the Church Commissioners and was illustrated by Denton.[48] It has now been converted to offices.

Figures 7, 81; Plate 4.

Hampshire (27)

Although there were about 60 landowners of over 3,000 acres in the county in 1871, there are few model farmsteads. Caird noted in 1851 that farm buildings were badly arranged and in poor repair. 'Landlords have given little attention to the wants of their tenants, and their agents have failed to perform a most important part of their duties'.[49] By the 1860s, the situation had improved slightly with rebuilding programmes on Lord Palmerston's New Forest estate at Broadlands, illustrated by Denton in 1864.[50] The Nicholson family were using some of their gin wealth to rebuild farms in the 1860s around their seat at Basing Park.[51] Two examples of the innovatory use of concrete are to be found at Grange Farm in Ashburton, built in 1878 and on the Peterson estate at Sway.

Herefordshire (17)

This is a pastoral county not associated with great estates. Its few model farmsteads place emphasis on cattle accommodation, as at Moccas, built 1783–84, where huge open-fronted hay stores occupy the upper floors above stables and cattle sheds,[52] and at Downton Castle and Uphampton Farm, both illustrated by Denton in the 1860s.[53] This emphasis on cattle accommodation is further emphasised by the early interest in covered yards to be found in the region.
Figures 61, 86.

Hertfordshire (25)

Like many counties near London, Hertfordshire never contained many major landed estates. Frederick Chancellor was responsible for two designs, and Denton designed his own farmstead for his farm at Manor Farm, Chisfield.[54] Because of its proximity to the London consumer market, the county is unusual for the number of late (post 1900) model (mostly dairy) farms and in particular those providing for the new food industries such as Ovaltine.[55]
Figure 102.

Isle of Wight (6)

There are two distinctive and important classes of model farmstead on the Isle of Wight. First, there is Norris Castle Farm, built for Lord Henry Seymour in *c.* 1798. It is a striking structure, hidden behind its castellated front with turrets at each corner. Symmetrically arranged around two yards, it is perhaps the grandest example of the open court layout generally accepted by the 1790s.[56] Secondly there are the model farmsteads created in the 1850s by Prince Albert on Queen Victoria's Osborne estate. Two, Alverstone and Barton Manor in Whippingham, are described and illustrated in J. C. Morton's book on the Prince Consort's farms. Alverstone is a small 'U'-shaped plan cattle unit and Barton Manor consisted of two open yards and a barn containing machinery powered by steam.[57]

Kent (21)

Although there were 57 owners of more than 3,000 acres in Kent in 1871, the small farm remained typical of the county and model farmsteads are not common. The most significant was Lord Torrington's farm at West Peckham, built in 1845 and described as 'without parallel in the county'.[58] Cattle were tied along six rows of mangers in a covered shed. The barn was powered by an underground shaft connected to a horse engine. The architect, George Devey was active in the county in the last quarter of the nineteenth century, designing farms at Cliffs End for Lord Granville and Penshurst for Viscount Harding as well as the Home Farm at Leigh.[59]

Lancashire (8)

Lancashire was generally regarded as a county of backward agriculture, and there were few planned or model farmsteads. Those who made money in industry chose to leave the area and invest in land elsewhere.[60] Indeed, in 1871 there were only 21 owners of more than 3,000 acres. J. Binns illustrated four farmsteads in 1851, all on a courtyard layout with open yards and drainage systems into liquid manure tanks.[61]
Figure 56.

Leicestershire (6)

There is very little evidence for model farmsteads in Leicestershire. Although there were some large estates such as those of the Duke of Rutland, Lord Stamford, Earl Howe and Lord Maynard, the majority of land was held by owner-occupiers of between 50 and 500 acres. Two-thirds of the county was pasture in 1851 [62] and farms commanded high rents without the landlord being obliged to invest in them. Where rents were lower, it was on the understanding that the tenant took on all the responsibility for improvement. Caird commented that the result was poorly drained land with inadequate buildings, and he regretted this lack of interest in improvement on the part of landlords.[63] Castle Farm at Belvoir contains a fine dairy designed about 1810 for the Duke of Rutland by James Wyatt.[64]

Lincolnshire (42)

Landed estates were an important feature of many parts of Lincolnshire, and some of them were very large. The Duke of Yarborough owned 55,000 acres, Henry Chaplin 23,000 acres, Christopher Turnor 20,000 acres, the Earl of Dysart 18,000 acres and the Marquis of Bristol 13,000 acres. All of them were responsible for extensive reclamation schemes in association with the building of some impressive farmsteads. Those of the Duke of Yarborough were built on reclaimed and newly enclosed land around Brocklesby in the 1770s and 80s. The Yarborough estates continued with the building of new steadings in the early-nineteenth century, one notable surviving example being Swallow Grange, built in 1826 around two yards. The buildings at Hall Farm, Blankney for the Chaplin family were designed by W. A. Nicholson in the early-nineteenth century and further reclamation resulted in new farms on the heath at Temple Farm, Scopwick Lodge, Thompsons Bottom and Green Man Farm.

Other farmsteads were built after 1850, particularly those for the Turnor estate and the Earl of Dysart which illustrate the gradual change in emphasis in farming practice. The distinctive Turnor design of the 1850s and 1860s, with stock divided from the outer U-plan of buildings by a walkway, was illustrated by Denton.[65] By the 1880s, when the Dysart estate was building, covered yards were thought to be more suitable and again a distinctive design with a central feeding passage between two covered yards was developed.
Figures 38, 72, 73, 96.

Norfolk (22)

Norfolk was a county famous for both its agricultural improvement and the publicity given to this by its great landowners, who were responsible for building a variety of model farmsteads across the county. The earliest (dating from the mid-eighteenth century) are those by William Kent at Houghton Hall, built on a two-storey cross plan with single-storey infills. Later are the semi-circular stable and barn blocks at Costessey Hall attributed to Sir John Soane.

The landowner whose name is inextricably linked with agricultural improvement in Norfolk is Thomas William Coke of Holkham who, in the 1790s, employed Samuel Wyatt to work on his estate buildings. He was responsible for the Great Barn at Holkham as well as the tenanted farmstead of Leicester Square and one for a small neighbouring estate at Crompton Hall. Two farmsteads of the 1830s include the Home Farm at Stratton Strawless, built as a dairy farm with a north-facing colonnade in front of the dairy,[66] and buildings at Starston Hall, illustrated by Loudon in 1844.[67] There are also several mid-century planned farmsteads, such as the remarkable buildings at Bylaugh, with covered yards, suggesting that improvement in the county was in no way limited to the early years of the century, but continued after Coke's lifetime.
Figures 11, 49, 52, 53, 54, 63, 65, 66.

Northamptonshire (63)

Northamptonshire was a county dominated by large estates. Nearly a third of the area was in estates of over 10,000 acres and there were 38 owners of more than 3,000 acres in 1871. However, according to Caird, 'many of them have no interest in their farms beyond the annual rent they receive, know nothing of the management of land themselves and do not employ an agent who does.' As a result 'their tenants, from deficient buildings and want of drainage are incapacitated from doing justice to their farms'.[68] There were of course exceptions to this general picture. The Spencers of Althorpe were well known for their interest in improvements, the third Earl Spencer being the first President of the Royal Agricultural Society of England. The Duke of Grafton was also influential, and in the 1830s erected well-planned sets of buildings on several of his farms. G. A. Dean was responsible for a set of buildings at Milton in the 1850s. The layout provided four open yards and one long bullock shed for tying stock.[69] His book (see p. 133) influenced the layout of Warren Farm, Aynho, built in 1848–52 for the Cartwright estate and dominated by its tall chimney.

A charming and unusual example of a *ferme ornée*, not built until the beginning of the twentieth century, survives at Aston Wold. It is in local vernacular style on a miniature scale and contains a dairy and cow stalls, stable, and poultry house around a small yard beside a pond.

Figures 57, 100.

Northumberland (78)

Northumberland was not only a county with a large number (58) of landowners of over 3,000 acres; it was also famous for agricultural improvement in the nineteenth century. The laying out of many new farms, often covering over 500 acres, involved much new building. The earliest include two farmsteads in the parish of Capheaton for the Swinburne estate and said to be designed by Daniel Garrett in the mid-eighteenth century. Plans by Garrett for a farm dated 1746 in Wallington, on Sir Walter Blackett's estate, show a simple courtyard design with the farmhouse on one side.[70] Cocklaw East, on the Beaufort estate, was designed by John Green of Newcastle in 1824 and the plans published by Loudon in 1833.[71] Green's plans for Newnham Barns show a huge farmstead with five yards and a barn in the centre.[72] The Duke of Northumberland was responsible for rebuilding farmsteads in the Alnwick area between 1805 and 1833. Four farmsteads, including the Home Farm, were designed by David Stephenson. In the 1840s John Grey was working for the Greenwich Hospital estates and his designs for a farmstead at Throckley (now in Tyne and Weare) were published in the *Journal of the Royal Society of England* in 1843. They show a conventional U-plan range divided into four cattle yards with pig sties under the front wall and a barn with a horse-engine house abutting behind. Similar plans for a steading in Outchester show the barn powered by a waterwheel. Water, horse or steam-powered barn machinery was part of the plan for many of these farms, in an area where mining and industry meant there was often a shortage of labour.[73]

Planned farmsteads continued to be built until the end of the century. As elsewhere, covered yards were adopted by the 1860s. Kilham Farm, in the parish of Thornington on the Tankerville estate, has a layout almost identical to that published under the name of 'Experimentia' in the *Journal of the Royal Society of England* in 1879. As late as 1913 A. D. Hall could write, in his *Pilgrimage of British Farming*: 'The most striking feature of Northumberland farming ... is the magnitude and excellence of the farm buildings – great blocks of well-built stone structures, dominated by a very factory-like

chimney',[74] features which can be seen north of the border through the southern uplands and Lothian counties of Scotland.
Figures 36, 37, 38, 39, 71; Plate 8.

Nottinghamshire (14)

Nottinghamshire, particularly the northern part, was dominated by large estates with 38 per cent of the land in the hands of owners of more than 10,000 acres. Of these, the Duke of Portland was described by Caird as 'one of the largest and best landlords in the kingdom', having been responsible for tile-draining much of his estate at his own expense. Few other Nottinghamshire landlords had either the means 'or the same taste for agricultural improvements'. As a result, farm buildings were 'imperfect and incommodious'.[75] Certainly, this is not a county of many model farmsteads. The earliest are those of Sir Thomas Parkyns on his estates in Bradmore and Bunny. In the 1720s and 30s, he rebuilt estate farmhouses and provided them with fine brick barns, but there is no evidence of fully planned farmyards. Unlike many other examples, these new farmsteads were built to serve open field farms and were not part of a process of enclosure.

Arthur Young commented on a group at Papplewick, which originated as a cotton mill and in 1783 were converted into farm buildings.[76] The most striking of the nineteenth century groups are the Gothic-style buildings at Kelham to the west of Newark and very visible from the main road to Mansfield. They were designed by Gilbert Scott for John Manners-Sutton of Kelham Hall.
Figure 12.

Oxfordshire (16)

Oxfordshire was not a county noted for agricultural improvement. Only on the light soils of the west was land held in large estates. Few of the landlords showed much interest in agriculture and their estates were run by agents with little knowledge of farming.[77] The earliest architect-designed farm buildings are the cattle shelters by William Kent as part of his landscaping at Rousham Park. They open onto pastures at the back and support a garden seat on the garden side. They have more relevance to the development of garden design than to farm buildings. Of much more significance is Lord Radnor's model farm at Coleshill which survives with remarkably few alterations (Figure 104). Planned by Edward Wells Moore, the Third Earl of Radnor's land agent for the Coleshill estate, it was built in 1852–4 under the supervision of the London architect George Lamb, who drew up the detailed plans and specification. The design provided ample cattle accommodation as well as piggeries and sheep feeding sheds with slatted floors. There is a covered manure house and tramways for delivering feed. Power was provided by a portable steam engine. They now serve as estate offices for the National Trust.[78] In 1857 Lord Macclesfield built a model dairy farm on his Shirburn estate, which still survives. Stonehill Farm, its exterior elevations designed by William Wilkinson of Oxford, had both open and closed yards and a steam engine to power farm and estate yard machinery.[79] At Buscot are the remains of the concrete buildings erected in 1869 for Robert Campbell, a wealthy Australian entrepreneur, as well as a farmstead designed by Frederick Chancellor for Lobbs Farm, Tetworth, the plans of which are in Essex Record Office.[80]
Figures 64, 104.

Shropshire (18)

Over 20% of Shropshire was in estates of more than 10,000 acres in 1871. The Marquis of Stafford, owning 17,000 acres, was one of those most interested in

FIGURE 104.
The Home Farm at
Coleshill, Oxfordshire.
(*The Builder*)

improvement. With the help of his agent, James Loch, he was responsible for draining, enclosing and amalgamating farms as well as building new farmsteads. Nine of those built between 1811 and 1820 were illustrated in Loch's book on the improvements, published in 1820. They all contained one or two yards, typically surrounded by a barn, shelter sheds, stables and cow byres. In some cases there was a paved way between the central yard and the buildings, and a few farmsteads had either steam or water-powered barn machinery. Although the buildings are plain and functional, many of the houses have the overhanging eaves of 'rustic' architecture. Of the later examples, the most impressive is that at Apley Park, built in 1875 with an ornate chimney and two covered yards roofed using huge laminated timber trusses for support.

The Attingham estate was built up gradually from 1700 and Attingham Hall built in 1782. Most of the farms were over 300 acres, and although the farms at Cronkhill, Berrington and Lower Betton were rebuilt in the late-eighteenth or early-nineteenth century, the fields were not rationalised. The home farm was partly rebuilt in the 1850s, but like most of the other steadings on the estate was not rebuilt as a model farmstead.[81]

Figures 2, 44, 45, 68, 69; Plate 15.

Somerset (26)

About a fifth of Somerset was held in estates of more than 10,000 acres in 1871, but, with the notable exception of the rich soils of the Vale of Taunton, this was a pastoral county of mainly small farms. However a few were built in the area around Bristol, where those with merchant-based wealth tended to settle, the most impressive of which was Eastwood Manor Farm in East Harptree. Home farm, Tyntesfield is a fine example of a late-nineteenth-century farmstead with covered yards for dairy cattle. It was built between 1881–83 for the Gibbs family whose wealth had been made in trade and

218

banking. The other main group of farmsteads were the fifteen created by Frederick Knight on Exmoor in the 1840s as part of his reclamation.
Figures 78, 98; Plate 19.

Staffordshire (88)

Over 30% of Staffordshire was recorded as being held in estates of over 10,000 acres in the 1871 census; and although only 33 landowners of more than 3,000 acres are listed, many of them were prominent improvers. These include the Marquis of Stafford, with lands both in Shropshire and Staffordshire, the Ansons (later Lords Lichfield) of Shugborough where Samuel Wyatt designed several farmsteads, and the Littleton estate at Penkridge and Teddesley where at least five were rebuilt at the end of the eighteenth century. Lord Bagot of Blythefield Hall spent £85,000 on 35 steadings between 1863 and 1893. Industrialists such as the Bass family of brewers also moved into the countryside, and in this case built farmsteads in the parish of Rangemoor. All periods of model farm building are well represented with several good eighteenth-century examples. The most spectacular is the group at Old Hall, Betley, built for Coke of Holkham's friend, George Tollett. It was on three levels, built into a hillside with water-powered barn machinery. Other more typical classical-style planned farmsteads include those at Sandon dated 1782. One of the finest groups is that at Shugborough, designed by Samuel Wyatt and housing the county agricultural museum. It exported cheese via the Trent and Mersey Canal to Birmingham, in addition to supplying Shugborough Hall. The stream that powered the threshing machine at Whitebarn Farm barn that also survives, continued over the railway to irrigate the kitchen gardens before filling the pond at Home Farm.[82] Seven plans for Staffordshire farmsteads were included in Loch's book on the improvements of the Marquis of Stafford. They were all built around one or two yards with barn machinery powered by water or horse-power. There are also examples of later model farmsteads. Greenhill Farm, Chebsy is dated 1857 and was primarily for milking cows with a barn over the cow house and machinery powered by a steam engine. Lawnhead Farm, Ellenhall, on the Litchfield estate is dated 1863 and is a U-plan group with a steam engine house.[83] Dunston Hall, Penkridge, built in 1870, has a wide cow house between two yards. Again in Penkridge, Drayton Manor was built in 1851 for the Littleton estate with a steam engine house and impressive buildings around a yard.[84]
Figures 27, 43, 44; Plates 1, 2, 3.

Suffolk (20)

Suffolk is traditionally an area of small farms, and except for Breckland in the west, was mostly enclosed early, so there were not the opportunities for reclamation and the creation of new farmsteads that existed in some other counties. However, the few planned and model farmsteads located cover a wide range of date and style. The earliest were built by the Duke of Norfolk at Fornham St Genevieve, and St Martin on the edge of the sandy brecks, where two similar farmsteads surround yards with the farm house on one side.[85] Both farmsteads have huge barns with two or three threshing floors, emphasising the fact that corn was hand threshed and mechanisation came to the county late. Three farmsteads date from the mid-nineteenth century. New buildings at Holton Hall are mentioned in Morton's *Farmer's Calendar* of 1864 and one at Broome is illustrated by Denton. In 1867 an impressive steading was built at Combs by the Webb family, whose wealth had been made in the local tannery. The yard is entered through an archway which led to a central walkway between two yards, the cattle yard on one side was covered while the horse yard was not. The pride the

family took in their farm is indicated by the fact that it was illustrated on the tannery bill head. It has recently been converted for housing. A notable late-nineteenth-century example is the Home Farm at Culford, remodelled by Lord Cadogan in the 1890s as a dairy farm. Model Farm, Easton was rebuilt in 1875 for the 12th Duke of Hamilton with a striking ornamental dairy. It is now a farm park. Finally, in the 1930s the Rothschild estate rebuilt the derelict village of Rushbrook and built a model farm there. It is a thatched dairy farmstead on a courtyard plan.
Figures 11, 97.

Surrey (28)

Caird described the farming of Surrey as being amongst some of the most backward in England, with a lack of capital being invested by landlord and tenant alike.[86] Farm buildings were rickety and land undrained, and it has remained an area with few planned and model farmsteads. Nearly all the recorded examples were built after Caird's visit. Home Farm at Albury, for example, was built for the Drummond estate in 1876, and its steam engine house survives.

Greater Felcourt Farm, Felcourt is a late example of a planned farmstead. Built between 1908–1914 for Hubert Sturdy it consisted of two covered yards within an E-planned farmstead. It was based on two prize-winning designs submitted to the Royal Agricultural Society competition of 1908. Of particular interest, however, was the experimental work that was carried out in 'electro-culture' on the farm. The theory was that by passing an electric current through wires suspended above the surface of a field the crops were induced to grow more quickly and luxuriantly. Although the electricity appeared to have some affect on rates of growth it was clearly not economical and the idea was finally dropped.[87]

Sussex

East Sussex (5)

Just under a quarter of Sussex was in estates of over 10,000 acres, and large farms were concentrated on the chalk soils rather than in the more pastoral Weald. Only a few model farms have been located in East Sussex, one notable surviving example being Sheffield Park in Fletchling, set around a yard with horse-powered barn machinery and designed by James Wyatt for Lord Sheffield in 1808.[88]

West Sussex (12)

The three main estates in this area are the Duke of Richmond's Goodwood estate, the Duke of Norfolk's Arundel estate and the Earl of Egremont's Petworth estate, all of which contain planned farmsteads. Stag Park Farm at Petworth, although incomplete, survives as a very impressive example, built around two yards. The farm which survives was created in 1782 out of a formerly wooded stag park. The Arundel farmsteads were built between 1837 and 1845 to courtyard plans. Later individual buildings within the park are of interest in that their roof trusses are of laminated wood.[89]

Warwickshire (7)

Although as many as 37 landowners with more than 3,000 acres were recorded in 1871, there were few model farmsteads built in this mainly pastoral area. The earliest example located is an early-nineteenth-century group at Haselor consisting of barn, granary, cart lodge, stable, loose boxes and piggeries. In 1854–6 Trinity College built a model farmstead for the Earl of Denbigh at Pastures Farm, Pailton,[90] and in 1867

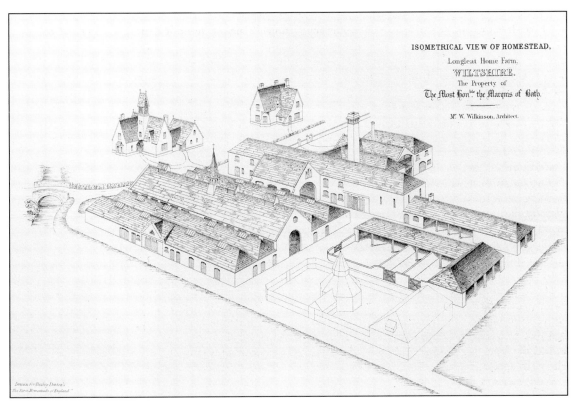

ISOMETRICAL VIEW OF HOMESTEAD,

Longleat Home Farm.

WILTSHIRE,

The Property of

The Most Honble the Marquis of Bath.

Mr W. Wilkinson, Architect.

FIGURE 105.

The Home Farm at
Longleat, Wiltshire.
(*The Builder*)

Dean published the plans of a farm he had designed for Mr Brooks near Leamington.[91]
The late-eighteenth-century Home Farm at Sandwell in West Bromwich, originally
built for the Earl of Dartmouth, is now the centre of farm park. The buildings, with
four pavilions to a U-plan, provide the setting for a farm museum and studies centre.[92]

Wiltshire (32)

Wiltshire is a county of contrasts, with small owner occupiers on the clay soils to the
north and large landowners concentrated on the chalks to the south, much of which
was open downland until the late-eighteenth century. There were forty landowners
with more than 3,000 acres in 1871. It would seem that they nearly all built planned
farmsteads, especially on their large, often newly-enclosed downland holdings. To the
west of Salisbury the Wilton, the Dinton and the Fonthill estates dominate the area.
On the heavier soils dairying was more important and this is reflected in the buildings.
Examples date from the eighteenth century, but by far the majority date from the
mid-nineteenth. Denton illustrated the elaborate set, designed by Wilkinson for
Longleat in 1860, containing a steam-engine house and covered yards costing £7000
(Figure 105).[93] He also reproduced plans of the much less expensive, although highly
decorative Italianate Bremerton Farm on the Earl of Pembroke's estates which was the
result of the influence of the eleventh Earl's Russian wife, Catherine Woronzov.[94] The
Earl owned 39,000 acres around Wilton and was responsible for a great deal of
building. Farms of 500 acres covered meadowland in the valleys as well as arable
chalkland, and so both dairying and cereals were catered for in his farm buildings. A
surplus of labour in the county meant generally that there was little incentive to
mechanise. The Neeld family built up their estates from 1828 around the village of

Grittleton in the north of the county and rebuilt most of the farms in the 1850s. They were mixed light land farms of between 150 and 300 acres. All contained large barns with opposing threshing doors for flail threshing.
Figures 79, 105

Worcestershire (12)
Worcestershire was a mainly county of small farms and so it is not surprising that it was an area with few model farms. The most impressive is that at Bredon Fields, Strensham, built in 1851, an extensive, complex plan with a later covered yard.

Yorkshire
Figures 19, 20, 40, 41, 42, 59, 70; Plates 5, 9.

East Riding of Yorkshire (47)
This was an area of large estates, many of which were owned by enthusiastic improvers, responsible between them for the enclosure of the Wolds and the creation of a formal rectilinear landscape of hedged fields. The most famous was Sir Christopher Sykes on his estates around Sledmere, where a fine group late-eighteenth-century farmsteads survive. Other owners such as the Duke of Devonshire around Middleton and Sir John Hotham at Lockington were also influential. Building continued into the nineteenth century with a farmstead at Sancton Hill being illustrated by Denton. The most impressive example is that built at Enholmes Farm, Patrington in 1849 by William Marshall, a flax spinner from Leeds. This huge complex, with five rows of cattle boxes, demonstrates a transitional stage between boxes in which cattle were stalled and covered yards in which cattle were kept loose. This arrangement with tramways connecting feed stores is similar to that illustrated in 1848 at Prince's Hall on Dartmoor.[95] Another particularly interesting group comprises the farmsteads designed by S. S. Teulon on Sunk Island and built for the Crown Estate around 1856. Only the buildings at Church Farm survive in anything like a complete form but the houses on seven other farms still stand.

North Yorkshire (62)
The old county of Yorkshire was by far the largest county in England. Even allowing for this, the 143 owners of more than 3,000 acres, spread across the three Ridings in 1871, makes it an area with one of the highest concentrations of substantial landowners in the country. The county exhibits a wide range of planned and model farmsteads, and in no other area are there so many dating from the period 1750–90. The most influential architect was John Carr, building farmsteads at Constable Burton in 1767 followed by several for Lord Holderness around the village of Hornby. For all their architectural pretentions, they are laid out on a courtyard plan in a manner publicised by the writings of Garrett. As in the Garrett plans, the house is nearly always incorporated in one side of the farm court. The model farm at Scarthingwell, built in the 1780s for Baron Hawke of Towton, was described by Arthur Young in 1793.[96] The buildings survive around three sides of a yard, with a barn and ox houses along one side and stables on the other two.[97] There is also a group of early-nineteenth-century farmsteads. Demesne and Howdale Farm, Fylingdales, were built in the 1820s. Both are of typical rectangular plan with the house taking up the shorter side. At Howdale the barn is across the opposing shorter end, with a horse-engine house attached, whilst at Demesne Farm the horse-engine is placed within the barn. A decorative dovecote is set above a gateway at Demesne Farm, and this decorative

approach is also found at Griff Farm, Rieveaulx, with a two-storey pyramidal roof granary in the middle of one long wall. By the 1830s, the house was being built away from the yard as at both Griff and nearby Danby Farm. Mid-nineteenth-century farmsteads are also well represented in the county. Examples are Aldborough Farm, Aldborough, 'altogether remodelled on improved principles' in the 1840s by Thomas Rickman for the Duke of Northumberland,[98] and Home Farm, Aldro, built in 1868 for Lord Middleton with two covered yards, a steam-engine house and an elaborate poultry yard. The buildings at White Hall Farm, Stanton Dale, curve back from the house in a way reminiscent of a plan published by Dean for 'A grass farm of 150 acres in extent'.[99] Cowhouses and stables are in the curving wings with yards for sheep, calves and pigs. Although open yards seem to have been the more usual design, covered yards survive at the home dairy farm at Beningborough Park (now owned by the National Trust) and at Birdsall as well as being described at Grinkle Park. Around Kirkleatham (Redcar and Cleveland) and on his west Yorkshire estate of Wombwell, Charles Turner had built new farms 'with convenient barns, stables, cowhouses etc. in the strongest manner'.[100] The landscape around Marske and Kirkleatham retains the strongly linear field pattern of these eighteenth-century enclosures with five planned farmsteads built between 1760 and 1770 by Charles Turner in Kirkleatham parish alone.[101]

South Yorkshire (10)
The work of the Marquis of Rockingham at Wentworth Woodhouse is particularly important in this county. Between 1750 and 1782, under the second Marquis, this estate became one of the most progressive in England, with many of his farms providing the food for the workers in his collieries and other industrial enterprises.[102]

West Yorkshire (28)
This county contains examples of the work of Daniell Garrett and John Carr, particularly on the Harewood estate where the first Lord Harewood employed Carr as estate surveyor to build farmsteads and a new village. Home Farm at Harewood survives as an impressive example of his work, dating from 1805.

223

Notes

Notes to Chapter 1: Beauty, Utility and Profit

1. Quoted in Lake 1989, 100.
2. RA Add 32/2020.
3. Thomas 1983, 254–6.
4. Norfolk Record Office WLS XXL VII/19 415 X 5.
5. Thomas 1983, 254–5.
6. Betham-Edwards 1898, 28; Robinson 1983, 6.
7. Belhaven 1699, Preface.
8. Robinson 1983, 4–10.
9. Daniels and Seymour 1990, 489.
10. Cobbett 1930 edn, III, 181.
11. Young 1771, II, 433.
12. Barrell 1972, 83.
13. He wrote a *History of the Poor* between 1793 and

1794 (Everett 1994, 125).
14. Ruggles 1788, 5–6.
15. Ruggles 1788, 7.
16. Kent 1775, 146.
17. Roberts 1997, 74.
18. Wade Martins 1980, 70.
19. Alnwick MS B/24/1.
20. Copland 1866, I, vii.
21. Browick 1862, 247–269.
22. Andrews 1852, 1, 7.
23. Macdonald 1981, 224.
24. Young 1770, 468–9. For a more general analysis of buildings as social objects see Markus 1993.

Notes to Chapter 2: Landlords, Tenants and the Farming Framework

1. Wade Martins 1990, *passim*.
2. Young 1764, 190.
3. Thirsk 1985, 5, part II, 572.
4. Mingay 1963, 20–21.
5. Wilson and Mackley 2000, 11–46.
6. Allen 1991.
7. Overton 1996, 8.
8. Chartres 1985, 406–501.
9. Caird 1852, 169.
10. Overton 1996, 147.
11. Overton 1996, 170.
12. Clay 1985, 163.
13. Caird 1852, 45.
14. Caird 1852, 49.
15. As defined by Rackham 1986, 4–5.
16. Caird 1852, 74.
17. Young 1771, II, 150.
18. Kent 1796, 123.
19. Bailey and Culley 1813, 23.
20. Caird 1852, 171.
21. Habbakuk 1953, 6, 92–102; Clay 1985, 217 and 228; Wade Martins and Williamson 1998, 127–141.
22. Young 1771, 150.
23. Quoted in Bettey 1993, 103.
24. Thompson 1963, 222.
25. Bailey and Culley 1813, 23.
26. Alnwick MS B/24/1.
27. Holkham MS Letter Books 1827, 86.
28. Young 1770, 468–9.
29. For a reassessment of the role of farmers and landowners in agricultural change, see Wade Martins and Williamson 1999.
30. Barrell 1972, 71.
31. Quoted by Wilmot 1990, 15.
32. Goddard 1983, 117–8.
33. Veliz 1959, esp. 19–27, 279–87.
34. 'A proposal for a Further Improvement of Agriculture by a member of the Bath Society', 1780, quoted by Hudson 1972, 2.
35. Hudson 1972, x–xi.
36. Goddard 1981, I, 246.
37. For the classic statement of this orthodox position see Chambers and Mingay 1966.
38. Wade Martins and Williamson 1999, 180–194.
39. Marshall 1787, I, 2.
40. Young 1813, 8.
41. Wade Martins and Williamson 1999 90–91; Marshall 1787, II, 274–6.
42. For a summary of these arguments, see Allen 1991, 236–254.
43. Marshall 1787, I, 2.
44. Rackham 1986, 1–5.

45. Daniels and Seymour 1990, 487.
46. 'In the landscape of benevolence, the gentleman occupies an estate whose resources are used to stimulate morality as much as prosperity' (Everett 1994, 16, 21).
47. Thirsk 1985, **V**, part II,553.
48. Harrison 1930, 76.
49. Laurence 1727.
50. Laurence 1727, 3.
51. English 1990, 172.
52. Quoted from Adam 1972, **2**, 267.
53. Richards 1973, 26.
54. National Library of Scotland Acc. 10225/58.
55. Robinson 1976, 276–281, 276–7.
56. Hughes 1949, 195.
57. Thompson 1963, 156–9.
58. Wade Martins 1980, 67.
59. English 1984, 29–46.
60. Elliot 1871, Book 1, Chapter 1.
61. Young 1770, 2, 470–473.
62. Lawrence 1801, 100.
63. Royal Archives Addl. MSS Geo 15.
64. PRO Works 44/10.
65. Spring 1963, 46.
66. Harroby MS vol 437, doc. 71, quoted by Appleby 1997, 103.
67. Sneyd MS S1972, quoted by Appleby 1997, 113.
68. Browick 1862, 248.
69. Wade Martins 1980, 79.
70. Brigden 1986, 204.

71. Browick 1862, 247.
72. Lake 1989, 119.
73. Wade Martins 1980, 79.
74. Bateman (final edn) 1883.
75. Thompson 1963, 112.
76. Wilson and Mackley 2000, 7.
77. Wilson and Mackley 2000, 3.
78. Bettey 1993, 130–131.
79. Bailey and Culley 1813, 205.
80. Young 1771, I, 274, 329, 334–5; II, 98–9, 242, 428, 435; III, p. 81.
81. Fletcher 1960–61, 421.
82. Young 1809, 20.
83. Wiliam 1986, 10.
84. Robinson 1983, 113–147.
85. Wiliam 1986, 13, 111, 176 and134.
86. RCAHMS 1967, II, 326–7 and plate 121.
87. Robinson 1983, 148–172; survey in progress by RCAHMS.
88. Cannadine 1995, 7–36.
89. Marchand (ed) 1933.
90. Stuart 1939, 36.
91. Toulier 1997, 204.
92. Information from Christine Toulier.
93. Cross 1980, 57–91.
94. Makhrov 1997, 171–183.
95. Tolstoy 1993 edn, 80.
96. Shvidkovskg 1996, 227–8.
97. Cannadine 1990, 21.
98. Deane 1867.

Notes to Chapter 3: The Philosophy of 'Improvement', 1660–1790

1. Bowden 1985, 118.
2. Clay 1985, 251.
3. Kent 1775, 8–9.
4. Wordie 1983, 483–505.
5. Beckett 1990, 35.
6. Overton 1996, 163.
7. Overton 1996, 165.
8. Markham 1635, 24–26.
9. Airs 1983, 51.
10. North 1988, 2, 15–25; North 1992, 6, 59–66.
11. Colvin and Newman (eds) 1981, 97.
12. Severn 1983, 7, 65–74.
13. Tyson 1979, 85–94.
14. Belhaven 1699, 29–32.
15. Robinson 1983, plate 16.
16. Palladio 1727, book 2, ch. 14.
17. Jones 1968, *passim.*
18. Wade Martins 1980, 148–9.
19. Quoted in Wade Martins 1988, 58.
20. Hunt 1797, 65.
21. Young 1770, II, 450.

22. Young 1770, II, 452.
23. Garrett 1747.
24. Colvin 1978, 332–4.
25. Grundy 1970, 2–5.
26. Newton 1972, 120.
27. Wragg 2000, 39–48.
28. Cited by Daniels and Seymour 1990, 497.
29. Colvin 1978, 610.
30. Robinson 1983, 135; Young 1771, II, 428–40, pls. 6 and 7.
31. Robinson 1983, 26.
32. Curzon MS, Robert Adam to Lord Scarsdale, 31st July 1760.
33. Sir John Soane's Museum, 40 28–30.
34. Sir John Soane's Museum, 42, 113–114.
35. Robinson 1983, 43.
36. Sir John Soane's Museum, 64/6/41.
37. Sir John Soane's Museum, 64/3/89.
38. Dean, 1999, p. 70 (note 21).
39. Colvin 1995, 1124–1128; Samuel Wyatt was studied by J. M. Robinson (1979). Samuel Wyatt's

agricultural buildings have recently been re-assessed by Judith Appleby (1997).

40. Young 1804, 20.
41. Robinson 1979, 35 and 52.
42. Appleby 1997, 1.
43. Appleby 1997, 200–213.
44. Taigel and Williamson 1993, 60; King 1974, 27–60.
45. Repton 1804, 93.
46. Young 1771, II, 329.
47. Robinson 1983, 124.
48. Robinson 1983, 93.
49. Appleby 1994, 27.
50. For a detailed exposition concerning the Whig and Tory views of landscape and 'improvement', see Everett 1994.
51. Williamson 1995, 123, quoting the *Journal of a Tour* by Edward Witts, 1777.
52. Ruggles 1788, 7.
53. Quoted in Loudon 1840, 84–5.
54. Lawrence 1801, 100.
55. Williamson 1995, 123.
56. Curwen 1809, 238.
57. Rowland Hunt 1797, 65.

Notes to Chapter 4: Patriotic Improvement, 1790–1840

1. Royal Archives, *Plan for the Improving of Windsor Great Park* by Nathaniel Kent.
2. Royal Archives, *Plan for the Improving of Windsor Great Park* by Nathaniel Kent.
3. Hunter 1803, 4, 172–188, 174.
4. Kent 1775, 146.
5. Royal Archives, Nathaniel Kent's *Journal*, 1.
6. Royal Archives, Addl. Mss. Geo./15.
7. Sir John Sinclair's speech to Parliament on 15th May, 1793, in *Annals of Agriculture* Vol. XXXI, 1793, 117, 128–143.
8. Overton 1996, 150–151.
9. Marshall 1796, 2, 318–9.
10. Loudon 1825, 426.
11. Loudon 1831, 449.
12. Robinson 1983, 161.
13. Wade Martins 1980, 90.
14. Waistell 1827, 2.
15. Waistell 1827, v.
16. Waistell 1827, plates XI and XII.
17. Waistell 1827, 2.
18. Hunt 1986, 935–966.
19. Wade Martins 1991, 50; Macdonald 1975, 24, 63–77; Hutton 1976, 25, 30–35.
20. Murray 1815, 59–60.
21. Hobsbawn and Rude 1970, 156.
22. Wade Martins and Williamson 1997, 275–295.
23. Tyson 1979, 85–89.
24. Barnwell and Giles 1997, 101.
25. Worgan 1811, 24–26.
26. Harvey 1988, 49–54.
27. Colvin 1978, 480–81.
28. English 1990, 147.
29. Jarrett and Wrathmell 1977, 108–119.
30. Hodgson 1827, 337.
31. Bailey and Culley 1805, 23.
32. Barnwell and Giles 1997, 68.
33. Newton 1972, 127.
34. Caird 1852, 371.
35. Newton 1972, 124.
36. Newton 1972, 173.
37. Newton 1972, 178–180.
38. Cobbett 1930 edn., II, 374–5.
39. Grey 1841, 190–192.
40. Colvin 1978, 779.
41. Alnwick MS B/24/7.
42. Alnwick MSS, uncatalogued.
43. Northumberland Record Office 1204/1–6.
44. Grey 1843, 11–12.
45. Colbeck 1847, 423.
46. Marshall 1788, II, 142: turnips were 'the most solid basis of Wold husbandry'.
47. Allison 1976, 150 and 153.
48. Strickland 1812, 40.
49. English 1990, 190.
50. English 1990, 190.
51. Popham 1986, 128–132.
52. Bannister 1994. I am grateful to Lord Middleton for permission to quote from this survey; Popham 1973.
53. English 1990, 48.
54. Bakewell 1820, 16.
55. Quoted by Richards 1973, 26.
56. Loch 1820, 180–181.
57. Bakewell 1820, 107.
58. Derbyshire Record Office D3772 E25/7.
59. Derbyshire Record Office D3772 E25/6.
60. Derbyshire Record Office D1564.
61. Derbyshire Record Office. Tithe map for Belper (1844) D2360/3/98a; plan by J. C. Hickling (*c.* 1850) D. 1564; roll 26 and plan by J. Beresford (1858) D. 1564, roll 11.
62. Storer 1998.
63. Holden 1990, 13.
64. Curwen 1809, frontispiece.
65. Curwen 1809, 239.
66. Bedfordshire Record Office R5/859/1.
67. Spring 1963, 24.

68. As Alexander Pope's poem, *Imitations of Horace* (2,2, lines 272–3), stated: 'The other slights for Women, Sports and Wines/All Townshend's Turnips and all Grosvenor's Mines'.
69. Parker 1975; Wade Martins 1980.
70. Wade Martins 1980, 94 and 101.

71. Young 1784, 382.
72. Young 1804, 20.
73. Holkham MSS Letter Books 1827, 86.
74. Wade Martins 1980, 132–3.
75. Wilson and Mackley 2000, 133
76. Young 1804, 238.

Notes to Chapter 5: 'Practice with Science', 1840–1875

1. Brockman 1974, 25–41.
2. Wade Martins 1980, 166–9.
3. Mingay 1994, 198.
4. Jenkins 1869, 461–70.
5. Holkham MS, Francis Blaikie (1816) 'Survey of the Holkham estate'.
6. Brigden 1986, 196–7.
7. Read 1858, 278.
8. Parliamentary Papers (1833) *Select Committee on the Present State of Agriculture* V. I qu. 2142.
9. Parliamentary Papers (1847–8) *Select Committee on Tenant Customs* VII, I.
10. Grey 1843, 2.
11. Caird 1852, 490–491.
12. Caird 1852, 97, 191, 301 and 438.
13. Caird 1852, 220.
14. Andrews 1852, 5.
15. Bearn 1852, 85.
16. Northamptonshire Record Office G/4101/1–3.
17. Copland 1866, vii.
18. Caird 1852, 170.
19. Caird 1852, 265.
20. Grey 1843, 3–4.
21. Wade Martins and Williamson 1997, 62.3, 275–295.
22. Hunt 1986, 943–5.
23. Caird 1878, 47.
24. Dean 1851.
25. Denton 1864, 2.
26. Andrews 1852, 6.
27. Pusey 1851, 35.
28. Thompson 1850, 186.
29. Giles 1999.
30. Spooner and Elliott 1850, 278.
31. Hobbs 1853, 325–6.
32. Andrews 1852, 5.
33. *The Builder* 23.12.1854; 15.12.1858; 21.7.1855 and 3.3.1860.
34. *Illustrated London News* XXXII (12.12.1858), 568.
35. Allibone 1991.
36. Essex Record Office D/Dqu29.
37. McCann 1998, 23.
38. Denton 1864.
39. Denton 1864, 20.
40. Denton 1864, 34.
41. Denton 1864, 81.

42. Denton 1864, 30.
43. Denton 1864, 67.
44. Wade Martins 1980, 171–173.
45. Brigden 1986, 33–35.
46. Dean 1867.
47. Brigden 1986, 61–63.
48. Hunt 1874, 211–232.
49. Gray 1971, 171–83.
50. Wade Martins 1980, 181.
51. Statutory List description.
52. Wiliam 1986, 40.
53. Royal Commission on Ancient and Historic Monuments of Scotland, unpublished survey.
54. Wade Martins 1996–7, 33–54.
55. Bannister 1994, 48; Booth 1971; Green 1846, 219–222.
56. North Yorkshire Record Office ZNK X/2/1/1711.
57. North Yorkshire Record Office ZNK X/2/1/1741.
58. North Yorkshire Record Office ZNK X/2/1/1711.
59. North Yorkshire Record Office ZNK X/2/1/1706.
60. North Yorkshire Record Office ZNK X/2/1/1998.
61. North Yorkshire Record Office ZNK M1/6/123.
62. Moscrop 1872,156–165.
63. Moscrop 1865, 88–99.
64. Grey 1841, 154.
65. Northumberland Record Office ZR1 49/8.
66. Northumberland Record Office ZR1 49/11.
67. Grey 1843,11.
68. Squires 1996, 49.
69. Denton 1864, plate XII.
70. Information from Shirley Brooks.
71. Bedfordshire Record Office R4/31.
72. Bedford, Duke of 1897, 226.
73. Bedfordshire Record Office R5/869/1.
74. Bedfordshire Record Office R5/869/1.
75. Bedford, Duke of 1897, 218–227.
76. Bedfordshire Record Office R5/869/1.
77. Caird 1852,441.
78. Cherry and Pevsner 1989, 580, 780–786.
79. Bedfordshire Record Office R5/869/1.
80. Tanner 1848, 489.
81. Bedfordshire Record Office R5/869/1.
82. Quoted in Wade Martins 1995, 128.
83. Bedford, Duke of 1897, 230–239.
84. Denton 1864, plates II and XX.

85. Thomas Andrew Knight (1759–1838) was a founder in 1804 of the Royal Horticultural Society and its president from 1811–1838; Orwin 1929, 8.
86. Smith 1856, 369.
87. Smith 1856, 356–62.
88. Orwin and Sellick 1970, *passim.*
89. Caird 1852, 89–90.
90. Course and Moore 1984, 107–114.
91. Thompson 1963, 237 and 1959, 95; Wade Martins 1980, 98–99.
92. Phillips 1996, 39.
93. Phillips 1996, 39.
94. Public Record Office WORK 44/10.
95. An unlocated article by John Tylor in *The Irish Farmers' Journal* for 1839, quoted in Green and Young's *Encyclopaedia of Agriculture* (1908), Vol. 2, 26; Johnston 1843, 57–63.
96. Morton 1842, 239.
97. Spring 1963, 46.
98. Morton 1842, 377–9 and 410.
99. Brigden 1986, 29–31; Downing 2000.
100. Morton 1863; Denton 1863, plate I; Spearing 1860, 1–46.
101. Public Record Office WORKS 44/10.
102. Morton 1863, 92–3.
103. Denton 1864, 10.
104. Dean 1867, plates 19–21.
105. PRO CRES 16–1 1851, 241.
106. Royal Archives, Privy Purse Letter Books, Vol. 2, 11.
107. Gurdon 1863, 165–168.
108. Brigden 1986, 192.
109. Lawson 1874, *passim.*
110. Lawson 1874, 153.

Notes to Chapter 6: Retrenchment, 1875–1939

1. Bedford, Duke of 1880, 181.
2. Fisher 1975, 16–17.
3. Brown 1987, 33.
4. Brown 1987, 37 and 46.
5. Staffordshire County Record Office D593 K/3/9/65; G. Menzies to the Duke of Sutherland, 6. September 1879, quoted in Perren 1973, 126.
6. Staffordshire County Record Office D593 K/5/2/16 749–50 in Perren 1973, 125.
7. Cannadine 1994, 47–48.
8. Wade Martins 1980, 183–4.
9. Perren 1970, 36–51.
10. Robinson 1988, 193–4.
11. Ojala 1952, 208.
12. Brown 1988, 45.
13. Perry 1974, 75.
14. Robinson 1988, 191.
15. Blundell 1882, 542.
16. Denton 1879, 774–781.
17. Denton 1879, 796.
18. I am grateful to Paul Barnwell and Colum Giles of English Heritage for this information; Barnwell & Giles 1997, 72–3.
19. Perren 1970, 48.
20. Scott 1885, iv, vi.
21. Scott 1885, 36–42.
22. Jenkins 1884, 126–246.
23. Jenkins 1884, 197.
24. Brigden 1986, 230.
25. Perry 1974, 49.
26. Sheldon 1879, 231; Scott 1885, iv 49.
27. William 1986, 97.
28. Barnes 1993, 29.
29. Barnwell and Giles 1997, 122.
30. Lake 1989, 31.
31. Cheshire Record Office DTW 2477/B/27.
32. Barnwell and Giles 1997, 123.
33. Sheldon 1879, 239.
34. Brunskill 1982, 109–111.
35. Bowen-Jones 1893, 571–620.
36. Grundy 1970, 2–5.
37. Denton 1864, plate XX.
38. Robinson 1988, 181.
39. Hubbard 1991, 63.
40. Bowen-Jones 1893, 618.
41. See report of the RCHME farm building survey on Hanby Lodge Farm, archived in the National Monuments Record, Swindon. I am grateful to Colum Giles and Paul Barnwell of English Heritage for drawing my attention to this information.
42. Brigden 1986, 76.
43. Robinson 1983, 88.
44. Morton 1868, 69–98.
45. Sheldon 1879, 346.
46. Sheldon 1908, 8.
47. Sheldon 1908, 10.
48. Report of the Judges 'Plans of Farm Buildings' *JRASE*, **69** (1908), 242.
49. Brigden 1992, 43.

Notes to Epilogue

1. Pusey, in editor's footnote to Roal 1845, 521.
2. Macdonald 1981, 218.
3. Brigden 1986, 192.
4. Read 1887, 27.
5. Browick 1862, 247–269.
6. Brigden 1986, 192.
7. Barnwell and Giles 1997, 146.
8. Read 1854, 258.
9. Perry 1974, 87.
10. Wade Martins 1980, 180.
11. Barnwell and Giles 1997, 149.

Notes to Appendix: County Synopses

1. Caird 1852, 441.
2. Robinson 1983, 145.
3. Caird 1852, 442.
4. Bedfordshire Record Office R1/1106/1.
5. Spearing 1860, 25.
6. Spearing 1860 29.
7. Denton 1864, plate XIV.
8. Caird 1852, 2.
9. Loudon 1833, 508–10.
10. Robinson 1983, 143.
11. Caird 1852, 2.
12. Denton 1864, plates II and XXI.
13. Denton 1864, plates VII, XXXIII and III.
14. Essex Record Office D/DQn29.
15. Brigden 1992.
16. Robinson 1983, 48,58,71,79 and 122; Barnwell and Giles 1997, 128–9 and 148–9.
17. Barnwell and Giles 1997, 130–1, 143, 149, 150 and 159, 170.
18. *Farmers Magazine*, **17**, May 1848, 379–382
19. Dean 1850, 559–562; Brigden 1986, 32–33.
20. Brigden 1986, 74–5; Denton 1864, plate XX; *Farmers' Magazine* 1853, Vol. 24, 383–4.
21. Denton 1864, plate XXV.
22. Barnwell and Giles 1997.
23. Karkeek, 1845.
24. Worgan 1811, 24.
25. Denton 1864, plate XII.
26. Caird 1852, 352–3.
27. Robinson 1983, 126.
28. Messenger 1975.
29. Appleby 1995, 25–34.
30. Robinson 1983, 121.
31. Pevner 1977, 317.
32. Robinson 1983, 141.
33. Marshall 1796, **2**, 2, 318–19.
34. Vancouver 1808, 472–3.
35. Caird 1852, 51.
36. Ruegg 1855, 409, 449.
37. Bell 1856, 99.
38. Caird 1852, 339.
39. Ewart 1850, 224–227.
40. Caird 1852, 134–5.
41. Essex Record Office D/DQn 29.
42. Essex Record Office D/DQn 29.
43. *Country Life* 13/5/39; Robinson 1983, 137.
44. Miller 1983; Brigden 1986, 193–5; Morton 1842, appendix.
45. Brigden 1988, 56.
46. Bravender 1850.
47. Caird 1852, 38.
48. Denton 1864, plate IV.
49. Caird 1852, 90.
50. Denton 1864, plate VIII.
51. Course and Moore 1984, 108–9.
52. Robinson 1983, 132.
53. Denton 1864, 57 and plate XXIV.
54. Brigden 1986, 37.
55. Brigden 1992, 35–45.
56. Robinson 1983, 133.
57. Morton 1863, 9 and 10.
58. Buckland 1845, 276.
59. Allibone 1991.
60. Garnett 1849.
61. Binns 1851.
62. Caird 1852, 213.
63. Caird 1852, 219–20.
64. Robinson 1983, 116.
65. Denton 1864, plate XIII.
66. Bacon 1844, 396–7.
67. Loudon 1844, 516–9.
68. Caird 1852, 416–7.
69. Dean 1867, plate 31.
70. Robinson 1983, 142.
71. Loudon 1833, 476.
72. Loudon 1833, 477.
73. Grey 1843, 11.
74. Hall 1913, 129
75. Caird 1852, 200.
76. Young 1770, I, 371; Robinson 1983, 134.
77. Caird 1852, 28.
78. Downing 2001.
79. *Illustrated London News* 12.12.1857, 585; Brigden 1986, 67–8.

80. Essex Record Office D/DQn 29.
81. Lake 1989 118–9.
82. Lake 1989, 114–17.
83. Peters 1969, 244–5.
84. Peters 1969, 238–9, 261.
85. Robinson (1983), 123–4; Arundel archives ACO 1729.
86. Caird 1852, 118.
87. Brigden 1991 18–19.
88. Young 1808 462–71, Robinson 1983, 137; Coutin 1990, 3–13.
89. Bannister 1994 34–53.
90. Bourne (n.d.).
91. Dean 1863, plate XXIX and XXX.
92. Robinson 1983 137.
93. Denton 1864, plate XVIII.
94. Denton 1864, plate XXII.
95. Tanner 1848, 489.
96. Young 1793, 10.
97. Hellier and Hutton 1987, 72–5.
98. Sturgess 1850, 289.
99. Dean 1844, plate II
100. Young 1771, II, 98–9.
101. Robinson 1983, 130
102. Robinson 1983, 142–3.

Bibliography

The following list includes the principal books and papers dealing specifically with farm buildings and agricultural background, but excludes less relevant texts as well as primary sources which are all cited in full in the footnotes.

JRASE; abbreviation for *Journal of the Royal Agricultural Society of England*

THASS; abbreviation for *Transactions of the Highland and Agricultural Society of Scotland*

Adam, R. J. (1972) *Sutherland Estate Management* (2 vols). Scottish History Society, Edinburgh.

Airs, M. (1987) 'Hovels or Helms: some further evidence from the seventeenth century'. *Vernacular Architecture*, **14**, 51.

Allen, R. C. (1991) 'The Two Agricultural Revolutions, 1459–1850'. In Campbell, B. and Overton, M. *Land, Labour & Livestock*. Manchester University Press, Manchester.

Allibone, J. (1991) *George Devey, Architect 1820–1886*. Lutterworth, Cambridge.

Allison, K. (1976) *The East Riding of Yorkshire Landscape*. Hodder & Stoughton, London.

Andrews, G. H. (1852) *Agricultural Engineering*, 1, *Buildings*. John Weale, London.

Appleby, J. (1994) 'Lord Harrowby's Dairy House at Sandon Home Farm'. *Journal of the Historic Farm Buildings Group*, 8, 26–33.

Appleby, J. (1995) 'Farm Building Designs for Lord Scarsdale at Kedleston Hall, Derbyshire'. *Journal of the Historic Farm Buildings Group*, 9, 25–34.

Bacon, R. N. (1844) *Agriculture of Norfolk*. Bacon & Co. Mercury office, Norwich.

Bakewell, T. (1820) *Remarks on a Publication by James Loch*. Longmans, London.

Bailey, J. and Culley, G. (1805) *General View of the Agriculture of Northumberland*. Board of Agriculture, London.

—— (1813) *General View of the Agriculture of the County of Cumberland*. Board of Agriculture, London.

Bannister, B. (1994) 'The Farm Buildings of the Dukes of Norfolk Arundel Estate, West Sussex'. *Journal of the Historic Farm Buildings Group*, 8, 34–53

Bannister, N. R. (1994) 'The Birdsall Estate: Historic Landscape Survey'. Unpublished report.

Barnes, P. (1993) *Norfolk Landowners Since 1880*. Centre of East Anglian Studies, University of East Anglia, Norwich.

Barnwell, P. and Giles, C. (1997) *English Farmsteads 1750–1914*. Royal Commission on the Historical Monuments of England, Swindon.

Barrell, J. (1972) *The Idea of Landscape and the Sense of Place*. Cambridge University Press, Cambridge.

Bateman, J. (1883) *The Great Landowners of Great Britain & Ireland*. Harrison, London.

Bearn, W. (1852) 'On the Farming of Northamptonshire'. *JRASE*, **13**, 44–113.

Beckett, J. V. (1986) *The Aristocracy of England*. Basil Blackwell, Oxford.

—— (1990) *The Agricultural Revolution*. Basil Blackwell. Oxford.

Bedford, Duke of (1897) *The Story of a Great Estate*. Murray, London.

Belhaven, Lord (1699) *The Country-men's Rudiment, or An Advice to the Farmers of East Lothian on how to Labour and Improve their Ground*. Heirs of A. Anderson, Edinburgh.

Bell, T. (1856) 'A Report on the Agriculture of the County of Durham'. *JRASE*, **17**, 86–122.

—— (1883) 'The Yorkshire Farm Prize competition'. *JRASE*, **2nd ser**, **19**, 506–580.

Betham-Edwards, M. (ed) (1898) *Autobiography of Arthur Young*. Smith, Elder, London.

Bettey, J. H. (1993) *Know the Landscape: Estates and the English Countryside*. B. T. Batsford, London.

Binns, J. (1851) *Agriculture of Lancashire*. Dobson & Son, Preston.

Blundell, J. H. (1882) 'The Berkshire Farm Prize Competition'. *JRASE*, **2nd ser**, **17**, 534–555.

Bourne, R. (n.d.) *1756 acres: A History of the People of Pailton*.

Bowden, P. J. (1985) 'Agricultural prices, wages, farm

profits and rents'. In Thirsk, J. (ed) *Agrarian History of England and Wales*. **5 (ii)**, 1–117, Cambridge University Press, Cambridge.

Bowen-Jones, J. (1893) 'Typical Farms in Cheshire and North Wales'. *JRASE*, **3rd ser**, **4**, 571–620.

Bravender, J. (1850) 'Farming of Gloucestershire'. *JRASE*, **11**, 116–171.

Brigden, R. (1986) *Victorian Farms*. Crowood London.

—— (1991) 'Richard Borlase Matthews and his Greater Felcourt 'Electro Farm'. *Journal of the Historic Farm Buildings Group*, **5**, 18–31

—— (1992) 'Bucking the Trend'. *Journal of the Historic Farm Buildings Group*, **6**, 35–48.

Brockman, H. A. N. (1974) *The British Architect in Industry*. Allen & Unwin, London.

Browick, T. (1862) 'On the Management of a Home Farm'. *JRASE*, **23**, 247–269.

Brown, J. (1987) *Agriculture in England, A Survey of Farming 1870–1947*. Manchester University Press, Manchester.

Buckland, G. (1845) 'On the Farming of Kent'. *JRASE*, **6**, 251–302.

Caird, J. (1852) *English Agriculture in 1850–51*. Longmans, London.

—— (1878) *The Landed Interest and the Supply of Food*. Cassell, Peter and Galpin, London.

Cannadine, D. (1990) *The Decline and Fall of the British Aristocracy*. Yale University Press, New Haven and London.

—— (1995) *Aspects of Aristocracy*. Penguin, London.

Chambers, J. D and Mingay, G. E. (1966) *The Agricultural Revolution*. B. T. Batsford, London.

Chartres, J. A. (1985) 'The Marketing of Agricultural Produce'. In Thirsk, J. (ed) *Agrarian History of England and Wales*, **5 (ii)**, 406–501. Cambridge University Press, Cambridge.

Cherry, B. and Pevsner, N. (1989) *The Buildings of England: Devon*. Penguin Books, London.

Clay, C. (1985) 'Landlords and Estate Management in England'. In Thirsk, J. (ed) *Agrarian History of England and Wales*, **7**, 119–251. Cambridge University Press, Cambridge.

Cobbett, W. ed. Cole (1930) *Rural Rides*. Peter Davies, London.

Colbeck, T. L. (1847) 'On the Agriculture of Northumberland'. *JRASE*, **8**, 422–437.

Colvin, H, (1978, 1995, 3rd edn) *Biographical Dictionary of British Architects, 1600–1840*. Yale University Press, New Haven and London.

Colvin, H. and Newman, J. eds (1981) *Of Buildings: Roger North's writings on Architecture*. Oxford University Press, Oxford.

Copland, S. (1866) *Agriculture, Ancient and Modern*. James Virtue, London.

Cross, A. G. (1980) *By the Banks of the Thames*. Newtonvill, Massachusetts.

Course, E. (1999) *Hampshire Farmsteads in the 1980s*. Southampton University Industrial Archaeology Group, Southampton.

Course, E. and Moore, P. (1984) 'Victorian Farm Building in Hampshire'. *Proceedings of the Hampshire Field Club and Archaeological Society*, **40**, 107–114.

Coutin, K. (1990) 'Lord Sheffield's Model Farm'. *Journal of the Historic Farm Buildings Group*, **4**, 3–13.

Curwen, J. C. (1809) *General Hints on Agricultural Subjects*. J. Johnson, London.

Daniels, S. and Seymour, S. 'Landscape Design and the Idea of Improvement 1730–1814'. In Dodgshon, R. A. and Butlin, R. A. (1990) *An Historical Geography of England and Wales*, 487–503. Academic Press, London.

Dean, G. A. (1844) *On the Construction of Farm Buildings*. Charles Henry Knight, Worthing.

—— (1850) 'On the Cost of Farm Buildings'. *JRASE*, **11**, 558–573.

—— (1851) *The Land Steward*. Atchley & Co., London.

—— (1867) *Selected Designs for Country Residences, Entrance Lodges, Farm Offices, Cottages, etc.*

Dean, P. (1999) *Sir John Soane and the Country Estate*. Ashgate, Aldershot.

Denton, J. B. (1864) *The Farm Homesteads of England*. Chapman & Hall, London.

—— (1879) 'Report of the judges of the farm plans sent in for competition at the London International Exhibition, 1879'. *JRASE*, **2nd ser**, **15**, 774–781.

Downing, R. (2000) 'The Coleshill Model Farm'. *Journal of the Historic Farm Buildings Group*, **14**, 9–22.

Duncomb, J. (1803) *General View of the Agriculture of Herefordshire*. Board of Agriculture, London.

Elliott, G. (1971 edn) *Middlemarch*. Riverside Edition, Yale University Press, New Haven and London.

English, B. (1984) 'Patterns of Estate Management in East Yorkshire c. 1840–1880'. *Agricultural History Review*, **32**, 29–46.

—— (1990) *The Great Landowners of East Yorkshire 1530–1910*. Harvester Wheatsheaf, Hemel Hempstead.

English Heritage (1998) *Conservation-led regeneration: the work of English Heritage*. English Heritage, London.

Everett, N. (1994) *The Tory View of Landscape*. Yale University Press, Newhaven & London.

Fletcher, T. W. (1960–61) 'The Great Depression of English Agriculture, 1873–1896'. *Economic History Review*, **2nd ser**, **13**, 417–432

Fisher, J. R. (1975) *Clare Sewell Read, 1826–1905*. Hull University Press, Hull.

Garnett, W. J. (1849) 'Farming of Lancashire'. *JRASE*, **10**, 1–51.

Garrett, D. (1747) *Designs for Farm Houses etc. for the*

Counties of Yorkshire, Northumberland, Cumberland, Westmorland and the Bishoprick of Durham.

Goddard, N. (1981) 'Agricultural Societies'. In Mingay, G. E. (ed) *The Victorian Countryside*, **1**, 245–269. Routledge & Kegan Paul, London.

—— (1983) 'The Development and Influence of Agricultural Newspapers 1780–1880'. *Agricultural History Review*, **31**, 116–130.

Gray, J. R. (1971) 'An industrial farm estate in Berkshire'. *Industrial Archaeology*, **8**, 171–83.

Grey, J. (1841) 'A View of the Past and Present State of Agriculture in Northumberland'. *JRASE*, **2**, 151–192.

—— (1843) 'On Farm Buildings'. *JRASE*, **4**, 1–17.

Grundy, J. E. (1970) 'Notes on the relationship between climate and cattle housing'. *Vernacular Architectur*, **1**, 2–5.

Gurdon, J. (1863) 'Co-operative farms at Assington, Suffolk'. *JRASE*, **24**, 165–8.

Habbakuk, H. J. (1953) 'Economic Functions of English Landowners in the seventeenth and eighteenth centuries'. *Explorations in Entreprenurial History*, **6**, 92–102.

Hall, A. D. (1913) *A Pilgrimage of British Farming*. John Murray, London.

Harrison, G. B. (ed) (1930) *Advice to his son by Henry Percy, ninth Duke of Northumberland, 1609*. Ernest Benn, London.

Harvey, N. (1984 2nd edn) *A History of Farm Buildings in England and Wales*. David and Charles, Newton Abbot.

—— (1988) 'The engine house of the oldest agricultural steam engine in the world'. *Journal of the Historic Farm Buildings Group*, **2**, 49–54.

Hatcher, J. (1990) *Richmondshire Architecture*. J. Hatcher, Richmond.

Hellier, R. and Hutton, B. (1987) 'A Model farm at Scarthingwell, near York in 1793 and 1986'. *Agricultural History Review*, **35**, 72–75

Hobbs, W. F. (1853) 'On covered home stalls'. *JRASE*, **14**, 325–6.

Hobsbawm, E. J. and Rude, G. (1969) *Captain Swing*. Lawrence and Wishart, London.

Hodgson, J. (1827) *History of Northumberland*. Thomas & James Pigg, Newcastle-upon- Tyne.

Holden, M. (1990) *Stacking Meadow Days*.

Hubbard, E. (1991) *The work of John Douglas*. Victorian Society, London.

Hudson, K. (1972) *Patriotism with Profit*. H. Evelyn, London.

Hughes, E. (1949) 'The Eighteenth-Century Estate Agent'. In Cronne, Moody & Quinn (eds) *Essays in British and Irish History*. Frederick Muller, London.

Hunt, E. H. (1986) 'Industrialisation and Regional Inequality of Wages in Britain, 1760–1914'. *Journal of Economic History*, **46** (**iv**), 935–966.

Hunt, G. (1874) 'On Concrete as a Building Material for Farm Buildings and Cottages'. *JRASE*, **2nd ser**, **10**, 211–232.

Hunt, R. (1797) 'Essay on the distribution of farms, farm buildings, etc'. *Communications to the Board of Agriculture*. Board of Agriculture, London.

Hunter, A. (1803) 'On His Majesty's Farms in Windsor Great Park'. *Georgical Essays*, **4**, 172–188. York.

Hutton, K. (1976) 'Distribution of Wheel Houses in the British Isles'. *Agricultural History Review*, **25**, 30–35.

Giles, C., (1999) 'Enholmes Farm, Partington'. *Journal of the Historic Farm Buildings Group*, **13**, 33–40.

Karkeek, W. F. (1845) 'On the Farming of Cornwall'. *JRASE*, **6**, 400–462.

Kent, N. (1775) *Hints to Gentlemen of Landed Property*. J. Dodsely, London.

—— (1796) *A General View of the Agriculture of the County of Norfolk*. Board of Agriculture, London.

King, R. W. (1974) 'Phillip Southcote and the Woburn Farm'. *Garden History*, **2** (**part 3**), 27–60.

Jarrett, M. G. and Wrathnell, S. (1977) 'Sixteenth- and Seventeenth-century Farmsteads, West Whelpington, Northumberland'. *Agricultural History Review*, **25**, 108–119.

Jenkins, H. M. (1884) 'Report on the Practice of Ensilage at Home and Abroad'. *JRASE*, **2nd ser**, **20**, 126–246.

Jenkins, J. M. (1869) 'Lodge Farm, Castle Acre, Norfolk'. *JRASE*, **2nd ser**, **5**, 461–70.

Jones, E. L. (1968) *The Development of English Agriculture 1815–1873*. Macmillan, London.

Lake, J. (1983) *The Great Fire of Nantwich*. Shiva Publishing, Nantwich.

—— (1989) *Historic Farm Buildings*. Blandford Press, London.

Laurence, E. (1727) *The Duty of a Steward to his Lord*. John Shuckburgh, London.

Lawrence, J. (1801) *The Modern Land Steward*. Symonds, London.

Lawson, W. (1874) *Ten years of Gentleman Farming at Blennerhasset*. Longmans, London.

Loch, J. (1820) *An Account of the Improvements on the estates of the Marquis of Stafford*. Longmans, London.

Loudon, J. C. (1825 and 1831) *Encyclopedia of Agriculture*. Longman Rees, London.

McCann, J. (1998) *The Dovecotes of Suffolk*. Suffolk Institute of Archaeology and History, Ipswich.

Macdonald, S. (1975) 'The Progress of the Early Threshing Machines'. *Agricultural History Review*, **24**, 63–77.

Macdonald, S. (1981) 'Model Farms'. In Mingay, G. E. (ed) *The Victorian Countryside*. **1**, 214–226. Routledge & Kegan Paul, London.

Makhrov, A. (1997) 'Earth Construction in Russia: A Scottish Connection'. *Architectural History*, **40**, 171–183.

Marchand, J. (ed) (1933) *A Frenchman in England 1784.* Cambridge University Press, Cambridge.

Markham, G. (1635) *The First Book of the English Husbandman.* W. Sheares, London

Markus, T. (1993) *Buildings and Power.* Routledge, London.

Marshall, W. (1787) *The Rural Economy of Norfolk.* 2 vols T. Cadell, London.

—— (1788) *The Rural Economy of Yorkshire.* 2 vols T. Cadell, London.

—— (1796) *Rural Economy of the West of England.* 2 vols G. Nichol, London.

—— (1799) *Minutes and Observations in the Southern Counties.* G. Nichol, London.

Messenger, P. (1975) 'Lowther Farmstead Plans'. *Transactions of the Cumberland and Westmorland Antiquarian and Archaeological Society,* **75**, 327–51.

Miller, C. (1983) 'Whitfield Example Farm, a Victorian model'. *Bristol Industrial Archaeological Society Journal,* **16**, 20–27.

Mingay, G. E. (1963) *English Landed Society in the eighteenth Century.* Routledge & Kegan Paul, London.

—— (1994) *Land and Society in England, 1750–1980.* Longmans, London.

Mitchell, B. R. (1988) *British Historical Statistics.* Cambridge University Press, Cambridge.

Morton, J. C. (1842 4th edn) *On the Nature and Property of Soils.* J. Ridgeway, London.

—— (1855) *Cyclopedia of Agriculture.* Blackie & Sons, Glasgow.

—— (1863) *The Prince Consort's Farms.* Longmans, London.

—— (1868) 'Town Milk'. *JRASE,* **2nd ser,** **5,** 69–98.

Moscrop, W. J. (1865) 'Covered Cattle Yards'. *JRASE,* **2nd ser,** **1,** 88–99.

—— (1872) 'On the Housing of Fattening Cattle'. *Transactions of the Highland and Agricultural Society of Scotland,* **4th ser,** **4,** 156–165.

Murray, A. (1815) *A General View of the Agriculture of Wiltshire.* Board of Agriculture, London.

Newton, R. (1972) *The Northumberland Landscape.* Hodder & Stoughton, London.

North, D. (1988) 'Some notes on the terminology of farm buildings in south-eastern England. *Journal of the Historic Farm Buildings Group,* **2,** 15–25.

—— (1992) 'Some Notes on the Terminology of Farm Buildings in Cornwall. *Journal of the Historic Farm Buildings Group,* **6,** 59–66.

Ojala, E. M. (1952) *Agriculture and Economic Progress.* Oxford University Press, Oxford.

Orwin, C. S. (1929) *The Reclamation of Exmoor Forest.* Oxford University Press, Oxford.

Orwin, C. S. and Sellick, R. J. (1970) *The Reclamation of Exmoor Forest.* David and Charles, Newton Abbott.

Overton, M. (1996) *Agricultural Revolution in England 1500–1850.* Cambridge University Press, Cambridge.

Palladio, A. translated by Ware, I. (1727) *The Four Books of Architecture.* (1965 edn with introduction by A. K. Placzek) Dover publications, New York.

Parker, R. A. C. (1975) *Coke of Norfolk, a Financial and Agricultural Study, 1707–1842.* Oxford University Press, Oxford.

Perren, R. (1970) 'Landlords and Agricultural Transformation, 1870–1900'. *Agricultural History Review,* **18,** 36–51.

Perren, R. (1973) 'The Landlord and Agricultural Transformation 1870–1900'. In Perry, P. J. (ed.) *British Agriculture 1875–1914,* 109–128. Methuen, London.

Perry, P. J. (1974) *British Farming in the Great Depression, 1870–1914.* David and Charles, Newton Abbott.

Peters, J. E. C. (1969) *The Development of Farm Buildings in West Lowland Staffordshire up to 1880.* Manchester University Press, Manchester.

Pevner, N (1977) *Buildings of England; Derbyshire.* Penguin Books, London.

Pevsner, N. and Cherry, B. (1973) *Buildings of England; Northamptonshire.* Penguin Books, London.

Pevsner, N. and Harris, J. (1989) *Buildings of England; Lincolnshire.* Penguin Books, London.

Pevner, N. and Neave, D. (1995) *Buildings of England; East Riding of Yorkshire.* Penguin Books, London.

Phillips, A. D. M. (1996) *The Staffordshire Reports of Andrew Thompson to the Enclosure Commissioners, 1858–68.* Staffordshire Record Society, Stafford.

Pitt, W. (1813) *General View of the Agriculture of Leicestershire.* Board of Agriculture, London.

Popham, J. (1973) 'Farm Buildings, Function and Form; the Birdsall Estate, North Yorkshire'. Unpublished thesis, University of York.

—— (1986) 'Sir Christopher Sykes at Sledmere'. *Country Life,* 16 January, 128–132.

Pusey, P. (1851) *What ought Landlords and Farmers to do?* J. Murray, London.

Rackham, O. (1986) *A History of the Countryside.* J. M. Dent, London.

Read, C. S. (1854) 'On the Farming of Oxfordshire'. *JRASE,* **15,** 189–275.

—— (1855) 'On the Farming of Buckinghamshire'. *JRASE,* **16,** 269–322.

—— (1858) 'Improvements in Norfolk Farming'. *JRASE,* **19,** 265–311.

—— (1887) 'Large and Small Holdings', *JRASE,* **2nd ser,** **23,** 1–28.

Richards, E. (1973) *Leviathan of Wealth.* Routledge & Kegan Paul, London.

Roal, J. (1845) 'On Converting a Mossy Hillside to Catch Meadows'. *JRASE,* **6,** 518–522

Roberts, B. K. and Wrathnell, S. (2000) *An Atlas of Rural Settlement in England.* English Heritage, London.

Roberts, J. (1997) *Royal Landscape: The Gardens and Parks of Windsor.* Yale University Press, Newhaven and London.

Robinson, J. M. (1976) 'Estate Buildings of the 5th and 6th Duke of Bedford at Woburn'. *Architectural Review,* **160**, 276–281.

—— (1979) *The Wyatts, An Architectural Dynasty.* Oxford University Press, Oxford.

—— (1983) *Georgian Model Farms.* Oxford University Press, Oxford.

—— (1988) *The English Country Estate.* Century/National Trust, London.

Royal Commission on Ancient and Historic Monuments of Scotland (1967) *Inventory of Ancient Monuments in Peeblesshire.* RCAHMS, Edinburgh.

Ruegg, L. H. (1854) 'Farming in Dorsetshire'. *JRASE,* **15**, 389–454.

Ruggles, T. (1788) 'Picturesque Farming' *Annals of Agriculture,* **9**, 1–15

Scott, J. (1885) *Text Book of Farm Engineering.* Part iv, *Buildings.* Crosby Lockwood & Co., London.

Severn, J. (1983) 'Sir Thomas Parkyns and his Barns and Farm Buildings at Bunny in Nottinghamshire'. *Journal of the Historic Farm Buildings Group,* **7**, 65–74

Sheldon, J. P. (1879) *Dairy Farming.* Cassell, Petter, Galpin & Co., London.

—— (1908 3rd edn) *British Dairying.* Crosby Lockwood, London.

Shvidkovskg, D. (1996) *The Empress and the Architect.* Yale University Press, New Haven and London.

Smith, R. (1856) 'Bringing Moorland into Cultivation'. *JRASE,* **17**, 356–62.

Spearing, J. B. (1860) 'On the Agriculture of Berkshire'. *JRASE,* **11**, 1–46.

Spring, D. (1963) *The English Landed Estate in the Nineteenth Century.* John Hopkins Press, Baltimore.

Spooner, W. C and Elliott, J. (1850) 'On the Construction of Farm Buildings', *JRASE,* **9**, 270–282.

Squires, S. (1996) 'Christopher Turnor, 1809–1886, and his Influence on Lincolnshire Buildings'. *Journal of the Historic Farm Buildings Group,* **10**, 49–51.

Strickland, H. E. (1812) *General View of the Agriculture of the East Riding of Yorkshire.* Board of Agriculture, London.

Storer, A. (1998) 'Report on Crossroads Farm, Blackbrook, Belper, Derbyshire'. Unpublished report for Derbyshire County Council.

Stuart, D. M. (1939) *The Daughters of George III.* Macmillan, London.

Sturgess, T. (1850) 'Farm Buildings'. *JRASE,* **11**, 288–299.

Taigel, A. and Williamson, T. (1993) *Know the Landscape: Parks and Gardens.* B. T. Batsford, London.

Tancred, T. (1850) 'On the Construction of Farm Buildings'. *JRASE,* **11**, 192–214.

Tanner, H. (1848) 'The Farming of Devonshire'. *JRASE,* **9**, 454–495.

Thirsk, J. (ed.) (1985) *The Agrarian History of England and Wales.* **V.** Cambridge University Press, Cambridge.

Thomas, K. (1983) *Man and the Natural World.* Allen Lane, London.

Thompson, F. M. L. (1959) 'Agriculture Since 1870'. *Victoria History of the Counties of England: A History of Wiltshire,* **4**. University of London, London.

—— (1963) *English Landed Society in the Nineteenth Century.* Routledge & Kegan Paul, London.

Thompson, H. S. (1850) 'Farm Buildings', *JRASE,* **9**, 181–92.

Tolstoy, L. (1993) *War and Peace.* Wordsworth Classics, London.

Toulier, B. (1997) 'Chateaux en Sologne'. *Cahier de l'Inventaire,* **26**. Paris.

Turner, M. E. (1980) *English Parliamentary Enclosure.* Dawson, Folkestone.

Turner, M. E., Beckett, J. V. and Afton, B. (1997) *Agricultural Rent in England 1690–1914.* Cambridge University Press, Cambridge.

Tyson, B. (1979) 'Low Park Barn, Rydal; the reconstruction of a farm building in Westmorland in the seventeenth century'. *Transactions of the Cumberland and Westmorland Antiquarian and Archaeological Society,* **2nd ser,** **79**, 85–94.

Veliz, C. (1959) 'Arthur Young and the Landed Interest 1784–1813'. Unpublished PhD thesis, University of London.

Wade Martins, S. (1980) *A Great Estate at Work.* Cambridge University Press, Cambridge.

—— (1988) *Norfolk: A Changing Countryside.* Phillimore, Chichester. (1990) *'Turnip' Townshend, Statesman and Farmer.* Poppyland, North Walsham.

—— (1991) *Historic Farm Buildings.* B. T. Batsford, London.

—— (1995) *Farms and Fields.* B. T. Batsford, London.

—— (1996–97) 'A Century of Farms and Farming on the Sutherland Estate 1790–1890'. *Review of Scottish Culture,* **10**, 33–54.

Wade Martins, S. and Williamson, T. (1997) 'Labour and Improvement': Agricultural Changes in East Anglia *c.* 1750–1870'. *Labour History Review,* **62.3**, 275–295.

—— (1998) 'The Development of the Lease and its Role in Improvement in East Anglia'. *Agricultural History Review,* **46**, 127–141.

—— (1999) 'The Roots of Change'. *Agricultural History Review Monograph.* British Agricultural History Society, Exeter.

Waistell, C. (1827) *Designs for Agricultural Buildings.* Longmans, London.

Wiliam, E. (1986) *The Historical Farm Buildings of Wales.* John Donald, Edinburgh.

Wilkinson, J. (1861) 'The farming of Hampshire'. *JRASE*, **22**, 239–347.

Williamson, T. (1995) *Polite Landscapes: Gardens and Society in Eighteenth-century England.* John Sutton, Stroud.

Wilmot, S. (1990) *'The Business of Improvement': Agriculture and Scientific Culture in Britain c. 1700–c. 1870.* Bristol.

Wilson, R. and Mackley, A. (2000) *Creating Paradise: The Building of the English Country House 1660–1880.* Hambledon, London.

Wordie, J. R. (n.d.??) 'The Chronology of English Enclosure, 1500–1914'. *Economic History Review,* **36**, 483–505.

Worgan, G. B. (1811) *General View of the Agriculture of Cornwall.* Board of Agriculture, London.

Wragg, B. ed. Worsley, G. (2000) *The Life and Works of John Carr of York.* Oblong, York.

Vancouver, C. (1808) *General View of the Agriculture of Devon.* Board of Agriculture, London.

Young, A. (1764) 'Common farmers vindicated from the charges of being universally ignorant'. *Museum Rusticanum,* **3**.

—— (1770) *The Farmer's Guide to Hiring and Stocking Farms.* W. Strachan, London.

—— (1771) *A Farmer's Tour through the North of England.* 4 vols W. Strachan, London.

—— (1784) 'A Minute of the Husbandry at Holkham by Thomas William Coke'. *Annals of Agriculture,* **11**, 382.

—— (1793) *General View of the Agriculture of Yorkshire.* Board of Agriculture, London.

—— (1804) *General View of the Agriculture of Norfolk.* G. & W. Nichol, London.

—— (1808) *General View of the Agriculture of Sussex.* Board of Agriculture, London.

—— (1809) *General View of the Agriculture of Oxfordshire.* Board of Agriculture, London.

—— (1813) *General View of the Agriculture of Suffolk.* C. Macrae, London.

Index

Adam, R. (architect) 30, 31, 53, 54–5, 65, 57, 58, 59, 72, 204, 211

Agricultural Revolution 2, 43, 111, 202

Albert, Prince Consort 69, 133, 161, 203, 208, 214

Albury, Surrey 220

Aldford Hall, Cheshire Plate 21

Aldborough, North Yorkshire 223

Aldro, North Yorkshire

Althorp, Northamptonshire 21, 223

Alnwick, Northumberland 66, 75, 80, 82, 83, 111, 203, 216
    East Brizlee Figure 38
    Park Farm Figure 37, Plate 8

American barn 177 Figure 89

Andrews, G. (agricultural engineer) 4, 118, 127

Annals of Agriculture 3, 14, 31, 66, 116

Anson family (later Lords Lichfield) 219

Apley Park Home Farm, Shropshire 136–7, 205, 218, Figures 68, 69, Plate 15

Arbuthnot, R. 31

Argyll 136, 160

Argyll, Duke of 30, 74

Armstrong, Lord 173

Arundel Estate, Sussex 138, 220

Ashburton, Hampshire 213

Aske, Olliver Farm, North Yorkshire 134, 138, Figure 70, Plate 16

Aston Wold, Northamptonshire 194, 217, Figure 100

Assington Estate, Suffolk 167

Attingham, Shropshire 218
    Cronkhill Farm 21, Figure 2

Aynho, Northampton 216

Badminton, Gloucestershire 64

Bagot, Lord 219

Bakewell, R. 31

Bank barns 39, 78, 199

Barker, J. (architect) 158

Beamish, Durham 213

Beatson, R. (writer) 72

Bedford, Duke of 5, 18, 20, 21, 24, 26, 27, 58, 104, 105, 111, 115, 118, 128, 130, 143, 146, 150, 160, 168, 170, 200, 201, 203, 205, 207, 208, 209, 211, 212

Bedfordshire 27, 104, 146, 173, 203, 205, 207

Belhaven, Lord 3, 30, 39

Belper, Derbyshire 94–9, 111, 203, 211

Cross Roads Farm, 96, 100
    Dalley Farm 97–100, Figure 47
    Wyver Farm 96–7, 100, Figure 45

Belvoir, Leicestershire 215

Beningborough Park, North Yorkshire 25

Bentham, J. 62

Benyon, Rev. 208

Berkshire 24, 154, 188, 208

Berwick, Lord 21

Betley, Old Hall, Staffordshire 219, Plates 1–3

Beverley, Lord 118

Birdsall, North Yorkshire 90, 225

Blackett, Sir William 48, 80, 203, 218

Blagdon, Northumberland 82, 90, 141, 158, 201, 203

Blaikie, F. (agent) 4, 13, 18, 21, 110, 116

Blankney, Lincolnshire 118, 215

Blennerhassett, Mechi Farm, Cumbria 166–8, 199, Figure 85

Blythefield Hall, Staffordshire 219

Board of Agriculture 13, 30, 37, 57, 67, 69, 72, 77, 203

Boulton, M. (engineer) 14, 58

Bridgwater Canal 90

Bristol, Marquis of 215

Broadlands, Hampshire 213

Brocklesby, Lincolnshire 215

Broome, Suffolk 219

Broughton Estates, Cheshire 209

Browick, Mr (agent) 4, 20, 21, 200

Buckingham, Duke of 17

Buckinghamshire 208

Buckland, Devon 73, 211

Bunny, Nottinghamshire 38, 203, 217, Figure 12

Burley Farm, Derbyshire 59, 60, Figure 26

Burlington, Lord 42, 46, 49

Burn Hall, Derbyshire 211

Burton, D (architect) 211

Buscot, Oxfordshire 136, 217

Bylaugh, Park Farm, Norfolk 125–7, 215, Figure 62

Cadland Farm, Surrey 57, 58, Figure 25

Cadogan, Lord 188, 200, 220

Caird, J. (writer) 11, 18, 80, 118, 120, 139, 147, 204, 208, 209, 211, 212, 213, 216, 217

Caithness, 30

Cambridgeshire 23–4, 26, 146, 151, 205, 209

Capheaton, Northumberland 216
Carr, J. (architect) 49, 53, 85, 224, 225
Cartwright Estate, Northamptonshire 217
Caterham, Surrey 76
Catherine the Great 31
Cattle housing 43, 75, 113, 117, 120, 121, 132, 146, 147, 176, 183, 200, 205
Cavendish, Lord 211
Chalfont Lodge, Buckinghamshire 208
Chancellor, F. (architect) 10, 115, 125, 128–9, 130, 192, 203, 208, 212, 214,
Channonz Farm, Tibenham, Norfolk 37, Figure 11
Chaplin, H. 118, 215
Charlton, Dorset 132
Chatsworth, Derbyshire 211
Chebsey, Greenhill Farm, Staffordshire 219
Cheese factories 173
Cheshire 26, 27, 62, 132, 173, 178–83, 199, 201, 205, 209
Chesterfield, Lord 18
Chignall, Stephen's Farm, Essex 128–9
Chillingham, Northumberland 80, 174
Chisfield, Hertfordshire 214
Chiswick, East House Farm, Northumberland Figure 36
Cirencester 213
Cirencester Agricultural College 213
Cliff End, Kent 214
Clubs and Societies, see farming clubs and societies
Coal mines 18, 48, 80, 81, 90, 180, 225
Cobbett, W. (writer) 3, 80
Cockerill, S. (architect) 213
Cocklaw, East, Northumberland 216
Coke, T.W. (see also Lord Leicester) 15, 22, 62, 68, 103, 105, 107–11, 217
Coleshill, Oxfordshire 5, 161, 168, 217
Combs, Suffolk 219
Commons 9, 23, 35
Concrete 134, 136, 170, 175, 200, 214, 219
Constable Burton, North Yorkshire 49, 51, 52, 224, Figure 20
Cooperative farming 167–8
S. Copland (writer) 4, 119
Corn Laws 75, 115, 117, 157, 204
Cornwall 24, 78–9, 210
Cornwall, Duchy of 210, 211
Corrugated iron 134, 170, 175, 200
Costessey Hall, Norfolk 215
Country Landowners' Association 205
Coutts brothers 10
Covered Yards 125, 128, 129, 134, 138, 139, 141, 146, 168, 170, 174
Cragside, Northumberland 173
Cranley Hall, Eye, Suffolk 37, Figure 11
Crompton Hall, South Creake, Norfolk 215
Crown Estates 128, 224
Culford, Suffolk 67, 188, 200, 220, Figure 97

Culley brothers 18, 80
Culzean Castle, Ayrshire 56, 57
Cumberland 12, 25, 211
Cumbria 25, 39, 64, 78, 100, 166–7, 168, 198, 199, 203, 210
Curwen, J. 67, 90, 100, 102, 111, 201, 211
Curzon, N. 53, 54–5, 59, 211

Dairies 59, 64, 66, 158, 216, 222
Dairy farms 11, 26, 29, 147, 173, 175–83, 189–90, 199–203, 223
Daintry family, Cheshire 201, 209
Darlington, Lord 3, 51, 212
Dartmouth, Earl of 221
Dartmoor, Tor Royal 211
Davy, Sir H. (scientist) 116
Day, J. (architect) 125
Dean, G. (architect) 21, 32, 120, 129, 130, 132, 133, 161, 164, 165, 167, 203, 208, 209, 216, 223
De Grey, T. 2
Denbigh, Earl of 220
Denton, J. (engineer) 19, 121, 129–30, 143, 161, 203, 208, 209, 210, 214, 215, 216, 224
Derbyshire 5, 92, 203, 211
Devon 5, 11, 146, 147, 151, 203, 211
Devonshire, Duke of 211, 224
Devey, C. (architect) 128, 214
Dinton Estate, Wiltshire 221
Dishley, Leicestershire 31
Doddington, Cheshire 62, 209
Dorset 24, 154, 212
Douglas, J. (architect) 180, 182–3, 205, 210
Dovecot 143, 225
Downton Castle, Herefordshire 214
Drainage 13, 16, 17, 19, 24, 25, 35, 36, 45, 68, 90, 100, 138, 151, 166, 171, 202
Drummond Estate, Surrey 220
Ducie, Lord 160, 213
Dundas family 138
Durham 3, 51, 53, 57, 77, 212
Dysart, Lord 170, 183, 187, 188, 203, 215

Easton, Suffolk 220
East Harptree, Eastwood Manor Farm, Somerset 134, 218
Ecclestone, Wrexham Road Farm 205, 210
Edgmond, Day House Farm, Shropshire Figure 43
Edinburgh 30, 92
Egremont, Lord 17, 222
Egmere, Norfolk 130, Figure 65
Electricity 222
Ellenhall, Lawnhead Farm, Staffordshire 219
Elliot, J. 123, Figure 61
Ely, Cambridgeshire 209
Enclosure 12, 19, 23, 35–6, 45, 49, 62, 68, 73, 80, 85, 90, 105, 198, 202
Enlightenment 1, 3, 64, 194

Englesfield, Berkshire 208
Enholme Farm, East Yorkshire 121, 123, 224
Essex 26, 62, 171, 205
Eversholt, Water End Farm 205, Plate 20
Example Farms 160
Exmoor 26, 113, 134, 151, 153, 158, 219
'Experimentia' 174, 175, 216, Figure 87
Express Diary Company 10, 192, 195, 205

Factory architecture 58, 95, 112, 118, 121
Farmhouses 44, 121
Farming clubs and societies 14, 15, 30
Fawley Court, Buckinghamshire 209
Felcourt, Surrey 220
Fenton, Northumberland 18
Ferme Ornée 62–3, 193–4, 216
Finchley, College Farm, Essex 192, 195, Figure 99
Fletchling, Sheffield Park, Sussex 220
Flookborough, Cumbria 211
Fonthill Estate, Wiltshire 221
Fornham St Genevieve, Suffolk 219
Fornham St Martin, Suffolk 219
France 31
Frogmore, Berkshire 60, 161, 162
Fylingdales, Desmesne Farm, North Yorkshire 222
    Howdale Farm 222

Gardner, J. (agent) 19, 118–19, Figure 57
Garrett, D. (architect) 46, 49, 53, 212, 218, 224, 225,
    Figure 18
George III 2, 4, 17, 20, 31, 68–9, 207–8
Germany 32, 138
Glendale, Northumberland 80
Gloucestershire 11, 24, 38, 64, 68, 160, 213
Goodwood, Sussex 21, 220
Graffham, Cambridgeshire 129, 209, Figure 63
Grafton, Duke of 19, 118–19, 203, 217
Graham, Sir J. 18, 210
Granville, Lord 214
Green, B. (architect) 134
Green, J. (architect) 83, 218
Greenwich Hospital farms 75, 80, 81, 83, 85, 142, 158, 203,
    216
Grey, J. of Dilston 81, 83, 85, 117–18, 120, 139, 142, 216
Grey, Earl of Bilton 80
Greystoke, Cumbria 25, 64, 100, 158, 198, 203, 211
    Bunkers Hill 64, Figure 30
    Fort Putman 64, Plate 6
Grinkle Park, North Yorkshire 225
Grittleton, Wiltshire 155–6, 201, 222

Haines Hill, Berkshire 208
Haldon, Devon 211
Halfpenny, W. (architect and writer) 31, 48
Hamels Park, Herfordshire 57

Hampshire 24, 118, 154, 213
Hampstead Heath, London 2
Harding, Viscount 215
Hawke, Baron of Towton 224
Hanley, Lincolnshire 183
Harewood, West Yorkshire 17, 66, 225
Harrowby, Lord 59
Haselor, Warwickshire 220
Heathfield, Lord 73, 211
Herefordshire 214
Hertfordshire 57, 195, 214
'High farming' 115, 116, 119, 127, 130, 136, 146, 170, 171,
    204
Hiorne, F. (architect) 64, 211
Holderness, Duke of 49, 138, 203, 224
Holkham, Norfolk 4, 5, 13, 19, 20, 21, 22, 44, 62, 66, 67,
    75, 103, 105, 107, 108, 109, 111, 115, 116, 130, 132–3, 158,
    161, 188, 200, Figures 49, 52, 66, Plate 11
Holland, H (architect) 18, 57, 207
Holton, Suffolk 219
Hornby, North Yorkshire 44, 49, 50, 203, 224
    Arbour Hill Farm 49, Plate 5
    Park Farm Figure 19
    Street Farm 49, Figure 19
Horse engines 18, 76, 77, 78, 100, 105, 146, 218, 221, 222
Hotham, Sir J. 224
Houghton, J. (writer) 34
Houghton Hall, Norfolk 215
Howard, H. 158, 203
Hudson, J. 10, 115, 116, 120
Huntington, Cheaveley Hall, Cheshire 182, Figure 93,
    Plate 20

'Improvement' 2–3, 14–15, 16, 45, 49, 66, 85, 138, 157,
    160, 194, 195, 198
Isle of Wight 214
Italy 32, 49, 51, 54, 59

Jones, I. (architect) 41

Kames, Lord 30
Kelham, Nottinghamshire 217
Kedleston, Derbyshire 53, 54–5, 58, 59, 211, Figures 22, 23
    Ireton Farm 54
Kent 11, 214
Kent, N. (writer and agent) 2, 4, 12, 13, 17, 20, 62, 68–9,
    116
Kent, W. (architect) 217, 219
Kilham, Northumberland 174, 216
Killerton, Devon 211
Kirkleatham, North Yorkshire 138–9, 225
Kings Langley, Hertfordshire 195–6, Figure 102
Kirtlington, Northbrook Farm, Oxfordshire 126, Figure 64
Knapp Farm, Herefordshire 124, 125, Figure 60
Knight, J. & F. 134, 151, 153, 155, 158, 220

Lake District, see Cumbria
Laminated timber 138, 200, 222
Lancashire 26, 29, 77, 120, 173, 214
Land agents 17–18
Land Improvements Companies 171
Land prices 35
Laurence, E. (writer) 17
Lawes, J.B. 116, 125
Lawrence, J. (writer) 20, 66
Lawson, W 167–8, 199, 211
Leamington, Warwickshire 221
Leases 9, 11–12, 36, 138
Leicestershire 1, 35, 118, 214
Leicester, Lord 18, 21, 130, 136, 158, 188, 200
Leigh, Kent 214
Leighton, Welshpool 29
Leveson-Gower 171, 175
Leyland family 80
Lightoler (architect and writer) 63
Lilleshall, Shropshire 25
Liming 13, 16, 17, 25, 36, 138, 153
Lincolnshire 12, 25, 26, 143, 170, 183, 187, 188, 203, 215
Linhays 79
Liscard, Cheshire 209
Little Ponton, Lincolnshire 183
Littleton Estate, Staffordshire 219
Liverpool 29, 178
Lockington, East Yorkshire 224
Loch, G. 18
Loch, J. 13, 17, 18, 31, 90, 92, 220, 221
London 10, 37, 38, 105, 120, 154, 171, 173, 180, 189, 190–2
London upon Tearn, Tearn Farm, Shropshire Figure 45
Longleat, Wiltshire 221
Lonsdale, Lord 64, 203
Loose boxes 124, 132
Loudon (writer) 73–4, 76, 203, 208, 217, 218
Lowther Estate, Cumbria 25
Low, David (writer) 30
Lucas West Estate, Bedfordshire 208
Luton Hoo, Bedfordshire 173, 208
L'vov (architect) 31, Figure 9
Lymm, Cheshire 132, 209

MacConnell, P. 213
Macclesfield, Lord 219
Maismore, Gloucestershire 213
MacVicar, J. 143
Malcolm, N. 16
Manchester 29, 178
Manure collection 43, 49, 51, 75 113, 117, 120, 123, 133, 147, 148, 177, 200, 219
Marketing 10
Markham, G. (writer) 37
Marlborough, Duke of 28
Marling 13, 16, 36, 68

Marshall, W. (industrialist) 123, 224
Marshall, W. (writer) 2, 13, 14, 15, 16, 73, 74, 100, 116, 211
Mechanisation 4, 18, 112–13, 143, 148, 151, 156, 160, 200
Mechi, J. 168
Methleigh Barton, Cornwall 24, 210
Mein, R. (agent) 151
Middleton, Lord, see also Willoughby family 79, 225
Middleton, East Yorkshire 224
Millbrook, Lower Farm, Bedfordshire Figure 74
Milton, Northamptonshire 217
Milton Abbott, Week Farm Devon 148–9, Figure 75
    Beara Farm 148, Figure 75
Moccas, Herefordshire 214
Moore, E. (agent) 161, 219
Morton, J. (writer) 160, 161, 167, 174, 190, 199, 214, 221
Moscrop, W. (agent) 139
Mucklow family 210

Naylor, J. 29
Neeld, J. 155, 223
Nesfield, W. (architect) 211
Netherby, Cumbria 210
Netherlands 32
Newnham Barns, Northumberland 216
New Horton Grange, Northumberland Figure 71
Nicholson, W. 155, 214
Norfolk 2, 4, 8, 11, 15, 16, 19, 37–8, 45, 68, 104, 171, 215
Norfolk, Dukes of 27, 64, 138, 211, 222
Norris Castle, Isle of Wight 214
Northamptonshire 19, 48, 118, 193–4, 203, 216
North, R. (writer) 37
North Rode, Cheshire 209
North Witham, Lincolnshire 188
Northumberland 24, 25, 77, 79, 80, 81, 82, 83, 118, 141, 171, 173, 174, 203, 216
Northumberland, Dukes of 4, 12, 17, 76, 80, 82, 83, 90, 111, 201, 203, 216, 225
Nottinghamshire 35, 38, 203, 217

Open fields 9, 14, 23, 35, 38
Ongar Park, Essex 213
Osborne House, Isle of Wight 214
Owen, R. 167
Outchester, Northumberland 85, 218, Figure 39
Oxfordshire 28, 161, 168, 217

Pailton, Warwickshire 220
Palk, Sir Lawrence 211
Palladio, A. (architect) 41–2, 43, 198, Figure 14
Palmerston, Lord 213
Pangbourne, Berkshire 188
Papplewick, Nottinghamshire 217
Parkland 3, 16, 21, 49, 62, 63, 66, 198, 202
Parkyns, Sir Thomas 38, 203, 217
Peel, Sir Robert 18

Pembroke, Earls of 26, 32, 155, 158, 221
Penkridge, Staffordshire 219
Penrhyn, Lord 29, 58
Penshurst, Kent 215
Peterson Estate, Hampshire 213
Petworth, Stag Park Farm, Sussex 220
Petre, Lord 62, 213
'Picturesque' 57
Pise 105, 146
Poling, Sussex 138
Portland, Duke of 219
Pondstock, Cornwall 210
Prices 11, 72, 75, 115, 170, 171
Pulford, Meadow House Farm, Cheshire 183
Pusey, P. 121, 161
Putteridge, Bedfordshire 208

Raby Castle, Durham 3, 51, 53, 212, Figure 21
Radnor, Earl of 5, 161, 168, 219
Railways 10, 113, 120, 173
Rangemoor, 221
Read, C.S. 116, 171, 201
Rent 10, 11, 23, 26–7, 35–6, 72, 75, 105, 138, 146, 157, 170,
    171, 180
Repton, H. 63, 66
Richmond, Duke of 222
Rickman, T. 225
Ridley family 82, 90, 139, 158, 201, 203
Rieveaulx, Griff Farm, North Yorkshire 223
Riots 45, 78, 146
Rivenhall, Essex 213
Road building 10, 19, 24, 25, 35, 49, 160
Rockingham, Marquis of 225
Rokeby, Durham 212
Rothamstead 116, 125
Rothschild, Lord 194, 208, 222
Rousham, Oxfordshire 63, 217
Royal Agricultural Society 15, 112, 116, 121, 123, 125, 160,
    161, 174, 176, 194
Royal Institution of Chartered Surveyors 205
Ruggles, T. 3, 66
Rushbrook, Suffolk 220
Russia 31–2
Rutland, Duke of 215
Ryder, N. 20, 59

Saint Cleer, Ford Farm, Cornwall 210
Salmon, R. (agent and architect) 5, 18, 105–6, 207, Figure
    50
Saighton, Saighton Lane Farm, Cheshire 183, Figure 94
Sancton Hill, East Yorkshire 224
Sandon, Staffordshire 20, 59, 61, 66, Figure 27
Sandwell, Warwickshire 221
Scarsdale, Baron, see Curzon
Scarthingwell, North Yorkshire 224

Scotland 30–1, 53, 57, 74, 77, 92, 189
Scott, G. (architect) 219
Scott, Prof. J. 174, 175, 176, 177, 178, Figure 88
Seymour, Lord 215
Sezincote, Gloucestershire 213
Sheep shearings 20, 104, 105–7
Sheffield, Lord 222
Shipley, Derbyshire 211
Shirburn, Oxfordshire 217
Shropshire, 27, 90, 151, 171, 175, 203, 217
Shugborough, Staffordshire 5, 54, 59, 62, 205, 219
Silage 160, 176, 192, 200
Sinclair, Sir J. 30, 69
Sledmere, East Yorkshire 12, 44, 67, 85, 90, 203, Figures
    40, 41
    Croome House Farm Plate 9
    Maramette Farm Figure 42
Smith, A. (economist) 30, 92
Smith, J. (architect) 92
Smith, R (agent) 134, 153
Smithfield 10, 43, 107
Smithson (agent) 138
Sneyd, Sir R. 18, 20
Soane, Sir J. (architect) 53, 57, 72, 204, 213, 217
Somerset 134, 173, 218
Somerville, Lord 14
South Creake, Leicester Square Farm, Norfolk 109, 215,
    Figure 54
Southcote, W. 62–3
Southill, Bedfordshire 208
Spencer, Lord 14, 217
Stacey Hill, Buckinghamshire 209
Staffordshire 13, 27, 49, 59, 90, 92, 111, 203, 219
Stafford, Marquis of 13, 17–18, 25, 27, 30, 90, 203, 219
Stanton Dale, North Yorkshire 225
Starston Hall, Norfolk 215
Steam power 76, 79, 90, 92, 113, 115, 121, 123, 133, 139,
    141, 151, 160, 174, 188, 218, 219, 222
Stephenson, D. (architect) 4, 82, 218
Stratton Strawless, Norfolk 215
Strensham, Bredon Field Farm, Worcestershire 224
Strutt family (Derbyshire) 5, 46, 94–6, 201, 203, 211
Sturdy, H. 222
Suffolk 11, 15, 37, 39, 57, 67, 146, 167, 183, 188, 205, 219
Sunk Island, East Yorkshire 26, 128, 224
Surrey 31, 56, 220
Sussex 11, 220
Sutherland 17–18, 27, 30, 92, 136
Sway, Hampshire 213
Swinburne, Lord 80
Swinburne Estate, Northumberland 216
Sykes, Sir C. 12, 79, 85, 203, 224

Tankervill, Lord 80, 174
Tattenhall, Cheshire 209

Tavistock, Devon 26, 115, 211
   Kilworthy Farm 147, 168, 211, Figure 76, Plates 17, 18
Taynton, Gloucestershire 213, Plate 4
Teddesley, Staffordshire 219
Tetworth, Oxfordshire 217
Teulon, S. (architect) 115, 128
Thompson, A. (agent) 18
Thorndon, Hatch Farm, Essex 62, 213
Thorney, Cambridgeshire 23–4, 26, 128, 130, 151, 209,
   Figures 7, 77
Thompson, H. 121
Threshing machines 72, 76, 77–8, 80, 100, 102, 112, 118,
   120, 184, 138, 143, 146, 148, 151, 168
Thriplow, Cambridgeshire 209
Throckley, Tyne and Wear 216
Tiverton, Ferney Lea Farm, Cheshire 210 Figure 91
Tollemache Estate, Cheshire 179, 183, 209
Tollett, G. 221
Torr, Mr (architect) 209
Torrington, Lord 215
Tortworth, Gloucestershire 21, 24, 160
Townshend, Lord 8, 15
Tramways 123, 124, 133, 134, 139, 168, 174, 188, 200, 219,
   224
Trebartha Barton, Cornwall 78–9, 210, Plate 7
Trentham, Staffordshire 25, 92, 111
Troutbeck, Townend Farm, Cumbria Figure 13
Turnbull, J. (architect) 20, 161, 164, 208
Turner, C. 225
Turnor, C. 26, 130, 143, 158, 203, 216, Figures 72, 73
Tyntesfield, Somerset 188, 190–1, 219, Figure 98

Uphampton Farm, Herefordshire 214
Upper Yatton Farm, Herefordshire Figure 86
Utilitarian 1, 22, 48, 62

Venice 41
Victoria, Queen 66, 117, 158, 215
Voelcker, Dr A. 125
Vulliamy, L. (architect) 214
Waddesden, Buckinghamshire 208
Wages 77
Waistell, C. (architect) 75, 76, 82, Figure 35
Wales 28
Wallington, Northumberland 48, 49, 80, 171, 203, 216
Wall's Court Farm, Gloucestershire 207
Walpole, H. 62
Warwickshire 220
Water power 72, 76, 78, 123, 134, 138, 153, 210, 211, 218,
   221
Watney, Dr H. 188
Watson, J. (architect) 174
Webb, J. (architect) 41

Wellington, Duke of 118, 208
Wentworth Woodhouse, South Yorkshire 225
Westminster, Duke of 27–8, 170, 173, 178, 201, 203, 205,
   209
Westonbirt, Gloucestershire 213
Weston Park, Staffordshire 49
West Peckham, Kent 214
West Sevington, Wiltshire Figure 79
West Wycombe Park 208
Whim, Peebleshire 30
Whitbread family 207
Whitfield Example Farm, Gloucestershire 160, 213, Figure
   81
Wighton, Wheycurd Farm, Norfolk Figure 53
Whitstone, Cornwall 210
Wilkinson, W. (architect) 128, 130, 161, 219, 223
Willoughby family, later Lords Middleton 90
Wilton, Wiltshire 32, 158, 221
Wiltshire 11, 26, 154, 155, 221
Wimpole, Cambridgeshire 57, 205, 209
Windmills 100–1, 151
Windsor, Berkshire 4, 17, 20, 68–9, 133, 158, 161–5, 167,
   203, 208, Figures 31, 32, 82
   Flemish Farm Figure 83
   Shaw Farm Figure 84
Wing, T. (agent) 151
Wispington, Lincolnshire 143
Woburn, Bedfordshire 5, 18, 20, 21, 26, 58, 66, 104, 105,
   107, 111, 115, 146, 147, 180, 200, 208, Figures 49, 51
   Crawley Heath Farm Figure 50
Woburn, Surrey 62–3
Wombwell, West Yorkshire 225
Worcestershire 224
Wright, T. (architect) 64
Workington, Schoose Farm, Cumbria 74, 100–1, 201, 211,
   Figure 48
Woronzo, C. 155, 223
Wurtenburg, Duke of 31
Wyatt, J. (architect) 216, 222
Wyatt, S. (architect) 5, 14, 58–9, 61, 62, 66, 69, 72, 107,
   109, 110, 132, 198, 209, 213, 217, 220, 221
Wyvill family 49–51

Yarborough, Lord 18, 215
Yorke, P. 57
Yorkshire 12, 17, 25, 49, 77, 79, 85, 123, 137, 173, 203,
   224–5
Young, A. (writer) 1, 2, 3, 5, 8, 12, 13, 14, 20, 25, 31, 36,
   45, 52, 96, 116, 201, 219, 224, Figure 16
Young, W. (agent) 17
Yule, J. (agent) 18